The Fragrant Vegetable

Also by Martin Stidham:

Yajio and *Rollicking Heroes* (Chinese translations)
Little Earth School: Education, Discovery, Celebration, with
Munzenrider, Newmann, Coffey, and DaSilva

Martin Stidham

The Fragrant
Vegetable

Simple

Vegetarian

Delicacies

from the

Chinese

Jeremy P. Tarcher, Inc.
Los Angeles
Distributed by St. Martin's Press
New York

Library of Congress Cataloging-in-Publication Data

Stidham, Martin, 1943-
   The fragrant vegetable.

Includes index.
   1. Cookery (Vegetables)   2. Cookery (Tofu)
3. Cookery, Chinese.   I. Title.
TX801.S75 1986   641.6′5   86-1941
ISBN 0-87477-378-4

Jeremy P. Tarcher, Inc.
9110 Sunset Blvd.
Los Angeles, CA 90069

Design by Renée Cossutta
Illustration by Ellen J. Drucker

Manufactured in the United States of America
10 9 8 7 6 5 4 3 2 1

First Edition

To Peter and Vivian

Contents

The Fragrant Vegetable

Temptations and Delights of Chinese Vegetarian Cuisine

For years now we have been reminded of the health risks in a meat-based diet. Rationally, we can accept the warning, but our appetites and tastebuds don't always acquiesce so readily.

Chinese vegetarian chefs have been answering this dilemma for centuries. With creativity and some very special, as well as some very common, ingredients, they have developed what is often viewed as a distinct branch of Chinese cuisine, one that uses no meat, fish, fowl, eggs, or dairy products.

The basic meaning of the Chinese term for vegetarian food implies "pure," "plain," and "simple." This is indeed the very perception that people often entertain toward meatless cooking. My first encounter with strictly vegetarian Chinese food was on a visit with friends to a Buddhist temple in the mountains of southern Taiwan. There were several hot vegetable and tofu dishes for dinner, with side plates of pickles, peanuts, and homemade tofu "cheese." The meal had a simplicity that seemed to me quite in keeping with the religious life. Yet, as I was to find out later, the chefs are also able to produce exquisite feasts that rival any nonvegetarian table. Many monasteries and temples have actually become famous for their food.

Because of the Buddhist injunction against the killing of any creature, monks and nuns are bound by their vows to total vegetarian diets. Pious Buddhist laymen may also abstain from meat, fish, and fowl—sometimes completely but at least twice a month (on the first and fifteenth), as well as throughout the entire seventh month of the year and during certain religious observances. During the centuries when Buddhism flourished in China, each household could prepare its own meatless meals for these "fasting" periods, and there were vegetarian restaurants that could serve up the most simple to the most lavish repast. In Suchow, superb vegetarian delicacies were even available on small pleasure boats that plied the surrounding waters, as these were used for excursions to temples in the nearby hills. Even today, scores of vegetarian restaurants thrive in cities like Taipei and Hong Kong.

Nearly every Chinese qualifies as some sort of epicure as well as amateur nutritionist. The average person on the street can tell you the health benefits of any given ingredient, and many people, the Cantonese in particular, avidly combine herbs with pertinent foods to build up stamina and maintain health, as well as to cure maladies. Chinese physicians have always prescribed a vegetarian diet as the most healthful of all and as the most basic of cures for any disorder. The physicians' special concern is with a "clean" diet—that is, one free of animal toxins. Many Chinese, especially older persons, recognize the health values of vegetarian eating, and gourmets find many of the creations as distinctive as meat dishes. Thus the following for meatless cuisine is potentially vast. This may be the guiding force that keeps the Chinese vegetarian tradition alive and flourishing, for with the secularization of most of China in recent years, the moral and metaphysical values that were of paramount influence in shaping this school of cooking have waned.

In the United States, more and more Chinese vegetarian restaurants are opening, and Americans are discovering the delights of this food. On a first visit to one of these establishments, we quickly realize that the fare is more than vegetables cooked in a Chinese style. One glance at the menu—maybe even a double take—reveals an array of unusual edibles: bean curd skin, wheat gluten, mung bean sheet, pressed tofu. Stranger still, there is a rather bewildering selection of the very things we thought we were going to avoid—"meatballs," "chestnut chicken," "ham," "sharks' fins," "whole fish." There are even some things we may have always hoped to avoid, like "brains." But after tasting these dishes, we're quick to marvel at how the chefs can satisfy our nutritional needs while regaling us with varied, meaty tastes and textures.

In a typical nonvegetarian Chinese restaurant or cookbook, even the "vegetable" dishes usually include some kind of meat. Vegetarian dishes, in the same tradition, frequently incorporate a "meaty" ingredient, but of course it is always from a vegetable source. (The word "meaty" is used here in a Chinese context, implying tender, well-cooked shreds, slices, or bite-sized morsels, rather than something like a steak.) This is where the tofu (bean curd) family plays a leading role —regular tofu, pressed tofu, tofu custard, bean curd skin, and other forms—all of which appear throughout this book.

Wheat gluten is another important protein, obtained by removing the starch from a flour dough, leaving behind the protein content, or gluten. Both tofu and gluten can be made at home, or you can buy them at the market.

Other favorite ingredients include dried black mushrooms (or shiitake) and bamboo shoots, as well as a full range of vegetables and legumes —fresh, dried, and preserved. A number of recipes here feature the fresh Oriental vegetables that are appearing more frequently in our markets, such as daikon, Chinese cabbage, and Japanese eggplant.

We are fortunate to have fresh produce readily available year-round. Imagine the isolated, winter-bound Chinese temples and villages, hard-pressed for fresh ingredients. They had to rely on items that would store for long periods, such as root vegetables; dried foodstuffs like black mushrooms, tree ear, lily buds, beans; preserved vegetables like Szechuan pickle and snow cabbage; nuts; bamboo shoots in their sheath. From wheat came gluten. And from dried soybeans came bean sprouts and tofu, which was also kept frozen—indeed, the tofu frozen in snowbanks by the monks of Mount Omei was so well known that visitors made a point of bringing some back home with them.

Supermarkets in the United States now carry these essentials, which means that you can prepare almost all the dishes if your local market and/or natural foods store has an Oriental section. If there is a Chinese or Japanese grocery nearby, shopping will be a cinch. A Shopping List is provided at the end of the book, including the Chinese names of all special ingredients. This can be convenient when you are asking for a particular item, as English names are often unclear or even unknown to Chinese grocers. Many ingredients can also be ordered by mail (see Shopping and Mail-Order Sources).

For specific shopping information, including the various names under which a given item is sold, as well as how to ready and store the products for these recipes, see Chinese Ingredients at the end of the book. Refer to this section especially if you have any questions about what kind of bamboo shoots, black mushrooms, and soy sauce to buy. Other frequently used or special ingredients may be described more fully in a chapter introduction or in a recipe where they principally appear; in these cases, the Chinese Ingredients section will refer you to the appropriate place.

When there is a chance that an ingredient may not always be readily available, a familiar alternate is usually suggested, which also gives you a chance to vary the recipe (green pepper for tree ear, lima beans for fava beans, and so on).

Mixing vegetables with "meat" makes these vegetarian dishes versatile enough to fit into almost any menu, whether you want a simple vegetable dish for the family dinner, something elaborate for guests, or a substantial one-dish meal when dining alone. You can even put on a complete vegetarian meal with the recipes (see Suggested Menus at the end of the book to help with this).

Those who are concerned about salt and oil intake will be glad to know that the dishes are neither extra salty nor oily. By Western standards, Chinese food often seems oversalted because it is usually seasoned to be eaten with rice. Indeed, a bit of rice along with other food has the effect of enhancing them both. These recipes aim for a happy medium —tasty enough to complement a swallow of rice, but good, too, just by themselves.

As for the oil content, most of the stir-fried selections contain only 2 or 3 tablespoons of oil for a dish that will serve three to four people. When you think about it, many people would consume the equivalent of this in the form of butter on a baked potato. The other dishes contain no oil at all except possibly a little sesame oil for enhancement; and, of course, there are no animal fats in any of the dishes.

For the sake of variety, some dishes are mildly hot. The spice is an optional embellishment you can successfully omit. Many Chinese vegetarians frown on spiced food, considering it of dubious health value and productive of undue stimulation of the system rather than tranquility. That is why you will not find liberal sprinklings of garlic or even green onion in these recipes. Chinese physicians, too, are stringent in restricting red pepper and garlic, as well as excluding monosodium glutamate. When the seasoning is light, this diet has a way of refining the palate and making one more sensitive to the subtleties of flavor in our foods.

On the other hand, if you like your food to bite you back, you are free to increase the amount of hot seasoning, and even add such condiments as hot pepper, garlic, Szechuan pickle, chile, and curry where desired. Many people in China would do the same, especially in regions where hot pepper is popular, such as Szechuan or Hunan.

Home style, restaurant, and temple styles of cooking are all represented in this book. Tastes from all the regions of China are present, too—Peking, Hunan, Szechuan, Shanghai, and Canton. Some of the recipes, although meatless, are not necessarily considered by Chinese as belonging to the "vegetarian" repertoire, simply because they may be everyday dishes, part of the regular diet of the population in general.

The cooking techniques are basic and already fairly well known to Americans. The section immediately following this introduction reviews cutting vegetables. Information on other techniques is given in the introductions to the chapters where they are predominantly used. For example, the method for salting and squeezing relish vegetables for ultra crispness is described in Chapter 1. Stir-frying is covered in Chapter 2. Instructions for steaming soups appear in Chapter 7. We are not accustomed in this country to preparing soups this way, so chances are the elegant clarity of the result, in both appearance and taste, will be a pleasant surprise.

The recipes can accompany American meals and, of course, non-vegetarian Chinese food. Start out by adding a single dish, no matter how simple, to your customary menus. The novelty and contrast can be an enhancement that makes everything taste better. Chinese vegetarian cooking offers a richly satisfying alternative to the usual pork, beef, fish, and poultry fare, besides providing deliciously varied ways to enjoy our abundance of fragrant, succulent vegetables. The temptations and delights of these simple, tasty delicacies from the Chinese await you.

On Cutting Vegetables

The aesthetic pleasure in eating is particularly heightened when the ingredients are appropriately cut. Skilled slicing affects nearly every sensory aspect of a dish, from visual appeal, to feel in the mouth, to taste. Neat, uniform shapes not only are pleasing to the eye, but help promote even cooking. This is especially important in stir-frying, where heat is high and cooking time short.

When a dish has two or more main components, it is customary to maintain matching shapes among them. There is a tactile element involved here. A jumble of diced, sliced, and julienned food in the mouth all at once could prove distracting and would not be conducive to a harmonious taste sensation. So, as a rule, shredded items go with shredded, diced with diced, and so on. When ingredients require different cooking times, they are either added in the appropriate order, or cooked separately first and later combined.

Sometimes the ingredient's basic character determines the fitting shape: you would not want large cubes of a potent item like Szechuan pickle, nor for a stir-fried dish would you julienne something as fragile as tofu. Sometimes shape is a matter of conformity to companion ingredients. Bamboo shoots, for example, are variously diced, sliced, and shredded; all are good, but the gastronomic experience is subtly different with each.

Most Chinese cooks use a cleaver, which has several advantages. Its broad surface is convenient for crushing (nuts), mashing (tofu, potato), pounding (carrot), and also for transferring ingredients to bowl or pan. Its weight can be utilized to do a lot of the work when mincing or chopping.

But use any knife you feel comfortable with. Sharpness is the key. Dull blades only mash and crush as they go. A good knife, by its clean cuts, will keep textures intact, thus retaining flavor. You can avoid bloodshed by anchoring things with your free hand, fingers curved. With fingernails facing the adjacent blade, you are well armored. By keeping the nails abutting, you can also help guide the knife.

If the vegetable is rounded, halve it lengthwise first, or slice off a side, then lay flat-side down for slicing. This works even for mincing something as small as a green onion. With bamboo shoots, be sure to slice and julienne *lengthwise.* Following the grain of the shoot promotes crispness. For information on cutting and slicing black mushrooms, see Chinese Ingredients.

To julienne: Slice the vegetable thinly, and stack the slices stair-step style from left to right so that each touches the board. Then cut into thin matchsticks (¼ inch), working from right to left. If necessary, cut the julienne strips into shorter lengths (1½ or 2 inches).

To shred: Same as for cutting julienne strips, but the slices should be as thin as possible; after stacking, cut into very fine shreds, then into shorter lengths (1 inch or so).

To dice finely: Cut into ¼-inch julienne strips, then cut the strips into ¼-inch dice.

To mince: Same as dicing, but on a Lilliputian scale.

Roll cut: Used on thin, more elongated vegetables as well as tubers and bamboo shoots to enhance appearance and to maximize surface area for cooking. Make a diagonal slice, then roll the vegetable forward a quarter turn before making another diagonal slice, and so on; quarter turn, slice, quarter turn, slice.

To mash: A cleaver or broad knife are good mashing instruments. For hints on mashing tofu (and potato), see Chapter 3, On Readying Tofu.

1   Crunchy Relishes

Just as a formal Chinese dinner starts with an elaborate plate of assorted cold delicacies, so an informal meal in a restaurant often begins with a cold relish or two, often served as a matter of course and sometimes on the house. In many restaurants, especially the smaller ones, there may be a cafeterialike display of cold foods and tasty, refreshing appetizers to enjoy while waiting for your hot food to arrive. You make your choice, and the small plates are sent to your table—Szechuan style cabbage relish, cucumber relish, sprouted fava beans, icicle radish, pickled garlic cloves, salt-boiled peanuts, pressed tofu in slices or strands, to name a few. There might be cold cooked vegetables, as well as shrimp and crab, cold cuts, preserved eggs. Some cozy eateries serve nothing but cold tidbits, for an evening snack perhaps, accompanied by a hot bowl of congee (rice gruel), or to be lingered over with wine.

In the morning, a similar variety of cold items appears on many a family breakfast table to be eaten with hot congee. At banquets in Suchow, relishes have even been served as a last course. A cold platter of soy-pickled cucumber, tofu "cheese," and cabbage relish with congee provides a palate-cleansing, refreshing end to a rich meal.

Preserved vegetables obviously are welcome during the winter when fresh produce can be scarce in China. In the summer, for lunch or dinner at home, a fresh, crisp vegetable often is cold-tossed with a dressing and sometimes another ingredient. These are not quite the same thing as salads. For even when leafy greens and root vegetables are eaten cold and uncooked, Chinese like to give them some kind of treatment to refine the rawness and improve the texture. The result has all the freshness of a salad but is usually crunchier, with enhanced flavor. Often it is similar to what we think of as a relish. This is because the liquid content of the ingredient has been reduced, either by the curing action of a little salt, or by blanching and pressing.

It is an easy and usually quick process. If the directions call for salting, place the chopped vegetable in a medium-sized ceramic mixing bowl, sprinkle with the required amount of salt, and mix well for a minute or so by hand, using a sort of repeated grasping motion that lightly "massages" it. After an allotted standing time, usually a half hour to an hour, rinse several times in cool water (if so directed) and squeeze out the liquid.

Do not be afraid of mashing the vegetable when squeezing. It will spring back into shape. The best way is simply to take a scoop of it in your right hand, cover with your left palm (or vice versa if you are left-handed), and press hard, letting the liquid drain out between your right fingers. You will find that the vegetable is now even more crunchy than when raw. Moreover, it will have a fine flavor with just the right amount of saltiness (most of the salt drains off in the rinsing and/or squeezing).

Transfer the vegetable to a serving bowl—again, ceramic or glass— or plate. Usually a small one is sufficient. All that remains now is to toss it with the dressing ingredients (not premixed). If you prefer, you can do this in another bowl, then transfer to the serving bowl or plate. The combination of soy sauce, sesame oil, and sometimes vinegar is as common a dressing in Chinese relishes as oil and vinegar for Western salads. (Please check the Chinese Ingredients section for more information on these ingredients. It is important to use the amber-colored Chinese or Japanese sesame oil, not the colorless health food-store variety. The soy sauce used in the testing of these recipes was Kikkoman.)

As with a salad, the predominant taste of the dishes changes with different vegetables. These relishes are tasty assets to just about any meal, and especially welcome to Americans who like a cold, crunchy course. Let them replace the salad in your regular menus. In a Chinese meal serve them as a cold side dish or as a first course. Don't feel limited to one relish. A variety, especially for guests, is always appealing. I suggest you pass them family style, with the hot food, or have them on the table as appetizers while you're doing the last-minute cooking. Provide little side plates for the relishes, if you like, or have portions already served up at each place when everyone sits down. A saucer per person is all that's needed, for these vegetables are condensed and take up much less space than a tossed salad.

When you are in the mood for a very light, clean-tasting collation, try one or two of these with plain hot rice or congee, and perhaps a soup. To make congee, simply place one part short-grain rice and nine or ten parts water in a pot, bring to the boil, reduce heat to low, cover partially, and simmer a little over an hour until the rice has fully blossomed and the consistency is gruellike (not too thick) or porridge-like, according to taste. Or you can use leftover cooked rice—three parts water to one part rice, for a cooking time of half an hour or more.

All of these recipes can be made ahead of time. Or in many cases you can start preparation as late as an hour or so before serving.

Most of the recipes in this chapter yield three or four small servings; for big eaters you might want to double them.

Sweet-and-Sour Chinese Cabbage Relish

Having a zestier flavor than lettuce yet still light and crisp, Chinese (Napa) cabbage makes a welcome appearance in any meal, especially when dressed with a clean, sweet tartness. In Chiao County of Shantung, these cabbages grow to enormous sizes, weighing over 40 pounds each. I like to use cider vinegar in this recipe instead of Chinese black vinegar, for reasons of color. This goes especially well with tofu dishes, like those in chapters 3 and 4, noodles, and stir-fried vegetables such as Curried Broccoli Stems or Asparagus (Chapter 2).

¾ pound (340 g) Chinese
cabbage (see Note)

1½ teaspoons (8 ml) salt

2 teaspoons (10 ml) sugar

1 tablespoon (15 ml) cider
vinegar or Chinese dark
vinegar

Note: Buy a 1-pound head of Chinese cabbage in
order to have ¾ pound after trimming. Discard
outer leaves if they are not firm and crisp.

Chop the cabbage by shredding, then turning and
cutting in a cross direction at ¼- or ½-inch intervals; you should have 4 to 5 cups. Place in a bowl
and sprinkle with salt. Mix well by hand for a minute or so, then set aside for at least a half hour.

Do not rinse. Squeeze handfuls of the cabbage
firmly to remove liquid, but leave it just slightly
moist, not bone-dry. Place in a small serving bowl
and toss with sugar and vinegar. Serve either at
room temperature or chilled.

Green-and-Gold Relish

*Garland chrysanthemum greens,
both raw and cooked, have a
bracing flavor. The bunches are
frequently seen in Oriental
groceries during cooler months.
Sometimes frilly, sometimes fuller
shaped, the leaf resembles that of
a familiar garden chrysanthemum.*

This is an eye-catching toss of deep green and
golden white. Garland chrysanthemum has a crisp,
clean pungency (see Garland Chrysanthemum or
Spinach with Wine and Soy Sauce, Chapter 2, for
more on this vegetable). It is a good choice for pre-
senting with a slightly spicy dish such as Noodles
with Sesame Sauce or Spicy Green Beans. Try to get
whole bamboo shoots or chunks, not presliced. They
are diced in this dish and their quality is important
to its success. Incidentally, when using spinach, do
not throw away the root ends. They have a vibrant
flavor and can be included here. They are also excellent tossed separately with a dressing of soy sauce
and sesame oil.

10 ounces (281 g) greens—
spinach or garland
chrysanthemum (see Note)

⅔ cup (170 ml) bamboo shoot
(preferably winter), diced

¼ teaspoon (1.5 ml) salt

½ teaspoon (3 ml) sugar

1½ teaspoons (8 ml) cider
vinegar or Chinese dark
vinegar

1½ teaspoons (8 ml) sesame oil

Note: Buy 11 ounces of greens (if stems of garland chrysanthemum are thick, buy 14 ounces) in order to have 10 ounces after trimming. Include stems of both vegetables; however, if garland chrysanthemum stems exceed ¼ inch in thickness, do not use them for this recipe since they may be too firm, tough, or stringy.

Wilt the greens by immersing them in a large pot of boiling water for 30 seconds (or steam in a vegetable basket, 1½ minutes for spinach, 2½ minutes for garland chrysanthemum, stirring once or twice). Rinse in cold water to stop the cooking. Divide into two or three bunches and firmly squeeze out the water. Chop each handful at ½-inch intervals, then turn and chop in a cross direction. Squeeze again if the greens are still watery, then loosen them by a light crumbling motion and place in a bowl.

Pour boiling water over the bamboo shoot to freshen it; rinse under cool water and dice finely (¼ inch).

Toss all ingredients together. Let sit a few minutes at room temperature, and test for seasonings, adding perhaps an extra ¼ teaspoon sugar with garland chrysanthemum. Serve chilled or at room temperature.

Snappy Cucumber Relish

You might think that cucumber is already crisp, until you try this and find the natural sweetness enhanced and the slices so crunchy they almost snap. The oil in this dressing is heated to give it a better flavor, ameliorating the "raw" oil taste, besides quickly sealing the vegetable. Cucumber is a very popular cold relish item with the Chinese, whether dressed with a hot sauce or tossed as a garnish with noodles. The small Oriental cucumber (*kyuri* in Japanese) is particularly crisp, with a tender skin like the hothouse (or English) cucumber. Oriental groceries might have it during the summer and fall—not to be confused with the baby pickling cucumber, however. It is sometimes not much bigger than a finger.

¾ pound (340 g) cucumber (see Note)

1 teaspoon (5 ml) salt

¾ teaspoon (4 ml) sugar

1½ tablespoons (22.5 ml) vegetable oil

½ teaspoon (3 ml) sesame oil

Note: You will need to purchase slightly over 1 pound of regular cucumber to obtain ¾ pound pared and seeded. Pare. Halve or quarter the cucumber lengthwise and scoop out or slice off the seeds. The English or Oriental cucumbers do not need to be skinned or seeded, so buy just slightly over ¾ pound. Halve or quarter them, or leave whole, depending on size.

Slice cucumber crosswise or diagonally (¼ inch thick, 2 inches long). Yield is about 3 cups.

Place cucumber in a bowl, sprinkle with salt, and mix-massage for a minute or two. Set aside for at least a half hour. Rinse several times in cold water; *firmly* squeeze handfuls of the cucumber to remove the liquid.

Dry the bowl and place slices back in it. Toss with sugar.

Heat vegetable oil to the smoking point. Pour the hot oil over the cucumber in the bowl and toss quickly. Add sesame oil. May be served right away or chilled first. Remove to a small serving bowl or small individual relish saucers.

"Crystal Icicles" Relish

Chinese icicle radish is large but more rounded than Daikon. When cooked, it resembles a turnip.

A cool-looking white, flecked with green onion and laced with a bit of vinegar, here is perhaps the crunchiest of all these relishes. If you choose entrees of distinct contrast, such as Eggplant Sautéed with Fried Gluten or Garlic, or Chinese Pumpkin or Yellow Squash with Pine Nuts—both soft and rich—this will stand out all the more. Daikon is the long, white radish that many supermarkets now carry year-round. The thicker Chinese icicle radish has a similar flavor and is sometimes green. Huge, 30-pound sizes grow in the northern Chinese province of Shantung. Throughout the country this is a staple vegetable, eaten raw, simmered in soups, stewed, or stir-fried. It is thought by the Chinese to have a "cooling" (calming) effect on one's system. The people of Tientsin attribute their robust health to their habit of eating icicle radish and drinking hot tea. The Empress Dowager Tsu Hsi is said to have been content eating radish flavored with soy sauce, while merely sniffing the aromas of the remaining 128 different dishes that arrayed her table at every meal.

1 pound (450 g) daikon or Chinese icicle radish (see Note)

1 teaspoon (5 ml) salt

½ teaspoon (3 ml) sugar

2½ teaspoons (13 ml) cider vinegar, more or less to taste

1 tablespoon (15 ml) green onion, minced

2 tablespoons (30 ml) vegetable oil

1 teaspoon (5 ml) sesame oil (optional)

Note: Buy a little over a pound of radish in order to have 1 pound after paring.

Pare the radish. Shred about 4 cups (loose), using a food processor or the coarse side of a grater. Place in a bowl and mix well by hand with salt; let stand 30 minutes to 1 hour. Rinse several times in cool water; squeeze firmly to extract liquid. Dry the bowl, replace the radish, and toss with sugar and vinegar (the vinegar presence should be perceptible but not overpowering; you can use 2 teaspoons for a very light effect or 1 tablespoon for a stronger one). Top with minced green onion.

Heat vegetable oil until very hot; pour it over the radish and quickly toss. May be further enhanced with sesame oil. Serve chilled or at room temperature.

Zesty Chinese Cabbage Stems

Save the frilly part of the cabbage for another recipe, such as Sweet-and-Sour Chinese Cabbage Relish, and here use only the firm, meaty stem portion. The flavor is gingery, garlicky, spicy-hot, or any combination of these flavors that suits your taste. Plan ahead for this, as it is best stored overnight.

1 pound (450 g) Chinese cabbage, stem part only (see Note)

2 teaspoons (10 ml) gingerroot, minced

2 cloves (large) garlic (optional)

1½ teaspoons (8 ml) chile oil (optional)

2 tablespoons (30 ml) vegetable oil

2 tablespoons (30 ml) water

¾ teaspoon (4 ml) salt

Note: To have 1 pound stems, buy a head of cabbage a little over 2 pounds in weight.

Trim off the frilly portion of the cabbage leaves and use the firm part only, a triangle shape. Cut into 1-inch squares; yield is about 5 cups.

Bruise the garlic.

Put all ingredients into a pan, adding cabbage last. Place pan over high heat. When the boil begins, stir-fry 4 to 5 minutes. Remove immediately to a ceramic bowl and cover with plastic wrap. Let cool, then refrigerate overnight. Remove garlic cloves before serving if desired.

Tangy-rich Carrot Relish

A more generous portion of sesame oil is used here than in other relishes, so this is an excellent choice when you want something gratifyingly rich. The piquant sauce is bound to perk up reluctant appetites. The carrots are crunchy but are given a good pounding to crack them open. The raggedy, broken texture helps hold the dressing, besides enhancing chewability. This is my favorite relish to eat with plain rice or congee.

¾ pound (340 g) carrots (see Note)

1 tablespoon (15 ml) sugar

2 tablespoons (30 ml) soy sauce

1 tablespoon (15 ml) cider vinegar or Chinese dark vinegar

2 tablespoons (30 ml) sesame oil

Note: Buy a little over ¾ pound carrots in order to have ¾ pound after paring. The carrots should be young, sweet, and juicy.

Peel carrots and cut up roughly into small, bite-sized pieces. Cover with heavy paper (such as a grocery bag) and a cloth; pound firmly with a mallet or the flat side, or blunt edge, of a cleaver to flatten and break open the pieces.

Toss the carrots with the remaining ingredients and let sit at least an hour before eating; toss occasionally. Serve chilled or at room temperature.

Green Peas or Soybeans in the Pod

These are fun to snack on with wine or beer. If you try green soybeans in the pod, you'll discover why Chinese call them "fuzzy beans": the pod has a smooth covering of fine fuzz. I have raised soybeans at home to eat this way; cultivation is the same as for any other bean, and their flavorful crunchiness is a special treat. Many Oriental groceries carry the frozen pods, intended specifically for this manner of serving. Fresh peas in the pod are good this way, too. What easier way could there be to serve them —you don't even have to do the shucking. To eat, just draw the peas or beans out between your teeth and discard the pod. Since this can be served hot as well as at room temperature, you might also enjoy it as an informal, very different vegetable dish. Provide plates for the empty pods, unless you want to be extra informal and let them pile up on the table!

1 pound (450 g) green peas in the pod, or ½ pound (225 g) green soybeans in the pod (see Note)

4 cups (1000 ml) water

1 tablespoon (15 ml) salt

1 teaspoon (5 ml) Szechuan peppercorns (optional)

Note: The same stores that carry frozen green soybeans in the pod will probably also have the same thing *without* the pod; these are for other recipes, such as soups and dishes like Crunchy Green Pepper and "Meat Shreds," or Feast of Delicacies.

If you are using frozen soybeans in the pod, do not defrost before using.

Place the peas or soybeans in a pot with water and salt. If you have them, include the Szechuan peppercorns, loose or tied up in a small cloth bag or square of cloth. Bring to the boil; reduce heat and cook at a gentle boil, covered, until done. Peas will take 5 to 15 minutes. Frozen soybeans may be ready as soon as the boil is reached or soon after (up to 5 minutes); fresh soybeans require about 20 minutes, or more if they are large. Keep testing and remove from the heat when *just* done, as they continue to cook a bit thereafter and are not good when overdone. Peas should be tender, soybeans tender yet crunchy. Drain, and remove bag of peppercorns (leave loose peppercorns to be discarded when eating). Serve hot or at room temperature.

Sun-dried Watermelon Rind and Tender Mushrooms

An unusual combination of ingredients, promising a refreshing change for summer palates. Watermelon rind is sun-dried for a day, then diced and steamed with mushrooms. It is tempting hot or cold as a little tidbit-type side dish. The watermelon rind stays slightly crunchy, while the mushrooms are juicy and soft. This is good when you want something slightly sweet and fruity in taste, perhaps with Chewy Stuffed Dumplings, Fried; or with a potato dish (Taro, Yuca Root, Mountain Yam, or Potato Temptation, Chapter 2).

1 cup (250 ml) watermelon rind, diced after drying (see Note)

¼ teaspoon (1.5 ml) salt

12 small fresh mushrooms, or 6 fresh and 6 presoaked black (or shiitake) mushrooms

½ teaspoon (3 ml) sugar

1½ teaspoons (8 ml) vegetable oil

1 teaspoon (5 ml) sesame oil

Note: Cut off and discard the hard skin of the watermelon rind. Set it out in the sun for one day to dry partially, turning at least once. It should shrink in size by about half, yet still be juicy inside. Dice finely to yield 1 cup.

Mix diced rind by hand with salt in a bowl; let stand 1 hour. Rinse several times and squeeze dry.

Place diced rind and mushrooms in a small heatproof bowl; mix in sugar and vegetable oil. Steam 5 to 10 minutes in the same manner as On Steaming Soups, Chapter 7). The watermelon rind should be crunchy, the mushrooms soft. After steaming, stir in sesame oil. Serve hot or at room temperature.

Szechuan Style Cabbage Relish

This relish is certainly the most ubiquitous and popular in all China. There is even a special earthenware pickling jar for it. Encircling the mouth of the jar is a shallow, water-filled trough, into which the lid fits like an upturned bowl, affording an airtight seal. Many a restaurant, no matter how small, keeps an ongoing batch in the works. It is especially favored as an appetizer or as an accompaniment to such specialties as boiled pot-stickers or noodles.

Szechuan is a Western province of China where red pepper frequently enlivens the food. The traditional hot, spicy flavor of this relish varies with individual taste; use as much or as little gingerroot and/or hot peppers as you like to do the job. Chiles can be chopped for a really hot effect; or for mere warmth, leave them whole with a slit down one side. If you omit the chiles and gingerroot altogether, the result will be a pleasant pickle flavor with the natural sweetness of the crisp vegetables in the forefront.

Green cabbage (not Chinese cabbage) is the principal ingredient, but other vegetables may be added for color (carrot) and variety (icicle radish). One batch requires several days' steeping. The brine should be reused, for each time the vegetables contribute their flavor, and it gets better and better.

1 medium head green
   cabbage

Marinade:

8 cups (2000 ml) water

2 tablespoons (30 ml)
   Szechuan peppercorns

3 tablespoons (45 ml) salt

2–3 tablespoons (30–45 ml)
   strong spirits (gin, tequila,
   kaoliang wine)

1 cup (250 ml) icicle radish,
   julienned (optional)

½ cup (125 ml) carrot,
   julienned (optional)

2–5 slices gingerroot (optional)

1–3 small fresh chiles (optional)

Discard limp outer leaves of cabbage. It is not necessary to separate leaves individually. Break the head into fairly large yet bite-sized pieces. Pat dry and let excess moisture evaporate.

To make marinade: Bring to a boil the water, peppercorns, and salt. Strain out the peppercorns as you pour the liquid into a plastic container (with airtight lid), ceramic bowl, or crock. Let cool to room temperature.

When the brine has cooled, add the alcohol, then cabbage and additional vegetables. Weigh these down with a clean, heavy ceramic object (I simply use a plate) or stone so that they remain submerged in the brine. Cover tightly with plastic wrap or airtight lid. Store in the refrigerator for at least three days before uncovering. The first one or two batches may seem a bit salty and raw-tasting; after that a mellow, richly mature character develops. It can store indefinitely if kept cold, airtight, and clean. Always use clean, dry utensils when removing the vegetables. You can remove as much as you want at a time and add new vegetables before the previous batch is used up.

To replenish the brine after several batches, add a little alcohol and a salt solution (½ teaspoon salt boiled with ½ cup water). The original marinade can be reboiled with additional water and salt, but this results in some flavor loss.

Variation: Shred the marinated cabbage or chop it coarsely, to yield about 5 cups, loosely packed. Toss with 1 tablespoon soy sauce, 2½ teaspoons sugar,

1 tablespoon vinegar (cider or Chinese dark), and 1½ teaspoons sesame oil. Serve at room temperature or chilled.

Mustard-hot Celery Relish

The hot mustard makes this a lively and invigorating relish—or if you want a mild taste, use just a dab. Dry mustard will be hotter than Dijon. The celery is flattened a little, all the better to drink in the dressing, then blanched and salted. Chinese celery, sometimes seen in Chinese markets, is very slender and long, yet it is not as meaty.

¾ pound (340 g) celery hearts or Chinese celery

½ teaspoon (3 ml) salt

½ teaspoon (3 ml) sugar

1½ teaspoons (8 ml) soy sauce

1 teaspoon (5 ml) premixed dry mustard or Dijon mustard (see Note)

1 teaspoon (5 ml) sesame oil

Pinch salt, to taste

Note: To prepare dry mustard, mix two parts powder with one part cold water in a small bowl. For this recipe, 2 teaspoons powder and 1 teaspoon water is about right. Place bowl on a rack (or on another small, upturned bowl as a stand) in a pot with some scalding, just-boiled water. Cover the pot and let stand several minutes. The moist heat develops the mustard flavor and aroma. This type of mustard dries if allowed to stand very long, so mix up the dressing right away and make up only what you need. Use 1 teaspoon of this mixture in the dressing, or less for a lighter flavor.

String the celery if necessary and cut lengthwise into narrow (¼-inch) strips. Pound or press with a heavy object such as the side of a cleaver to break it open. (With Chinese celery, omit all the above steps except stringing.) Cut into 1-inch lengths. You should have about 3 cups.

Wilt celery by steaming in a vegetable basket 3 minutes (or immerse celery in a pot of boiling water till the second hard boil is reached). Cool in cold water to halt cooking. Squeeze firmly to remove liquid. You should have about 2 cups at this point.

Place regular celery in a small mixing bowl, and sprinkle with ½ teaspoon salt (omit this step with Chinese celery). Mix-massage by hand for a minute; let stand a half hour, stirring occasionally. Rinse 5 times with cool water. Divide into several handfuls and *firmly* squeeze out liquid.

Toss the celery with sugar, soy sauce, mustard, and sesame oil. Test for salt and add a pinch or so if needed. Let stand at least 30 minutes at room temperature or in the refrigerator, tossing occasionally.

Tofu "Cheese"

These small cubes are occasionally served as a condiment, thus their inclusion here with the relishes. The name suggests their consistency, which is like that of a soft cheese. Cubes of tofu or pressed tofu are fermented on a bamboo rack, then packed into earthenware jars and aged with different flavorings, such as salt and wine or red rice (red rice is used in making some wines; the lees are used by Chinese in southeastern China in marinating chicken, fish, and even cocks' crowns). The taste will vary with the wines of different locales. If the tofu "cheese" is of particularly good quality (such as that flavored with Guilin's San Hua Wine) it may be shipped far and wide. There are other names for this product, such as "preserved bean curd" on the jars or little brown pottery crocks in which it comes. Several varieties are available—white (plain and mild); red (salty and more pungent); and spicy (laced generously with chile).

Because the flavor is quite potent, all you will want is a tiny dab on the tongue at a time, just enough to smack your lips over and enjoy with a mouthful of rice. I recommend the plain, white kind if you are trying this for the first time. Include it in a simple snacking meal of rice or congee; one or two crisp vegetable relishes (a sweet or tart one like Sweet-and-Sour Chinese Cabbage Relish or Snappy Cucumber Relish); a dish of peanuts; and Eggplant with Fried Gluten or Chestnuts (Chapter 6). With a hot meal, too, tofu "cheese" will provide a touch of variety. Try it when you are having a sweetish stir-fried dish from Chapter 2, such as Fresh and Black Mushrooms with Delicacies, or Braised Chinese Cabbage with Delicacies.

1 cube tofu "cheese" per
person

Sugar

Sesame oil

Place each cube (or half of one if cubes are extra large, as with some red tofu "cheeses") on a small saucer. Sprinkle with sugar to taste and add ¼ to ½ teaspoon sesame oil.

Pungent Bean Sprouts

Quickly blanched, the bean sprouts retain their fresh crunchiness. They take on a robust savor from the steeping liquid, which is flavored with red tofu "cheese," often labeled "preserved bean curd (red)," at Chinese groceries. See the preceding recipe for more information on tofu "cheese." Red tofu "cheese" plays a part in Chinese dips and various dishes. For example, the cavity of Cantonese suckling pig is rubbed with it and other seasonings before being roasted.

No oil is added to this relish, so it makes a fine companion for entrees containing fried gluten, or deep-fried foods like tofu, Spicy Green Beans, and Shredded Black Mushroom "Eel." It has a rather unexpected sweetness, an inherent quality of the bean sprouts that is not always appreciated when they are eaten raw.

8 ounces (224 g) mung bean
sprouts or soybean sprouts
(see Stock—Basic Recipe)

5 cups (1250 ml) water

1 teaspoon (5 ml) salt

1½ tablespoons (22.5 ml) soy
sauce

1 tablespoon (15 ml) red tofu
"cheese"

¼ teaspoon (1.5 ml) sugar

Bring the bean sprouts and water to the boil. Remove from the heat. With a slotted spoon, transfer the bean sprouts to a small but deep ceramic bowl. Reserve the cooking liquid.

Add 1 teaspoon salt and 1½ tablespoons soy sauce to the cooking liquid.

In a separate small bowl, dissolve 1 tablespoon red tofu "cheese" in a little of the cooking liquid; pour this mixture over the bean sprouts. Add ¼ teaspoon sugar. Pour in enough of the cooking liquid to cover the bean sprouts. Cover tightly with plastic wrap and let stand a couple of hours or more; then chill if desired. To serve, remove the bean sprouts from the soaking liquid.

Sweet-and-Sour Relish Sticks

An array of green, white, and orange that adds color and refreshing tartness to meals, this relish brings together cucumber, icicle radish, and carrot. It takes a few hours to marinate and is best if left overnight in the refrigerator.

4 ounces (112 g) each: carrot, daikon or Chinese icicle radish, and cucumber (see Note)

½ tablespoon (7.5 ml) (heaping) salt

2 tablespoons (30 ml) sugar

2 tablespoons (30 ml) cider vinegar

Note: Buy a little over 4 ounces carrot and radish, and 5 ounces regular cucumber, in order to have 4 ounces after trimming. English (hothouse) and Oriental cucumber can be used whole, without peeling or seeding. Regular cucumber should be pared (leave a few strips of skin for texture and color) and seeded. Pare carrots and radish.

Cut all three vegetables into small sticks: ¼ × ¼ × 2 inches for carrot and radish, thicker for cucumber. Place in a bowl, sprinkle with salt, and mix-massage for a minute or two. Let stand at least 1½ hours, mixing occasionally. Rinse five times with cold water. Toss with sugar and vinegar till sugar dissolves. Let marinate at least 2 hours, stirring occasionally. For best results, refrigerate overnight, covered tightly with plastic wrap.

Succulent Black Mushrooms and Cashews

These are not what we usually think of as relishes, but they are perfect for a cold appetizer plate in combination with any of the preceding recipes. Make separate arrangements on a colorful platter or sectioned dish. If you add other delicacies—baby corn spears (canned or steamed fresh; see Chinese Ingredients) and slices of Crispy Fried "Duck" or Chinese "Ham" garnished with cilantro or watercress (see Chapter 5)—this makes not only a tantalizing first course for guests but also a complete cold supper with hot congee or rice. The raw cashews are sold in Chinese markets and health food stores. Though browned in oil and sprinkled with sugar while still hot, they are not oily or sweet; the light sugaring enhances the rich nut flavor. Of course, you can salt them instead, or simply use canned nuts, which require no preparation. Both cashews and mushrooms are good hot and will stay warm quite awhile after cooking. They do not have to be teamed up; you can serve them individually. The mushrooms make a fine hot side dish in any meal.

12 black (or shiitake) mushrooms, presoaked

1 tablespoon (15 ml) soy sauce

1 teaspoon (5 ml) sugar

1 teaspoon (5 ml) rice wine

1 cup (250 ml) raw cashew nuts

Vegetable oil to cover cashews

Sugar

To prepare mushrooms, arrange them upside down in a small heat proof bowl. In a separate bowl mix together the soy sauce, sugar, and rice wine. Sprinkle this mixture evenly over the mushrooms and toss. Place bowl on a rack in a steamer and steam 5 minutes.

To prepare cashews, place raw nuts in a small heavy pot and cover with vegetable oil. Place this over medium heat, and allow the nuts to brown slowly, stirring occasionally. When browned, remove the nuts with a slotted spoon. Drain on paper toweling, at the same time tossing with sugar (¼ teaspoon). Remove to a serving plate or small bowl.

2

Home Style Vegetables and Legumes

A Chinese friend of mine, on first arriving in the United States, saw an artichoke for the first time in her life and was so spellbound by this vegetable, its taste, and the whole process of eating it, that she sent off a shipment by air express for her father in Taiwan to enjoy.

Americans react with similar wonder at the fresh greens and odd-shaped vegetables that bedeck the shelves of Chinese markets and, increasingly, many supermarkets in the United States. Giant white radishes, baby and elongated eggplants, myriad varieties of leafy cabbage, fava beans in pulpy pods, foot-long (and longer) green beans, wedges of pale green winter melon . . . it's a varied and healthy bounty waiting to be enjoyed, and at very economical prices. These Oriental vegetables are intriguing to most everyone and baffling to many. After "What is that?" surely the most common question is, "How do you fix it?"

Think of the newcomers as just different versions of the standbys you're used to. Many of them are good raw with a salad dressing. Others readily adapt to cooking styles you normally use, and make refreshing substitutes in your old recipes. What could be simpler than simmering roots or melons, such as daikon or winter melon, in stews and soups? Steam or sauté the leafy vegetables, like Chinese cabbage or baby bok choy, and season them with flavorings of your fancy. Experiment a little.

When a vegetable first comes into season at the market, Chinese cooks, like cooks everywhere who appreciate fresh ingredients, begin to plan dishes for it. Restaurants will feel the need to make a somewhat elaborate presentation, combining it with other vegetables or meats. But home cooks know that the best way to enjoy a fresh vegetable is often the simplest—in a quick, unadorned stir-fry, or braised with soy sauce.

Of all the cooking styles or methods used in Chinese cooking, stir-frying is certainly the most basic and oft employed. Following is a quick rundown of the technique. No special utensils are required, not even a wok. In fact, if your stove is electric, you should use a skillet. The recipes in this chapter are mostly stir-fried, or stir-fried and braised. Since stir-frying involves speed and close timing, measurements are repeated in the instructions of each recipe so that you will not have to keep referring back to the ingredients list.

In case the star ingredient is unavailable or you can't venture beyond your neighborhood market for it, familiar substitutes are suggested that produce quite similar and equally delicious results. With a little practice you will quickly get the improvisational knack and should be able to woo and win over any vegetable in the market, Oriental or not, with tantalizing Chinese accents.

These recipes are fuss-free evidence that there is no more satisfying delicacy than a simple and well-prepared vegetable. Typical of home style cooking, they are basic dishes yet open to a great variety of elaboration. A good example of what you can do by way of adding other ingredients is Braised Chinese Cabbage with Delicacies. Serve these vegetable dishes on a small platter, family style, or divide into individual portions in the kitchen.

Unless otherwise stated, each recipe yields three generous portions, or four smaller.

On Stir-frying

There is nothing esoteric or even difficult about stir-frying unless you are an incorrigible slowpoke. Even then there is hope, if you simply follow the recipe directions and have everything within easy reach before you begin cooking.

The most important thing is to relax, adding a dash of salt here, a splash of soy sauce there. Don't worry too much about proportions, even though the recipes list exact amounts and timing. There's plenty of room for experimentation and your own intuition, if not sheer inspiration! With a little experience, you'll catch on and can stir-fry just about anything on your own, with easy confidence.

For proper and even cooking, try to keep a fairly uniform shape among the principal ingredients of a dish (see On Cutting Vegetables). Match sliced with sliced, diced with diced, etc. Usually when there are two or more main ingredients, they are used in more or less equal amounts, by volume. Incidentally, if you make sure that the ingredients are well drained and even patted dry after washing, much spattering and spraying of hot oil can be avoided. A wok with its high sides and deep basin affords some protection. With a skillet, you will find that a three-sided, collapsible aluminum shield saves considerable cleanup work. Some cooks—both here and in China —have a portable or sheltered, permanent stir-frying setup outdoors (hot plate, for example), which certainly helps keep the kitchen cleaner. Some of the best food I've ever had was cooked in a pan over a little charcoal brazier right outside the back door.

If your stove is gas, use either a skillet or a wok. In some cases a skillet is preferable, such as when browning foods like spring rolls.

On an electric stove, be sure to use a skillet. Your pan must be in direct contact with the heat, and an electric burner cannot reach up the sides of a wok as gas flame can. For these recipes a 10- or 11-inch frying pan is fine. An 11-inch size is preferable with leafy vegetables, such as Chinese cabbage or garland chrysanthemum; but these cook down quickly, so you can manage with a 10-inch. I often use an 11-inch nonstick Creuset skillet. Cook on your large, 7-inch electric burner. A smaller one is all right if you have no choice, but settings will probably have to be one above those specified—high for medium-high, etc.—coupled sometimes with longer cooking, as when the recipe requires high heat.

Preheating the pan over high heat—before adding the oil—is said to reduce sticking of foods to the pan. I haven't noticed that it makes much difference, but I do it anyway to be sure of having a completely hot pan (and before the oil gets overheated). When you're stir-frying a couple of dishes in succession, preheating will dry the pan from a quick washing after the first dish.

Many Chinese chefs favor peanut oil, which is flavorless yet expensive. Home cooks find corn oil or good grades of vegetable (salad) oil just as satisfactory. When the pan (skillet or wok) is hot, put in the oil and wait another minute or so, swirling it around to coat the sides, until it is well heated. Then add the ingredients.

On an electric stove, it is usually necessary to lower the heat to medium-high just before or after adding the first ingredient. When using a wok, it will probably not be necessary to lower the flame: do all the stir-frying over high. When braising (adding liquids after stir-frying or browning), leave the heat at medium-high, or lower it to medium.

Upon tossing the first vegetables into the pan, do not be alarmed at the immediate hissing, sizzling, and crackling. This is unnerving, but natural, for the oil is hot. Likewise, liquids such as soy sauce, water, and wine will instantly boil and send up steam. These effects are somewhat intimidating to the un-initiated, those used to slower, gentler methods of cooking. But after the first intrepid attempts, you will expect it and discover the rewards—wonderful, juicy textures.

On the other hand, if you are too miserly with your fire, you will reap limp, raw, or grease-sodden results; if you are too slow or timid with your hand, the results may be burned. Hot oil seals in juices while sealing *out* oil. The quick cooking retains textures. And with the subsequent addition of a little liquid, such as soy sauce and water, which has a quick steaming (or braising) and cleansing effect, the final result is not only flavor-packed but non-oily.

Stir-frying is usually done with speed, to keep the food in frequent contact with the hot pan and to avoid burning. In a wok, it is accomplished by scooping and tossing with a Chinese spatula, which is like a pancake turner with sides, and from which the foods fall naturally. In a skillet, of course, such a method is messy as well as inappropriate. So, instead, try distributing ingredients back and forth with a regular pancake turner *held upside down*. This sounds odd, but give it a try.

Even if liquids and seasonings (soy sauce, salt, sugar, wine, water) are to be added in quick succession, do not mix them together beforehand to be poured in all at once. If you like, measure them out ahead, but introduce each separately, possibly even with a few turns of the spatula, before adding the next. They are better absorbed this way; the temperature is kept at a reasonably constant level; and it is the most natural, spontaneous, and accurate way of cooking. It allows you to respond to the needs of the moment and your own developed instinct for the right amount of seasoning under the conditions. (When testing the mixture for salt, by the way, taste the *liquid* in the pan, not the solid food. And you will note that a little sugar is added in most of these recipes, not so much to sweeten as to refine or heighten the flavor—replacing monosodium glutamate. Sugar is usually added toward the end, rather than earlier, to avoid burning.) The most efficient way is to measure out these additions just as you add them to the pan. Since spooning from a dish is much neater and quicker than pouring into a spoon from a bottle or container, store your seasonings in small bowls or jars.

Each recipe allows you sufficient time to measure out and add the various seasonings—granted, of course, that they are in the immediate vicinity. For example, if a recipe says, "Add 2 tablespoons soy sauce, ¼ teaspoon salt, and ½ teaspoon sugar; stir-fry 1 minute," you should spoon soy sauce over the top, then add the salt, then the sugar (perhaps stirring once or twice after each), *then* stir-fry for a minute.

When adding wine (Chinese rice wine or Japanese saké), the directions usually say, "Swirl wine around the side of the pan." This method is in fact more appropriate to a wok, where the wine is easily introduced around the side, at or just above food level. Upon contact with the hot metal, the wine immediately steams up, infusing the food with its vaporous bouquet. In a skillet, just add wine quickly around the pan in a wide circular motion. Very small portions are required to accomplish this subtle method of flavoring and imparting aroma.

Sometimes the pan juices are thickened with cornstarch just before removing from the heat. To prepare the cornstarch, dissolve it in cold water in a small bowl, mixing with your fingers. Do *not* pour the mixture over the food. Rather, first stir a little of it into the liquid at one side of the pan; then give everything a few turns to combine well. Although the proportions given here are as accurate as foreseeable, to avoid overthickening always add just a little of the mixture at a time (first half, then as much of the remainder as necessary). Usually the result should have the consistency of a light gravy.

Often a final step, either before or after removing the pan from the heat, is to add a little sesame oil. Dispensed in very small quantities, this provides a fine, appetizing aroma and enhances flavors. Dribble a few drops over the top or stir it in. Note that only the amber colored kind processed from roasted sesame seeds is to be used—and *not* overused, for it is very rich and strong in flavor.

Braised Chinese Cabbage with Delicacies

I could happily consume this whole dish all by myself without anything else. Even if you leave out the delicacies, the Chinese cabbage has a delicious savor, almost as if it had been cooked with meat. For variety, you can add baby corn spears, chestnuts, ginkgo nuts, or lily buds (fresh ones are usually not available here, but you can use dried ones). See Chinese Ingredients for more information on all these. This is a braised dish that you can start ahead of time, then do a final heating just before serving.

1¼ pounds (562 g) Chinese cabbage (see Note)

4 ounces (112 g) baby corn spears; or ½ cup (125 ml) precooked ginkgo nuts; or ½ cup (125 ml) cooked chestnuts; or ¼ cup (60 ml) (loose) dried lily buds, presoaked (optional)

3 tablespoons (45 ml) vegetable oil

1 tablespoon (15 ml) water (if needed)

1 tablespoon (15 ml) (generous) soy sauce

⅛ teaspoon (.5 ml) salt

¾ teaspoon (4 ml) sugar

Note: Buy a 1½ pound head of cabbage in order to have 1¼ pounds after trimming.

Shred the cabbage by cutting crosswise into thin strips.

To prepare baby corn spears, fresh or canned, slice lengthwise thinly, about three slices per spear. Yield is about 1 cup, loose. To prepare fresh ginkgo nuts, see Chinese Ingredients; canned nuts need only to be drained and rinsed. To prepare chestnuts, see Chestnut "Chicken," Chapter 5. To prepare dried lily buds, squeeze dry and nip off any hard stems.

Heat a wok or large (11-inch) skillet over high; add 3 tablespoons oil and bring it to the smoking point before putting in the cabbage—the stem part first, then frilly; stir-fry 2 minutes. Reduce heat to medium-high. If the pan is dry, stir in 1 tablespoon water, but most cabbage gives off enough juice itself so this should not be necessary. Add baby corn spears if using them. Add 1 generous tablespoon soy sauce and ⅛ teaspoon salt. (If you are making this ahead, cover now and turn off the heat. Before serving, add ginkgo nuts, chestnuts, or lily buds; bring to the boil, add ¾ teaspoon sugar, and continue to stir-fry until the cabbage is very tender, then serve.) Cover and cook, stirring occasionally, until the cabbage is very tender—about 6 minutes. Add ginkgo nuts, chestnuts, or lily buds. Return heat to high, sprinkle with ¾ teaspoon sugar, and stir-fry another minute or two.

Garland Chrysanthemum or Spinach with Wine and Soy Sauce

You can easily spot a resemblance to the leaves of the familiar garden flower, but these are feathery and finer. Some Chinese groceries occasionally have the leafy bunches or stems in season (spring and fall). Japanese markets are sure to have them—under the name *shungiku*—for this is a popular ingredient in sukiyaki, with a taste that is pleasantly pungent. Spinach takes on new life, too, when prepared in this manner, invested with an intoxicating bouquet of rice wine and soy sauce. I suggest this simple dish when you're planning others that require extra time, such as Boiled Pot-stickers, Open-face Steamed Dumplings *(Shao Mai),* or the viands in Chapter 5.

10 ounces (281 g) garland chrysanthemum greens or spinach (see Note)

2 tablespoons (30 ml) vegetable oil

½ teaspoon (3 ml) sugar

1 teaspoon (5 ml) rice wine

1 tablespoon (15 ml) soy sauce

Note: Buy 11 ounces garland chrysanthemum greens or spinach (14 ounces garland chrysanthemum if stems are thick) in order to have 10 ounces after trimming.

When using spinach, chop it crosswise, including stems (and the pungent root ends if desired), at roughly 1½-inch intervals. Garland chrysanthemum can be chopped in the same way if the stems are not thick; if stems are over ⅓ inch thick, strip off the leaves and use them whole, without stems. (Save the thicker stems for munching; these would not cook through if included with the leaves.)

Heat a wok or 11-inch skillet over high. Add the oil; when very hot, put in the vegetable, reduce heat to medium-high or medium, and stir-fry 1 minute until wilted. Sprinkle on ½ teaspoon sugar; then 1 teaspoon rice wine and 1 tablespoon soy sauce; stir-fry 30 seconds. Remove from the heat immediately to avoid overcooking.

Fresh and Black Mushrooms with Delicacies

Two kinds of mushrooms are simmered with an extra ingredient of your choice—crunchy tree ear, aromatic green pepper, luscious ginkgo nuts, or tender bean curd sticks. This is very tasty with light-flavored and filling foods such as potato, squash, or noodles. It is equally welcome as a complement to hot dishes like Hot Pepper Tofu with "Pork."

12 black (or shiitake)
  mushrooms, presoaked

12 large fresh mushrooms

4 tree ears, presoaked; 1 cup
  (250 ml) green pepper; or
  ⅓ cup (85 ml) ginkgo nuts;
  or 1 bean curd stick
  (20-inch [500mm]),
  presoaked

2 tablespoons (30 ml)
  vegetable oil

⅓ cup (85 ml) soaking liquid
  from black mushrooms

1 tablespoon (15 ml) soy sauce

Pinch salt

½ teaspoon (3 ml) (scant) sugar

1 teaspoon (5 ml) cornstarch
  dissolved in 2 teaspoons (10
  ml) water (with ginkgo nuts
  or bean curd stick only)

½ teaspoon (3 ml) sesame oil

Steam fresh mushrooms in a vegetable basket three minutes; rinse with cold water.

Tear the presoaked tree ears into small pieces, yielding 1 cup, loose. If using green pepper, cut it into 1-inch squares. If using ginkgo nuts or bean curd sticks, see Chinese Ingredients for prepatory steps. Cut softened bean curd stick into 1-inch lengths.

Heat a pan over high. Add 2 tablespoons oil. When the oil is hot, reduce heat to medium-high. Add in succession—stirring briefly after each addition—the green pepper, black mushrooms, fresh mushrooms, and tree ear (or ginkgo nuts or bean curd sticks). Add ⅓ cup mushroom liquid, 1 tablespoon soy sauce, and a pinch of salt (omit salt with ginkgo nuts). Cook at a fast simmer, stirring frequently, until only 2 or 3 tablespoons liquid remains—2 minutes or so. Sprinkle on a scant ½ teaspoon sugar; if using ginkgo nuts or bean curd sticks, stir in cornstarch mixture. Stir-fry until the pan is nearly dry or the sauce is thickened—less than a minute. Top with ½ teaspoon sesame oil.

Braised Long or Green Beans with Black Mushrooms

Long beans, light or dark green, are a foot or more in length.

If you like your green beans tender yet still with good, juicy, and not watery character, try this quick, simple dish—with or without black mushrooms (see Variation). Fresh green (string) beans are superb fixed this way, as are dark or light long beans. These are thinner than string beans and a foot or more in length.

¾ pound (340 g) long beans or green beans

7–8 black (or shiitake) mushrooms, presoaked

3 tablespoons (45 ml) vegetable oil

½–¾ cup (125–180 ml) soaking liquid from black mushrooms

½ (scant) teaspoon salt

1½ teaspoons (8 ml) soy sauce

½ teaspoon (3 ml) (scant) sugar

Pat beans dry after washing (to reduce spitting oil) and cut into 1½-inch lengths.

Cut black mushrooms into ¼-inch strips.

Put 3 tablespoons oil into a preheated (high heat) pan. When the oil is hot, put in the beans, reduce heat to medium-high, and stir-fry 1½ minutes. Stir in black mushrooms. Add ½ cup water if you are using green beans; ¾ cup if you are using long beans more than ¼ inch thick. Sprinkle on a scant ½ teaspoon salt and 1½ teaspoons soy sauce. Reduce heat to medium, cover, and cook, stirring frequently, until the beans are tender but still with texture (6 to 7 minutes; 8 to 10 if long beans are thick). Stir in a scant ½ teaspoon sugar, and serve.

Variation: Omit black mushrooms and soy sauce. Use 1 pound beans and ¾ teaspoon salt. Proceed as above.

Luscious Fava or Lima Beans with Bamboo Shoot

Fava beans, well-liked in the Middle East and some European countries, come in bright green pods 5 to 6 inches long. After shucking and skinning, the beans are also bright green, resembling limas in shape.

Fresh fava beans (also called broad or horse beans; in China one of their early names was Buddha's beans) come well-padded in big green pods. Watch for them from spring through fall at Chinese and Italian groceries. Feel the pods to make sure you are getting several fair-sized legumes, for sometimes they contain but a couple of miniature specimens. Shucking and skinning the beans takes some time but is well worth it: they are a splendid emerald green, rich-tasting and smooth-textured. Persons prone to laziness might balk at the skinning, since these jackets are actually edible. But they are bitter and a bit tough, so the dish is better off without them. With bamboo shoot, this is a mixture of gold and green, crunchy and soft.

1½ cups (375 ml) fresh, skinned fava beans; or 7½ ounces frozen lima beans (see Note)

2 tablespoons (30 ml) vegetable oil

½ cup (125 ml) bamboo shoot, sliced

⅓ cup (85 ml) water

¼ teaspoon (1.5 ml) salt

½ teaspoon (3 ml) sugar

½ teaspoon (3 ml) sesame oil (optional)

Note: You need about 3 cups shucked, *un*skinned fava beans to yield 1½ cups after skinning. To skin, immerse the shucked beans in a pot of boiling water for 1 minute; drain, rinse under cold water, and with the help of a knife remove the skins. Frozen limas need only to be defrosted.

Heat 2 tablespoons oil in a preheated pan over high; put in the beans, reduce heat to medium, and stir-fry 1 minute. Add ½ cup sliced bamboo shoot and ⅓ cup water (½ to ⅔ cup with large fava beans). Cover and cook 5 or 6 minutes (8 to 10 minutes with large favas), stirring occasionally. Add ¼ teaspoon salt and ½ teaspoon sugar; increase heat to high and stir-fry until the pan is nearly dry—less than a minute. Add ½ teaspoon sesame oil if desired, and serve.

Fava or Lima Beans in Mustard Sauce

Fava beans are found in Middle Eastern and some European cookery but are largely ignored here, which is a pity, for they have a bright flavor and dense, silken texture. Chinese also use them to make an excellent bean sauce, superior to the soybean-based types. A popular snacking dish is the sprouted dried beans, cooked in salted water served at room temperature. This recipe is an equally pleasing side dish or hot vegetable. Preparing limas couldn't be easier. It takes a bit of extra trouble to ready the favas, but the result is definitely worth it. See preceding recipe for more information. The mustard taste in this recipe will be hotter if you use dry rather than Dijon.

2 cups (500 ml) fresh, skinned fava beans; or 10 ounces (281 g) frozen baby limas (see Note 1)

2 tablespoons (30 ml) soy sauce

1 teaspoon (5 ml) premixed dry mustard or Dijon (see Note 2)

2 teaspoons (10 ml) sesame oil

Note 1: You will need 5 to 6 cups raw, *un*skinned fava beans to yield 2 cups after cooking and skinning. To do this, steam them in a vegetable basket until *very* tender, then pinch them out of their jackets. Baby limas do not need defrosting. Simply steam them until tender (15 minutes).

Note 2: To prepare dry mustard, see Note in Mustard-hot Celery Relish, Chapter 1. For this recipe, 2 teaspoons powder mixed with 1 teaspoon cold water is about right.

Toss steamed beans with remaining ingredients and serve hot or at room temperature.

Hashed Icicle Radish or Turnip

This long pole of a white root is sold in supermarkets under its Japanese appellation, daikon or dycone. Of course it is good raw, but when cooked it resembles the turnip and may be even milder and juicier. The Chinese icicle radish (also called Chinese radish) is also white-skinned but bulkier. It is available in Chinese groceries. (See page 14 for illustrations.) On paper this recipe may sound rather plain, but if you try it with good, sweet, and *juicy* turnips or radish, you may find your impression changing to "scrumptious." Serve it when you want a crunchy vegetable dish with an assertive flavor, as with Tender Greens and Deep-fried Tofu. During the last half of stir-frying, please note that it is important to alternate stir-frying with firm pressing or mashing in order to promote complete, quick cooking.

1 pound (450 g) firm daikon or Chinese icicle radish, or turnips (see Note)

2½ tablespoons (37.5 ml) vegetable oil

1 tablespoon (15 ml) soy sauce

Pinch (large) sugar

2 teaspoons (10 ml) green onion, minced

⅛ teaspoon (.5 ml) (generous) salt

Note: Purchase a little over 1 pound vegetable in order to have 1 pound after skinning. Pare.

Shred radish very thinly, using a food processor or the coarse side of a grater. (Lacking these, use a potato peeler.) Yield should be 4 cups, loosely packed.

Heat a pan over high; add 2½ tablespoons oil. When oil is hot, put in the vegetable and stir-fry 2 minutes; turn heat to medium-high and continue to stir-fry 1½ minutes, pressing frequently and firmly with spatula or pancake turner. Sprinkle on 1 tablespoon soy sauce, a large pinch of sugar, 2 teaspoons minced green onion, and a generous ⅛ teaspoon salt; mix and mash another minute or so.

Baby Corn Spears with Mushrooms and Tree Ear or Green Pepper

Baby corn spears are wonderfully sweet and delicious when fresh, but just try to find a produce market that carries them! It is possible to use the canned product, sold in Chinese markets and in the gourmet sections of supermarkets. But a better alternative is to cut fresh corn right off the cob. Of course, the corn will be in kernels this way, not tiny spears (see Variation). Try to find ears with small, firm, light-colored kernels that pop out at you when pressed.

1 cup (250 ml) fresh or canned young corn spears, whole (see Note)

3–4 tree ears, presoaked; or 1 cup green pepper (¾-inch squares [19 mm])

10 black (or shiitake) mushrooms, presoaked and sliced; or 1 cup (250 ml) sliced fresh mushroom (¼ inch [7 mm]) if using fresh corn spears

2½ tablespoons (37.5 ml) vegetable oil

1½ tablespoons (22.5 ml) soy sauce

⅓ cup (85 ml) soaking liquid from black mushrooms

½ teaspoon (3 ml) sugar

½ teaspoon (3 ml) cornstarch dissolved in 2 teaspoons (10 ml) water

¼ teaspoon (1.5 ml) sesame oil

Note: If using canned "baby corn on the cob," make sure it contains no flavorings such as vinegar; if salt has been added, adjust soy sauce accordingly.

Slice corn spears lengthwise thinly, about three slices per spear, to yield about a cup.

Tear the presoaked tree ears into small pieces, discarding the tough stems. Yield is about ¾ to 1 cup, loose.

When using fresh mushrooms, use soaking liquid from several black mushrooms and save the black mushrooms for another recipe.

Heat a pan over high; add 2½ tablespoons oil. When oil is hot, turn heat to medium-high and put in the baby corn spears; stir-fry 2 minutes. Add the mushrooms and stir-fry 30 seconds. Add tree ear or green pepper; stir-fry 30 seconds.

Add 1½ tablespoons soy sauce, then ⅓ cup mushroom liquid and ½ teaspoon sugar. Cook several minutes, stirring frequently, until only 2 to 3 tablespoons liquid remain in the pan. Stir in the cornstarch mixture; when thickened slightly, remove from the burner and mix in just a little sesame oil —¼ teaspoon.

Variation: Purchase about four ears fresh corn. Hold cob vertically and cut downward to slice off the kernels, to yield 1½ cups.

Use 1 heaping cup fresh mushrooms sliced ¼ inch thick.

Except for oil, other ingredients are same as above but are added in different order: Heat 3 tablespoons oil over high. When oil is hot, reduce heat to medium-high. Add in succession—stirring briefly after each addition—tree ear or green pepper, mushrooms, and corn. Then proceed as above, adding soy sauce, etc.

Curried Broccoli Stems or Asparagus

Chinese broccoli, deep green in color, has slender stems with a few large leaves and sometimes tiny yellow or white flowers.

Spiced up with a little curry, or seasoned just with soy, this is a vegetable dish with invigorating flavor. Besides the stem of either Chinese or American broccoli, you can use fresh asparagus. Chinese broccoli resembles a small version of collard greens in appearance. For this recipe it is preferable to buy the type that is mostly stem, ¼ to ½ inch in diameter (thicker stems may require peeling), with a few large, dark green leaves near the top. Sometimes there are little yellow or white flowers as well, but don't let this guide you, for several other vegetables sport a similar decoration. It's not likely you'll want to gather enough American broccoli to make a whole recipe (you'll need six to nine stems), but it's possible to mix it with Chinese broccoli or asparagus. Don't ever throw away these delicious stems.

When using curry powder, try to find a Madras mixture. Many Chinese markets sell good brands of Indian curry.

¾ pound (340 g) broccoli
stems (Chinese or
American), or fresh
asparagus (see Note)

2½ tablespoons (37.5 ml)
vegetable oil

1½ teaspoons (8 ml) curry
powder (optional)

1 tablespoon (15 ml) soy
sauce

¼ cup (60 ml) water

1½ teaspoons (8 ml) rice wine

½ teaspoon (3 ml) sesame oil
(omit this if using curry
powder)

Note: Purchase about 1¼ pounds Chinese broccoli
in order to have ¾ pound after trimming. Or buy
six to nine large stems American broccoli.

To prepare Chinese broccoli, strip off leaves and use
stems only (without flowers, which will scorch unless
included toward the end of frying). Slice diagonally
¼ inch thick and 1½ inches long.

To prepare American broccoli stems, break off the
flowerets and save for another recipe. Pare the stems
and cut into thin strips (¼ × ¼ × 1½ inches).

To prepare asparagus, discard tough, fibrous base
part. If very thin (¼-inch diameter), cut into 1¼-
inch lengths. If thicker, slice diagonally ¼ inch
thick and 1½ inches long.

Heat a pan over high; add 2½ tablespoons oil.
When oil is hot, put in the vegetable, reduce heat to
medium-high, and stir-fry about 5 minutes for asparagus, 7 minutes for broccoli. Add optional 1½ teaspoons curry powder, 1 tablespoon soy sauce, then
¼ cup water; stir-fry another minute. Swirl 1½
teaspoons rice wine around the edge of the pan, stir
to mix, and remove from the heat. Sprinkle ½ teaspoon sesame oil over the top (omit this if using
curry).

Juicy Winter Melon or Cucumber

Winter melon is so mammoth that it is usually sold
by the slice or wedge, often cut to your require-
ments. It usually shows up in Chinese and Japanese
markets in the early fall. The flesh is snow white and
bland, a popular soup item (see Broth with Winter
Melon, Chapter 7). In soups and stews it might be
simmered as long as ten hours, and the result is
thought to be almost as beneficial as some slow-
cooked medicinal brews in cleansing and purifying

the system (for smokers, etc.). At banquets the seeded but unskinned melon is sometimes used as the soup bowl itself, with top removed and decorative motifs cut into the rind. The whole is then steamed with stock and tasty ingredients in the cavity. In this recipe it is braised, with optional black mushrooms and tree ear (see Variation). You may be surprised at how juicy cucumber tastes this way, too.

1¼ pounds (562 g) winter melon or cucumber (see Note)

2 tablespoons (30 ml) vegetable oil

½ cup (125 ml) water

1½ tablespoons (22.5 ml) soy sauce

½ teaspoon (3 ml) (scant) sugar

½ teaspoon (3 ml) sesame oil (optional)

Note: Purchase about 2 pounds winter melon or cucumber in order to have 1¼ pounds after skinning and seeding.

Cut winter melon into ½-inch-thick slices. Cut seeded cucumber lengthwise into inch-wide strips. Put in a pot with water to cover, and cook over medium heat, covered, until just tender (about 10 minutes). Drain well in a colander and pat dry on paper towels.

Heat a skillet over high; add 2 tablespoons oil. When oil is very hot, put in the melon or cucumber; brown it lightly on one side, then turn and brown on the other side, reducing the heat to medium-high as necessary to avoid scorching. When lightly browned, remove strips to a chopping board and cut into bite-sized pieces. Return these to the pan with ½ cup water and 1½ tablespoons soy sauce. Bring to a simmer, reduce heat to medium, cover and cook, stirring once or twice, until the melon is very soft and only a little liquid remains in the pan—about 3 minutes. Turn heat to high; sprinkle on a scant ½ teaspoon sugar and ½ teaspoon sesame oil; stir to mix, and remove from the heat.

Variation: Just before adding liquids, stir in five black (or shiitake) mushrooms, presoaked and sliced, and ½ cup tree ear, presoaked and torn into small pieces. Instead of water, use soaking liquid from black mushrooms.

Taro, Yuca Root, Mountain Yam, or Potato Temptation

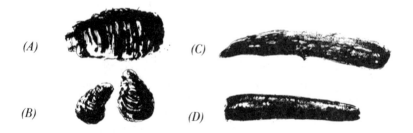

(A)

(B)

(C)

(D)

Oriental tubers offer textural and flavorful alternatives to the familiar potato. Taro (A) is a bulky, dark-skinned root 6 inches or more in length. Baby taro (B) is only 2½ to 3 inches long. Yuca (C), also called cassava and mountain yam, is long and yamlike with woody skin. Naga imo (D) is also long but with potato-colored skin.

You have several choices here, each quite different in flavor and texture. It is worth seeking them all out if you are a tuber lover. The trusty old potato takes very well to this recipe, cubed and temptingly flavored with soy and green onion.

The taro is a big, dark skinned, burly root. If you have tried the taro fritters at dim sum teahouses, you know that it is rich and delicious. There is a baby taro (*hsiao yu tou* in Chinese, *sato imo* in Japanese) that is preferable, but of course more trouble to pare. Street vendors in China cook it in a syrup to make a rib-sticking, warming, cold-weather sweet. This tuber is also used to make wrappers for steamed pot-stickers.

Yuca root (also called cassava) is shaped like a giant yam, with woody, barklike skin. It has an intriguing, wild sweetness and dense chewiness.

In Japanese markets you are apt to see a similarly long and thick root, but more regular in shape with white, potato-colored skin, called *naga imo.* White inside, it has a natural creaminess. Chinese may call both this and yuca by the term *shan yao,* which means mountain yam or potato.

You can be busy with one or two other entrees while this is cooking, as it requires minimal watching. Potato fans will know what to serve it with—almost anything, except rice, of course. This recipe provides a couple of extra portions, enough for five or six people, and it can be reheated.

1½ pounds (675 g) taro, *yuca root, naga imo,* or potatoes

3½ tablespoons (52.5 ml) vegetable oil

1–2 cups (250–500 ml) water

1½ tablespoons (22.5 ml) soy sauce

½ teaspoon (3 ml) salt

1 tablespoon (15 ml) green onion, minced

1½ teaspoons (8 ml) sugar

Peel your choice of tuber (potato can be left unpeeled if desired, but scrub well). Dice into ½-inch cubes. Heat an 11-inch skillet over high (a 10-inch skillet can be used but will be crowded). Put in 3½ tablespoons oil. When oil is hot, reduce heat to medium-high, put in the vegetable, and stir-fry 2 minutes. Add 1 cup water with potato or *naga imo;* 2 cups for taro or yuca. Cover, reduce heat to medium, and cook without uncovering until tender—about 15 minutes (25 to 30 minutes for taro or yuca, stirring twice). Add 1½ tablespoons soy sauce, ½ teaspoon salt, 1 tablespoon minced green onion, and 1½ teaspoons sugar (1 teaspoon or none for yuca). Turn heat to high and stir-fry until well mixed and remaining liquid is reduced to a saucelike consistency.

Variation, without soy sauce: Stir-fry the vegetable 2 minutes as above, then sprinkle on 2 tablespoons minced green onion and 1 teaspoon salt. Pour in 1 cup water with potato or *naga imo;* 2 cups with taro or yuca. Cover, reduce heat to medium, and cook 15 minutes without uncovering (25 to 30 minutes for taro or yuca, stirring twice). Turn heat to high and stir-fry 1 minute until any remaining liquid in the pan is thickened.

Amaranth or Spinach with Garlic

Amaranth comes in stems or bunches, abundantly filled out with soft, dark green leaves that are often purple-red on the border or underleaf. Its appearance in Chinese markets is sporadic; early summer and fall are perhaps the most predictable times. The flavor is rich, even potent, and the consistency like spinach when cooked—here with light garlic overtones.

10 ounces (281 g) amaranth or spinach (see Note)

1–2 cloves garlic

2 tablespoons (30 ml) vegetable oil

1½ teaspoons (8 ml) rice wine

¼ cup (60 ml) water

¼ teaspoon (1.5 ml) salt

Note: Buy 11 ounces vegetable (if amaranth stems are thick, buy 12 ounces) in order to have 10 ounces after trimming. Discard thicker amaranth stems (over ⅛ inch). Spinach stems, both thick and thin, should be included. Chop the vegetable crosswise at 1½-inch intervals (as well as root ends if desired).

Bruise the garlic.

Heat a wok or 11-inch skillet over high; add 2 tablespoons oil. When oil is hot, put in the crushed garlic. Add the vegetable, reduce heat to medium-high, and stir-fry 1 minute or until it wilts. Add 1½ teaspoons wine and ¼ cup water. Cover, reduce heat to medium, and cook 2 minutes or until tender, stirring once or twice. Stir in ¼ teaspoon salt and remove from the heat. Before serving, remove the garlic cloves.

Young Luffa Gourd with Gingerroot

This vegetable takes top award for marvelous shapes. Tapering to pointed ends, it has ribbed, dark green, rough skin and an almost hexagonal shape (see page 147 for illustration). Its other English names—pleated squash and Chinese okra—don't quite hit the mark, but no description of appearance can really do it justice. To some people it looks like a species of cactus. With its tasty, lush flesh, it is hard to believe there is any connection with those dried scrubbing loofahs, which are the skeletons of this gourd.

A traditional sun-dried preparation is possible in this recipe (see Variation) but can prove inconvenient. Instead, a quick salt curing produces excellent results. This dish can be made ahead and served at room temperature, or steamed just before mealtime for a hot vegetable dish. It is an attractive light green in color, and the tenderness as well as the ginger-vinegar seasoning recommend it for serving with "meaty" dishes or when you want something just a bit tart.

1 pound (450 g) luffa gourd (see Note)

1 teaspoon (5 ml) salt

1½ tablespoons (22.5 ml) vegetable oil

½–1 teaspoon (3–5 ml) cider vinegar or Chinese dark vinegar, to taste

¼ teaspoon (1.5 ml) sugar

¼ teaspoon (1.5 ml) (packed, generous) gingerroot, minced or grated

½ teaspoon (3 ml) sesame oil

Note: In order to have 1 pound luffa after skinning, you will need to purchase about 2 pounds.

Skin the luffa, quarter lengthwise, then cut crosswise at ¼-inch intervals. Place in a medium-sized bowl and mix-massage with 1 teaspoon salt. Let stand 1½ hours, mixing now and then. Rinse three or four times. Squeeze firmly to remove liquid. Place in a small heatproof bowl and toss with 1½ tablespoons vegetable oil. Place on a rack in a steamer and steam 5 minutes. After steaming, stir in remaining ingredients and serve hot or at room temperature.

Variation: Skin and quarter the luffa. Massage with 1 teaspoon salt for a couple of minutes. Place in an open basket or on a rack (so that it does not sit in its juices) and set out in the sun for one day to dry partially. Turn the strips two or three times during this period. Then proceed as above, slicing and steaming.

Chinese Style Refried Beans

This is a thick, rich concoction, with an enticing hint of sesame and garlic. Use either garlic cloves or Tientsin preserved cabbage, which adds a bit of vegetable "crunch" (see Chinese Ingredients). The taste will vary, of course, with the bean you use. If you want to try dried fava beans, you can find them in Chinese markets, but I prefer dried lima, pinto, or kidneys for this. For variety you can also include diced tomato. A humble yet highly enjoyable meal might feature this with rice, one or two relishes (try Sweet-and-Sour Chinese Cabbage Relish), and Spicy Three Shreds Soup.

½ pound (225 g) dry beans—lima, pinto, kidney, or fava

4 ounces (112 g) fresh or canned tomato (1 small) (optional)

1 tablespoon (15 ml) (packed) Tientsin preserved cabbage; or 2 cloves garlic

4 tablespoons (60 ml) vegetable oil

2 tablespoons (30 ml) soy sauce

1 cup (250 ml) water

½ teaspoon (3 ml) sugar

2 teaspoons (10 ml) sesame oil

Soak the dry beans overnight (24 hours for favas, which then need to be skinned), then rinse several times. Steam in a vegetable basket or cook in water until tender (this could take 1 to 1½ hours). You should have 3 cups cooked beans.

Dice the optional tomato to yield ½ cup.

Mince the Tientsin preserved cabbage, or bruise two cloves garlic.

Heat a pan over high; add 4 tablespoons oil. If using garlic, stir-fry it while the oil is heating; when it starts to brown, remove and discard. Put in the beans, turn flame to low, and stir-fry 30 seconds. Then begin to press the beans firmly until they are mashed (about 2 minutes), scraping the pan occasionally to prevent burning. Stir in optional tomato. Add 2 tablespoons soy sauce (and a dash or two more when using garlic), 1 cup water, ½ teaspoon sugar, and 1 tablespoon (packed) Tientsin preserved cabbage. Combine thoroughly; cover, turn heat to medium-high, and cook 4 minutes without uncovering. Stir in 2 teaspoons sesame oil, turn heat to high, and continue stirring until the consistency is thick (2 minutes).

Chinese Pumpkin or Yellow Squash with Pine Nuts

With toasted pine nuts, this dish is richly epicurean. But even unadorned, the various golden squashes are delicious, and this is a quick way to cook them. Chinese pumpkin *(nan kua)* is called *kabocha* or "Japanese pumpkin" in Japanese groceries, and I have seen it called Hokkaido pumpkin in health food stores. It is round like a pumpkin but more squat, and usually small with green or green-and-yellow skin. Sometimes you can buy a half, which is about the right size for this recipe.

Good sources for pine nuts include natural food stores, nut shops, and Italian food shops. They are often stored in a large jar and sold by the ounce. Ask for a sample taste, as some are devoid of flavor.

1 pound (450 g) Chinese pumpkin or yellow squash (banana, acorn, butternut)

4 tablespoons (60 ml) vegetable oil

⅓–½ cup (85–125 ml) water

½ teaspoon (3 ml) salt

1 teaspoon (5 ml) sugar

¼ cup (60 ml) toasted pine nuts (optional)

½ teaspoon (3 ml) sesame oil

After peeling, julienne the squash or pumpkin—rather thickly for soft varieties such as banana, more finely (⅛ inch) for acorn, butternut, and Chinese pumpkin. Yield is a little over 4 cups.

Heat a pan over high; add 4 tablespoons oil; when oil is hot, put in the squash or pumpkin. Reduce heat to medium-high and stir-fry 3 to 4 minutes. Add ⅓ cup water (½ cup for acorn or butternut), ½ teaspoon salt, and 1 teaspoon sugar. Turn heat to medium, cover, and cook until tender, stirring occasionally—3 to 4 minutes for Chinese pumpkin and banana squash, longer for acorn or butternut (perhaps 10 minutes). A minute or so before removing from the heat, stir in the pine nuts. Before serving, add ½ teaspoon sesame oil.

Spicy Green Beans

Deep-frying seals in the beans' juiciness. Then they are quickly sautéed with the spicy ingredients, including Szechuan pickle, which gives an unusually crunchy character to the dish.

¾ pound (340 g) green beans (see Note)

Vegetable oil for deep-frying

1½ tablespoons (22.5 ml) vegetable oil

1 teaspoon (5 ml) (heaping) each, minced: garlic and gingerroot

2½ tablespoons (37.5 ml) (packed) Szechuan pickle, minced (optional)

1 teaspoon (5 ml) soy sauce

1 tablespoon (15 ml) water

1 teaspoon (5 ml) rice wine

Pinch salt (omit this if using Szechuan pickle)

1 teaspoon (5 ml) cornstarch dissolved in 2½ tablespoons (37.5 ml) cold water

Note: Buy a little over ¾ pound beans in order to have ¾ pound after trimming. Wash, string, and trim beans. Pat with cloth or paper toweling to dry thoroughly. Cut beans into approximately 2½-inch lengths.

Heat oil for deep-frying. After it is hot, keep heat around medium-high or medium. Deep-fry the beans (in two or three batches if your pot is small) for 2 to 3 minutes or until skin begins to pucker and turn white in spots. Remove with a slotted spoon and drain on paper toweling.

In a preheated pan over medium, put 1½ tablespoons vegetable oil. When oil is hot, put in garlic, gingerroot, and Szechuan pickle; stir-fry 15 seconds till aroma rises. Add beans and stir just to mix (15 to 30 seconds). Add a large pinch of salt if not using Szechuan pickle; add 1 teaspoon soy sauce, 1 tablespoon water, and 1 teaspoon rice wine; pour cornstarch mixture over the top and stir-fry until beans are coated (1 minute). Remove from heat and test for salt.

Noodles with Sesame Sauce

Some of the most authentic local specialties in China are to be had not in restaurants or even homes but in those small mini-diners and portable stands that have traditionally clustered around temple precincts, shopping districts, and city gates. These may offer but a single item—spring rolls or steamed dumplings, soybean custard, or a soup of deep-fried tofu with bean threads. If the food is really good, the street vendor's reputation will spread, and customers will come from far and wide just for a taste. In some cases, the dishes have gone on to become nationwide favorites. A couple of examples of this are Hot Pepper Tofu with "Pork" (see Chapter 4) and these *"don don"* noodles from Szechuan. Rich and filling, they are a specialty often favored between meals and eaten in small portions. A fine, round wheat noodle is traditionally used, but you can be just as satisfied with the flat, narrow kind or a thicker round variety. These are sold fresh, in packages, in the refrigerated sections of Chinese markets and many supermarkets. Or use a dried Chinese flour noodle.

If you serve this as part of a meal, which I like to do in cold weather, it is good with green beans or a soup like Asparagus and Mushroom Soup. Have your other dishes ready before starting on this. Prepare the sauce while the noodles are cooking (or beforehand) so that you can toss them together and serve immediately. The sesame paste is sold in Chinese markets; or use roasted (not raw) sesame tahini found in health food stores. If you like fiery foods, the addition of a little chile oil should be appealing, and this can be toned down—or up—to taste. Be sure to garnish with Tientsin preserved cabbage if available (see Chinese Ingredients). It gives a piquant, crunchy quality to the dish. You can also top with a sprinkling of finely ground roasted peanuts.

3 tablespoons (45 ml)
  sesame paste or roasted
  sesame tahini

2 tablespoons (30 ml) soy
  sauce

2 tablespoons (30 ml)
  water

½ teaspoon (3 ml) rice wine

2 tablespoons (30 ml)
  sesame oil

6 ounces (170 g) noodles
  (3 cups [750 ml] after
  cooking)

½–¾ teaspoon (3–4 ml) chile
  oil (optional)

1½–2 tablespoons (22.5–30 ml)
  (packed) Tientsin
  preserved cabbage or
  1½ teaspoons (8 ml)
  green onion, minced

2 tablespoons (30 ml)
  finely ground roasted
  peanuts (optional)

To prepare a smooth sauce, first place sesame paste or tahini in a small bowl. Add soy sauce gradually, 1 tablespoon at a time, stirring until well blended. Then stir in water, rice wine, and sesame oil.

Boil the noodles till tender. Drain and toss immediately with the sesame sauce. If desired, add chile oil. Divide into individual portions, on small plates or in bowls, and top with Tientsin preserved cabbage or minced green onion and optional ground peanuts.

Bean Thread Noodles

This is like a dish of fine noodles, except that the bean threads ("cellophane noodles") are transparent, with a slick, silky feel on the palate. They are dried and can be found in small cellophane packages among the Chinese products in supermarkets. Soaking is required before use; some brands take a little longer than others for this step. I prefer using cold water 3 to 4 hours, since this does not "cook" them. Or you can cover with boiling water for a shorter period, 15 to 30 minutes. The important thing is to cook them until just tender; when overcooked they are apt to dissolve. They also tend to mass together during frying. To avoid this, cut them into shorter lengths after soaking and draining. This also makes them easier to eat.

Another product made from mung beans (starch is extracted from ground mung beans through a water process, then dehydrated) is mung bean sheet—thin, round, and milky colored. Fresh, it is very tender and is often tossed in strips with cucumber and a dressing. Alas, I have yet to see the fresh sheets sold in the United States. The dried version is a bit tough for a cold dish, but it is good cooked. In the Variation below you can prepare another noodlelike dish, but again with an unusual slick quality. Some stores also sell precut dried strips in packages.

Serve either of these dishes whenever you want a plate of noodles. For lunch (one to two persons) they make a hit with Sweet-and-Sour Relish Sticks. To serve three to four persons, add a soup, perhaps Spinach and Tofu Potage with Black Bean Sauce.

4 ounces (112 g) bean
  threads

6 black (or shiitake)
  mushrooms, presoaked

2–3 tablespoons (30–45 ml)
  peas or green soybeans,
  fresh or frozen

3 tablespoons (45 ml)
  vegetable oil

¾ cup (180 ml) soaking liquid
  from black mushrooms

½ cup (125 ml) bamboo
  shoot, julienned

2 tablespoons (30 ml) soy
  sauce

½ teaspoon (3 ml) sugar

Pinch salt

½ teaspoon (3 ml) sesame oil

Cover the bean threads with cool water and let stand 3 to 4 hours. Or for a shorter soaking period, cover with boiling water and let sit 15 to 30 minutes. Drain, and cut into 4-inch lengths.

Cut mushrooms into narrow strips.

It is not necessary to defrost frozen green soybeans or peas. Fresh ones should be parboiled until almost tender.

Heat a pan over medium-high; add 3 tablespoons oil. When oil is hot, put in the bean threads and stir-fry 30 seconds; work quickly, scraping the pan to prevent sticking. Pour in ¾ cup soaking liquid from mushrooms. Add the bamboo shoot, mushrooms, and green soybeans or peas. Season with 2 tablespoons soy sauce, ½ teaspoon sugar, and a pinch of salt. Cook at a rapid boil, stir-frying until no excess liquid remains. Test for salt. Then remove from the heat and stir in ½ teaspoon sesame oil.

Variation: Use two dried mung bean sheets, 10-inch diameter (or 4 ounces precut strips). Pour boiling water over them to more than cover, and steep 30 minutes. Rinse in cool water and drain. The sheets will be slick and gelatinous; do not fret if they tear during handling. Cut the sheets into long strips, roughly ¾ to 1 inch wide. You should have about 2 cups strips, loose. Prepare a cornstarch mixture of 1 tablespoon cornstarch to 1 tablespoon cold water. Prepare as above, but after cooking at a rapid boil 1 to 2 minutes to reduce the liquid, stir in just enough of the cornstarch mixture (start with half) to thicken the sauce. Remove from the heat and add 1 teaspoon sesame oil.

Fried Noodles with Garden Vegetables

There are so many kinds of Chinese noodles and noodle dishes that a fascinating (and very filling) book could be written on the subject alone. Restaurants, stalls, and even portable stands specialize in them everywhere in China. There have even been vegetarian noodle houses. Especially in the north, a noodle dish—soup, stir-fried, or tossed with sauce

—is often the whole meal. In Yangchow you might have a choice of dozens of different delicacies— meat, nuts, fish, vegetables—to accompany your soup noodles, as a topping or side dish. And noodles are not always hot. In summer they are served cold with savory sauces for dipping or tossing.

My favorite type of noodle is knife-cut. I've enjoyed these even in roadside stands. The adroit chef, holding a firm ball of dough in one hand and sharp blade in the other, slices off short, sharp-edged noodles in a quick forward motion, letting them drop right into the boiling water. I've even heard of ambidextrous masters who could do this with a blade in each hand and the dough on their head.

Many establishments hand-cut their own noodles, often very thin and fine, from a folded slab of dough. Or they may be hand-pulled to order—fine and round, thin and flat, broad and flat, and so on. The dough can be stretched into a rope, swung, and twisted between the maker's two hands until gluten elasticity allows it to be looped in two, pulled long, and looped again over and over, the number of strands multiplying exponentially. The most sublimely skilled masters can produce an amazing 2,000-some strands from a single small ball of dough. No doubt the world's most rarefied, these are called dragon's beard noodles and are as fine as a hair.

On birthdays, many Chinese customarily eat a bowl of long-life noodles—or rather, *noodle*, since it is just one strand, perhaps five feet long, filling the bowl, to symbolize long life. There are noodle makers who can cut the dough as they revolve it on a plate and end up with a single noodle that fills the whole cooking pot.

Some noodles are short and pointed on both tips, or pointed on one end and broad on the other, like a willow leaf.

Some varieties are traditionally served in small bowls that hold little more than a mouthful—some people want just a taste; for others, part of the pleasure is having one leisurely serving after another, with time in between for aftertaste mixed with anticipation and mounting appetite. Noodles are a popular noontime order at Southern Chinese teahouses.

They are likely to be egg noodles, or even shrimp noodles. Cantonese often deep-fry them before including them in soups or stir-fried dishes.

For this recipe try a dried, thin, flat Chinese noodle (labeled "udon" by some brands and available in supermarkets) or fresh packaged noodles sold in Chinese markets and some supermarkets. (Don't use the deep-fried, crispy type.) For lunch, with fruit, this is all you need when serving three persons.

8 ounces (224 g) noodles

2 teaspoons (10 ml) sesame oil

7 black (or shiitake) mushrooms, presoaked

2 large cloves garlic

1 small carrot (2 ounces [56 g])

2 leaves Chinese cabbage

¾ cup (180 ml) fresh mushrooms, sliced

½ small green pepper

½ cup (125 ml) bamboo shoot (preferably winter), julienned

1 small tomato (5 ounces [140 g])

3 + 2 tablespoons (45 + 30 ml) vegetable oil

2 tablespoons (30 ml) soy sauce

Salt to taste

Boil noodles but leave them underdone by several minutes. Drain in a colander. Transfer to a mixing bowl and toss with 2 teaspoons sesame oil to prevent sticking. You should have 3 heaping cups, loose. Set aside.

Cut black mushrooms into narrow strips.

Slice garlic.

Julienne the carrot finely.

Shred Chinese cabbage by cutting firm portion crosswise into narrow strips. Cut frilly part into wider, 1-inch strips. Keep stem and frilly parts separate.

Sliver green pepper, then cut slivers into 2-inch lengths.

Cut tomato into very thin wedges (sixteenths).

Put 3 tablespoons oil into a preheated pan over high. When the oil is hot, reduce heat to medium-high. Add ingredients in the following order, stirring 5 to 10 seconds after each addition, just to mix: garlic, carrot, firm part of Chinese cabbage, black and fresh mushrooms, green pepper, bamboo shoot. Add noodles and pour remaining 2 tablespoons oil over the top; stir-fry 30 seconds to combine. Add tomato, 2 tablespoons soy sauce, and frilly part of Chinese cabbage; stir-fry till well mixed. Remove from heat and test for salt, adding a dash or more to taste. Serve immediately.

3

"Meat Without Bones"– Tofu

"All the virtues of meat with none of the toxins."

This assessment of tofu, or bean curd, was made by no less a personage than the father of modern China, Sun Yat-sen. The qualities he cited are the very ones that have made tofu a mainstay in Chinese vegetarian cooking. In fact, this high-protein food, with a consistency ranging from firm to custardy, has been part of Chinese cuisine as far back as the second century B.C. Tradition has it that a man named Liu An invented the process. Though not especially complex, it is an ingenious one when you consider that the ingredients are but soybeans, water, and a coagulant. As one Chinese writer has said, "If the inventor of tofu were living today, he would win the Nobel Prize for Science." And —one is tempted to add—the prize for Peace, considering the pleasure and nourishment that this food gives to rich and poor alike, from gourmets to ascetics, from infants to the aged, in temples, restaurants, and homes throughout the world. It has been a major protein source not only for vegetarians in China but for the general population, for whom meat has always been a luxury.

In China, it would not be uncommon to spend the whole eating day, from early morning to midnight, with tofu and its related products. One of the most popular breakfasts is a hot bowl of soybean milk with a deep-fried Chinese cruller sandwiched inside a crusty wheat bun. In the markets, tofu appears fresh daily (so it does not have to be stored in water). The exposed slabs, straight out of the pressing mold, are cut into 2- to 3-inch squares, which are less than an inch thick (the thickness of the slab). Lunch could easily include tofu in a soup, vegetable, or meat dish.

Various forms of tofu provide some of the most common snacking foods, such as pressed tofu slices and pressed tofu strands *(gan sz)*. These are enjoyed with wine and other cold appetizers, not only in restaurants but in streetside stands with their tables and chairs out in the open. The highly odiferous "stinking" tofu *(chou doufu)* is made by fermenting tofu or pressed tofu, or allowing it to grow moldly, then deep-frying it. Usually eaten with a hot sauce, this is available at movable carts equipped with their own braziers and woks. In Anwei, two-inch-long mold is allowed to grow on cakes of tofu, which are then grilled, boiled, or deep-fried. In Guilin, famous for fantastical mountain scenery that has inspired centuries of Chinese painters, street vendors offer a temple dish called "monk's tofu," which has a porous, honeycomb texture from being stewed for long periods. It too is eaten with a hot sauce, which it soaks up like a sponge.

Come dinnertime, tofu might again appear in a great variety of forms. The subtle, unassertive flavor is actually an advantage, making this food a ready companion for almost any vegetable, meat, fish, or seasoning. It is featured in soups and fillings, and is even filled itself—slices of regular tofu or deep-fried puffs are slit and stuffed with a variety of tasty mixtures. Tofu is a common feature in fast stir-fried dishes and slow-cooked stewpots. Uncooked, with a dressing, it is also delectable. Soybean custard is often eaten cold as a late-night snack with a sweet syrup, or with salty and piquant seasonings.

Numerous highly unusual dishes have been invented around tofu. One of the most bizarre was found in a locality of Anwei province, where a large block of tofu was put in a pot of cold water along with tiny live fish. This was heated, causing the fish to seek escape from the mounting temperature by burrowing into the cool tofu. Ready-stuffed, the block would then be removed and steamed with mushrooms in stock. If this seems cruel, it was certainly an isolated practice, and to balance the impression we might recall that on the lake waters of Hangchow, pious people would purchase a live fish for the express purpose of releasing it, thereby gaining karmic merit for saving a life!

The popularity that tofu has achieved in the United States within just the past few years is vivid testimony to its manifold values. (In English it is alternately called bean curd, soybean curd, soybean cake, or Chinese bean cake. The Mandarin word is "dofu"; "tofu" is the Japanese.) It is available across the country now, not just in Oriental and health food stores, but in most supermarkets.

In spite of its virtues, one occasionally hears objections from American shoppers, who claim, "It doesn't have any taste." Often they aren't far from wrong: the practice in this country of packing tofu in water, with preservatives, drastically impairs its delicate, perishable flavor. The purpose, of course, is to prolong shelf life and facilitate transport. Certainly we should be glad to get it this way rather than not at all. But can you imagine the outcry that would go up if meat came to us in cartons of water?

Fortunately the condition is reversible. By a very simple procedure—draining and wrapping slices of the tofu in paper towels to extract most of the excess water—you can obtain squares that are very similar to the fresh product in both taste and consistency. See below, On Readying Tofu, for detailed directions.

Of course, it is possible to enjoy fresh tofu. One way is to make it yourself. The procedure takes several hours yet is well worth the trouble. Or you can seek out one of those rare shops that sell it fresh. Occasionally in Chinese markets here, tofu squares are available in bulk (the same that are sold to restaurants), stacked in a large, lined carton box. Snap them up, for they are the freshest you may ever see. The water in the box contains no preservatives, and the tofu is not as waterlogged as that in sealed cartons, for it has been pressed more and is not as absorbent.

A quick rundown of the procedure for making tofu will give you an idea of the many related foods that can enrich your diet and eating pleasure.

Producing tofu: Presoaked dried soybeans are ground and cooked in abundant water, which is then strained to yield a thin, yellowish liquid called (in English usage) soybean "milk" or soymilk. The film that forms on the surface of heated soybean milk is bean curd skin (see Chapter 5). Solidifying soybean milk with an agent such as calcium sulfate or magnesium chloride produces soybean custard. When soybean custard is pressed to reduce it in bulk by about half, removing some of its liquid content, the result is tofu. When tofu is pressed to remove almost all the moisture, pressed (or dry) tofu is obtained (see next chapter). Pressing soybean custard into a thin sheet yields bean curd sheet (see Chapter 5). Bean curd "cheese" (also called fermented or preserved bean curd) is tofu or pressed tofu that has been fermented and aged with flavorings.

Most of these are represented in recipes throughout this book, in this chapter and in Chapters 4, 5, and 7). You will experience how easy it is to cook with tofu and how amazingly versatile it is. You can toss it cold with a sauce, brown or deep-fry it, stir-fry and braise it with other vegetables, mash it for fillings, press it for a really meaty texture, simmer it in soups, and create special "viands" (employing bean curd sheet and bean curd skin) that simulate and rival even the most delectable meats.

The recipes in this chapter yield three to four servings.

On Readying Tofu

American tofu typically comes in a 14- to 16-ounce block packed in water in a sealed carton. For stir-frying and for use in fillings, purchase either regular or firm tofu. The label will usually give this information, but if it does not, you can probably assume it is "regular." (Because of its fragility, the "soft" or "silken" kind is usually reserved for use in dishes that are simmered or steamed, such as soups.)

Immersed in water, tofu will keep for a week or more in the refrigerator, if you change the water daily. Flavor loss is rapid, however.

To ready tofu for these recipes, first rinse the block by running several changes of tap water into the carton around the tofu (or use boiling water). Drain well.

Then slice the block crosswise, vertically, to obtain (usually) four slices, averaging ¾ to 1 inch thick. Depending on the size of the block, the slices will be roughly 2½ to 3 inches square, weighing 3 to 4 ounces each.

Lay out a double thickness of several paper towels; arrange the tofu slices side by side at one end, and wrap the toweling around them several times securely; let stand several minutes. It is also helpful to set a light weight on top, such as a cutting board or glass bread pan (which, incidentally, is a good container for storing the tofu). You may have to change the towel wrapping as many as six or seven times. When the slices seem more or less dry and do not yield moisture to the toweling, they are ready to use.

This may sound like a lot of bother, but it takes a half hour at most. The benefits are a significant improvement in flavor and an enhanced texture, ensuring better, more authentic-tasting dishes. The tofu also becomes easier to handle and cook with, for it holds together better. In dishes where tofu is to be browned, this drying step is absolutely essential.

Do not prepare tofu in this manner unless you intend to use it the same day, for it does not keep well.

To mash tofu: When tofu is used in fillings, balls, etc. (see recipes at the end of this chapter), it is usually mashed. First remove excess moisture, as directed above. Then place the slices flat on a cutting board. Mash them one by one. Start at the right end of each slice, pressing firmly with the flat side of a cleaver or broad knife held at an angle; work gradually to the left, pushing the knife toward the right as you press. Then turn the tofu 90 degrees and repeat the process, perhaps also chopping it a little. This is an easy way to mash potatoes, too.

On Browning Tofu

Several of these recipes call for browning cubes of tofu in oil before adding the other ingredients. Be sure to use regular or firm (not soft) tofu. Follow the directions for readying tofu, above, so that the wetness is removed. If you find yourself tempted to skimp on the number of towel changes, remind yourself of this simple truth: doing it right will mean the difference between easy success and total, disheartening failure!

A generous amount of oil facilitates the browning (most of it is drained off later). The oil must be quite hot before adding the tofu and must be kept hot while browning. To prevent sticking, shake the pan just after putting in the cubes; continue shaking it at intervals, or nudging the tofu with a Chinese spatula or pancake turner. If sticking occurs, keep the crust scraped from the pan. Turn when browned. Ideally there should be a light golden color on all sides, but at least on top and bottom. If you find that browning occurs quickly and easily, you may be able to stir-fry the whole time. But most likely you will have to brown top and bottom first, then stir-fry for 30 seconds or so to complete the other sides.

If you experience some difficulty in getting your tofu to brown, chances are you did not remove enough moisture with the paper towels. Next time, you might try the following initial step: Bring a pot of water to the boil. Immerse the tofu slices, then turn off the heat and let sit 30 minutes. Drain, and follow the same procedure for removing moisture as described in "On Readying Tofu." This parboiling is a practice followed by some cooks to remove any (albeit slight) chemical taste as well.

On Deep-frying Tofu

Deep-fried tofu is especially suited for stir-fried dishes, stews, and soups. It holds together well, readily soaking up the sauces or stock. The golden crust makes for better chewing than plain tofu. Some Chinese eat it cold, slit open and seasoned with soy sauce, vinegar, and sugar. In the puffy type, fillings can be inserted through a tiny hole.

Deep-fried tofu is available in Oriental markets and delicatessens in a variety of forms—square, rectangular, and triangular, with textures ranging from light and airy to firm and heavy. These are packaged and refrigerated under different names, including tofu puffs, fried bean curd, raw fried tofu, fried soy bean cake, and *age* (Japanese). A cube form is sometimes sold in bulk in Chinese markets.

For the sake of freshness and more certain quality, it is worthwhile to make your own. Use it below in Tender Greens and Deep-fried Tofu, and Three Delicacies and Deep-fried Tofu; or in soups (Deep-fried Tofu Soup with Bean Threads, Chapter 7).

To deep-fry tofu, use regular or firm tofu, any amount you like, cut into squares or slices, each 2½ to 3 inches square by approximately ¾ inch thick.

To obtain a nice brown crust, it is sometimes helpful to soak the slices in a saline solution of 1 teaspoon salt per 1½ cups water for 15 minutes; rinse twice and drain. (You can try omitting this step and proceeding as below, to see if your tofu browns well without it.)

Follow directions for On Readying Tofu, earlier in this chapter. Then cut each square into four small triangles by slicing diagonally from each corner to its opposite corner.

Heat oil for deep-frying. Put in triangles a few at a time and fry to a light golden color. Agitate them slightly at first, as they tend to stick to the bottom before floating to the top; then turn occasionally until evenly browned. Keep the heat between high and medium-high; if the oil should get too hot, remove the pot from the burner for a minute. Do not overfry or the crust will be hard, not tender. Drain the tofu on paper towels.

Wrapped in plastic, deep-fried tofu will keep in the refrigerator for a week or so, but in this case (and with any purchased fried tofu products) you should freshen it before use by dunking in boiling hot water, then rinsing and squeezing.

Note: Do not expect your homemade deep-fried tofu to be like the light, puffy commercial product; the latter employs a kind of tofu made especially for the purpose, in which the soybeans are ground and cooked differently than for regular tofu.

Tofu Dressed with Gingerroot and Green Onion

This is a tofu dish that can be ready in short order and one that will please everybody. Just toss bite-sized cubes of tofu with the dressing and a little minced gingerroot or crunchy Szechuan pickle. The pleasant spiciness suits it for companion entrees of all types, particularly something crunchy like Hashed Icicle Radish or Turnip. Making it ahead will give you plenty of time for a more involved, last-minute recipe like Spring Rolls.

If you ever find yourself with access to fresh cedar buds in spring (the trees may grow in your area), seize the opportunity to enjoy a very special garnish (to replace the green onion). They are thought by some Chinese to have medicinal qualities, effective in treating and preventing any number of ailments.

16 ounces (450 g) regular or firm tofu

2 teaspoons (10 ml) gingerroot or Szechuan pickle (or 1 teaspoon [5 ml] each), minced

1 tablespoon (15 ml) green onion, minced; or 2 tablespoons (30 ml) fresh cedar buds, chopped

3 tablespoons (45 ml) soy sauce

2 teaspoons (10 ml) sesame oil

See On Readying Tofu, earlier in this chapter. Cut the tofu into roughly 1-inch cubes and place in a bowl. Toss gently, using chopsticks, with the remaining ingredients. Toss two or three times at intervals until the dressing is absorbed. This should take only a few minutes at most.

Tofu with a Rich Sesame Sauce

Another sumptuous way to serve cold tofu. The thick, rich, hearty sauce is made with Chinese sesame paste (*jr-ma jiong* in Oriental markets) or toasted sesame tahini. The latter is sold in jars at health food stores. Avoid the "raw" type also sold in Middle Eastern groceries. The label you want should indicate "toasted" or "roasted." Here is another perfect dish for a garnish of fresh cedar buds if available. This recipe will serve four or five persons generously.

1½ pounds (675 g) regular or firm tofu

2 tablespoons (30 ml) green onion, minced; or fresh cedar buds, chopped

3 tablespoons (45 ml) sesame paste or roasted sesame tahini

4 tablespoons (60 ml) soy sauce

1 tablespoon (15 ml) sesame oil

See On Readying Tofu, earlier in this chapter. Cut tofu into approximately 1-inch cubes and place in a medium-sized serving bowl. Sprinkle with minced green onion.

For a smooth sauce, first place 3 tablespoons sesame paste or tahini in a small bowl. Add soy sauce gradually, 1 tablespoon at a time, stirring until well blended. Then stir in the sesame oil. Pour this mixture over the tofu, and toss carefully (with chopsticks, so as not to break it up). Can be served at once; or allow to stand an hour or so at room temperature, stirring occasionally.

Easy Browned Tofu with Soy Sauce

For a hot dish that really enhances the subtle texture and flavor of tofu, there is none better or more simple. It is a good place to start if you're browning tofu for the first time, since there are no other main ingredients to worry about. After the browning, all you have to do is sprinkle on a little soy sauce and salt.

16 ounces (450 g) regular or firm tofu

4 tablespoons (60 ml) vegetable oil

1 tablespoon (15 ml) soy sauce

Dash salt, to taste

½ teaspoon (3 ml) sesame oil

Important: See On Readying Tofu and On Browning Tofu, earlier in this chapter. Cut tofu slices into sixths (roughly 1-inch cubes).

Heat a skillet over high; add 4 tablespoons oil. When oil is hot, put in the tofu, reduce heat to medium-high, and brown tofu lightly on top and bottom (or on all sides). Without removing the tofu, lift pan from the heat and spoon out remaining oil. Return pan to the stove (medium or medium-high heat); sprinkle 1 tablespoon soy sauce over the top. Stir-fry until well mixed and the pan is dry—about a minute. Test for salt, adding a dash or more as needed. Remove from the heat and add a few drops of sesame oil.

Savory Browned Tofu with Leek or Green Onion

Juicy morsels of browned tofu, lavished with chopped green onion or shredded leek. The "long onion" or Welsh onion, which is bigger than a green onion yet smaller than a leek—in fact, it looks like a cross between the two—is sometimes to be found in Japanese markets. Its full-flavored yet refined taste and texture make it ideal for this dish.

16 ounces (450 g) regular or firm tofu

1 leek (white part, 1 × 4 inches [25 × 100 mm]), or Welsh onion, or 10 small green onions

4 tablespoons (60 ml) vegetable oil

1½ tablespoons (22.5 ml) soy sauce

1½ tablespoons (22.5 ml) water

½ teaspoon (3 ml) sugar

Important: See On Readying Tofu and On Browning Tofu, earlier in this chapter. Cut tofu into bite-sized cubes (about 1 inch), six to eight per slice.

Pound leek or Welsh onion to flatten slightly, then sliver lengthwise into very fine shreds. Cut these into 1-inch lengths; you should have about ½ cup, packed. If you are using green onions, simply cut them into 1-inch lengths.

Heat a skillet over high; put in 4 tablespoons oil. When the oil is hot, put in the tofu, turn heat to medium-high, and brown it top and bottom, or on all sides. Without removing the tofu, lift pan off the heat and spoon out all but 1 tablespoon oil. Add the leek (or Welsh or green onion) to the tofu in the pan; stir-fry gently over medium or medium-high for 1 minute. Sprinkle 1½ tablespoons soy sauce over all, then 1½ tablespoons water and ½ teaspoon sugar. Turn heat to high; continue to stir-fry until the pan is dry (1 minute).

Five-spices Browned Tofu and Black Mushrooms

In a slightly thickened sauce, faintly aromatic with spices, this pair of tender delicacies goes down very smoothly. Five-spices powder (the mixture varies— see Chinese Ingredients) is stocked by stores that carry Oriental goods. One little jar or plastic bag should last you a thousand years, for it is very strong. Use it in excess and your food will taste like Chinese medicine. Use it with delicate restraint, and the effect will be heady and exotic. This recipe yields four to five servings.

1¼ pounds (562 g) regular or firm tofu

10 black (or shiitake) mushrooms, presoaked

4 tablespoons (60 ml) vegetable oil

¾ cup (180 ml) soaking liquid from black mushrooms

½ teaspoon (3 ml) sugar

2 tablespoons (30 ml) soy sauce

Pinch five-spices powder

2 teaspoons (10 ml) cornstarch dissolved in 1 tablespoon (15 ml) water

½ teaspoon (3 ml) sesame oil

Important: See On Readying Tofu and On Browning Tofu, earlier in this chapter. Cut each tofu slice into quarters, 1¼ inches square or so.

Leave the mushrooms whole, or cut them in half if large.

Heat a skillet over high; put in 4 tablespoons oil. When oil is hot, reduce heat to medium-high, put in the tofu, and brown it lightly on top and bottom or all sides. Without removing the tofu, spoon out all but 1 tablespoon oil. Return pan (with tofu) to medium-high heat; add mushrooms and stir briefly. Add ¾ cup mushroom liquid, ½ teaspoon sugar, 2 tablespoons soy sauce, and a *small* pinch of five-spices powder. Cook over medium-high 2 to 3 minutes, stirring occasionally, or until liquid is reduced by half. Blend in cornstarch mixture; cook, stirring, until the sauce is slightly thickened, another minute. Serve topped with ½ teaspoon sesame oil.

Crunchy Tree Ear or Snow Peas and Soft Browned Tofu

You would think some wonderful folktales might exist about trees with ears. Able to hear the secrets of the surrounding world, they would grow wiser than all the other trees in the forest. "Ear," of course, describes the shape of a certain fungus that grows on tree trunks. According to recent medical reports, this popular ingredient in Chinese cooking is beneficial in promoting the blood's clotting properties. The ancients thought of it as so nutritious that they sometimes called it tree or wood chicken. The springy, chewy texture contrasts nicely with the soft, browned tofu in this recipe. It soaks up the five-spices powder and soy sauce like a sponge, magnifying the flavors, so remember to go very light on the aromatic powder. Snow peas are a perfect, snappy counterpart to the tofu as well. Do not include five-spices powder if using them.

16 ounces (450 g) regular or firm tofu

2–3 tree ears, presoaked; or 1 cup (250 ml) fresh snow peas (3 ounces [84 g])

4 tablespoons (60 ml) vegetable oil

2 tablespoons (30 ml) soy sauce

2 tablespoons (30 ml) water

½ teaspoon (3 ml) sugar

Dash salt, to taste

Pinch five-spices powder (with tree ear only)

½ teaspoon (3 ml) sesame oil

Important: See On Readying Tofu and On Browning Tofu, earlier in this chapter. Cut each tofu slice into sixths or eighths.

Tear the tree ear into very small pieces to yield ½ cup, loosely packed. If using snow peas instead, string them and pat dry; leave whole.

Heat a skillet over high; add 4 tablespoons oil. When oil is hot, put in the tofu, reduce heat to medium-high, and brown it lightly on top and bottom or on all sides. Without removing the tofu, lift the pan off the heat and spoon out all but 1 tablespoon oil. Return the pan to medium heat; add the tree ear or snow peas and stir-fry briefly. Sprinkle on 2 tablespoons soy sauce, 2 tablespoons water, ½ teaspoon sugar, a dash of salt, and—only with tree ear—a *small* pinch of five-spices powder. Turn the heat to high and stir-fry 1 to 2 minutes, until the pan is nearly dry. Do not let snow peas get overdone; they should be tender yet still fairly crisp. Remove from the heat and add ½ teaspoon sesame oil.

Tofu and Black Mushrooms Simmered with Lily Buds

A type of tiger lily bud, slender when dried and therefore called "golden needle" in Chinese, lends unique tang to this dish. Buy them packaged in Chinese markets; the more golden the color, the better. Soak until soft, pinch off any hard ends, then tie in pairs, knotted in the center. The knot improves texture and promotes eye appeal, as well as keeping in the pollen. Unlike the four preceding recipes, the tofu is not browned here. Everything is cooked in a little mushroom liquid, which is then thickened into a gravy.

12 ounces (337 g) regular or firm tofu

10 black (or shiitake) mushrooms, presoaked

⅓ cup (85 ml) (loosely packed) dried lily buds, presoaked

1 tablespoon (15 ml) (packed) salted-dried bamboo shoot tips, presoaked and shredded (optional) (see Note)

2 tablespoons (30 ml) vegetable oil

½ cup (125 ml) soaking liquid from black mushrooms and bamboo shoot tips

1 tablespoon (15 ml) (generous) soy sauce

¼ teaspoon (1.5 ml) salt

½ teaspoon (3 ml) sugar

1 teaspoon (5 ml) cornstarch dissolved in 2 teaspoons (10 ml) water

1 teaspoon (5 ml) sesame oil

Note: See On Salted-dried Bamboo Shoot Tips, Chapter 5. If you are using these, omit salt and use only 1 level tablespoon soy sauce.

See On Readying Tofu, earlier in this chapter. Cut each slice of tofu into sixths.

Cut the mushrooms into halves or thirds.

Tie lily buds in pairs. You should have fifteen to twenty knotted pairs.

Into a preheated pan on high heat, put 2 tablespoons oil. When oil is hot, reduce heat to medium-high; add mushrooms and dried bamboo shoot tips; stir-fry 30 seconds. Add lily buds and tofu; stir just to mix. Pour in ½ cup soaking liquid and sprinkle with appropriate amounts of seasoning—1 generous tablespoon soy sauce, ¼ teaspoon salt, and ½ teaspoon sugar (if you are including dried bamboo shoot tips, use only 1 tablespoon soy sauce and omit salt). Cook over medium-high, stirring two or three times, to reduce the liquid—about 2 minutes. Blend in the cornstarch mixture at one side of the pan, then stir-fry gently until you have a slightly thick gravy. Remove from the heat and add 1 teaspoon sesame oil.

Honeycomb Tofu

When tofu is boiled at length, either in water or in stewing stocks, it becomes porous. You can try the procedure in this recipe for such a texture, or you can go ahead and use unboiled tofu. Either way, the dish has a pert, fruity taste, compliments of a little tofu "cheese," preserved gingerroot, and soy-pickled cucumber (see Chinese Ingredients for purchasing information on all these; they are easily found at Chinese markets).

16 ounces (450 g) regular or firm tofu

1 teaspoon (5 ml) white tofu "cheese" + 1 tablepoon (15 ml) packing liquid

2 tablespoons (30 ml) marinated gingerroot, julienned

2 tablespoons (30 ml) soy-pickled cucumber, julienned

3 tablespoons (45 ml) vegetable oil

½ teaspoon (3 ml) sugar

½ teaspoon (3 ml) sesame oil

Cut the tofu into inch-thick slices. Place in a pot or skillet, cover with water, and boil till the pan is nearly dry. Then cover with water again and repeat. If time is short you can omit this step.

See On Readying Tofu, earlier in this chapter. Cut each tofu slice into quarters.

Combine 1 teaspoon white tofu "cheese" with 1 tablespoon of the liquid in which it is packed.

Heat a pan over high; add 3 tablespoons oil; when oil is hot, add the tofu and brown lightly. Without removing tofu, spoon out remaining oil from the pan. Return pan (with tofu) to medium heat. Add the gingerroot and cucumber; stir-fry 30 seconds. Pour the tofu "cheese" mixture over the top; sprinkle with ½ teaspoon sugar. Mix well, then remove from the heat and add ½ teaspoon sesame oil. Serve hot or cold.

Tender Greens and Deep-fried Tofu

As appetizing to the eye as it is to the palate, this dish is best if you prepare your own deep-fried tofu —which can be done even a day or more in advance. For the greens, I suggest spinach (save the root ends for snacking, or include them in this recipe). If you live near a Chinese market, try baby mustard cabbage, a princely little vegetable that is so attractive and tasty that the hearts often appear whole in banquet dishes (see illustration on page 150 and Chinese Ingredients).

12 pieces deep-fried tofu

10 ounces (281 g) baby mustard
   cabbage or spinach

 2 tablespoons (30 ml)
   vegetable oil

⅛ teaspoon (.5 ml) salt

 1 tablespoon (15 ml) soy sauce

See On Deep-frying Tofu, earlier in this chapter. Freshen deep-fried tofu by pouring scalding hot water on top, then rinse and squeeze to remove liquid (omit this step if you have just made it). Use 12 small triangles. Slice larger pieces thickly.

Separate the leaves of the greens. Wilt them by plunging into a large pot of boiling water; after 30 seconds, drain and cool under running water to stop the cooking and hold color. (Or steam in a vegetable basket—1½ minutes for spinach, 2 to 2½ minutes for baby mustard cabbage, stirring once; then rinse in cold water.)

Divide into two or three handfuls and squeeze to remove liquid, but leave slightly moist. Chop, then loosen the packed greens and squeeze again if necessary.

Heat a pan over high; add 2 tablespoons oil and *half* the salt (2 large pinches). When the oil is hot, put in the chopped vegetable; reduce heat to medium and stir-fry 30 seconds. Add the deep-fried tofu, 1 tablespoon soy sauce, and the rest of the salt (2 large pinches); if the pan seems too dry, add also 1 to 3 tablespoons water. Turn heat to high; stir-fry 1 minute or until the pan is nearly dry.

Three Delicacies and Deep-fried Tofu

This recipe puts special emphasis on dried ingredients and thus offers good contrast for fresh vegetable dishes. The dried bamboo shoot has a piquant taste and chewy rather than crunchy texture, so the result will be different from using a fresh or canned shoot. This dried product is available in cellophane bags in most Chinese markets. Do not confuse it with the salted-dried tips used in many dishes in Chapter 5.

10–12 pieces (bite-sized)
deep-fried tofu

6 strips (8-inch [200 mm]
length) dry bamboo
shoot

6 black (or shiitake)
mushrooms, presoaked

2–3 tree ears, presoaked

3 tablespoons (45 ml)
vegetable oil

2 tablespoons (30 ml) soy
sauce

1 teaspoon (5 ml) sugar

½ cup (125 ml) mushroom
soaking liquid

Salt to taste

½ teaspoon (3 ml) sesame
oil

See On Deep-frying Tofu, earlier in this chapter. Freshen deep-fried tofu by pouring scalding water on top, then rinse and squeeze dry (omit this step if you have just made it). If the pieces are large, cut them into bite-sized triangles or cubes. You should have ten to twelve of these.

Soak the dry bamboo shoot in warm water 3 hours or until soft. Cut into 1½-inch lengths.

Slice the mushrooms to bite-size.

Tear the tree ear into very small pieces, discarding the hard stem, to yield about ½ cup, loose.

Heat a pan over high; add 3 tablespoons oil. When oil begins to smoke, reduce heat to medium-high; add in succession the mushrooms, bamboo shoot, tree ear, and deep-fried tofu, stirring briefly after each addition. Sprinkle on 2 tablespoons soy sauce and 1 teaspoon sugar; pour in ½ cup mushroom liquid. Cook, stirring occasionally, about 4 minutes or until only 1 tablespoon liquid remains in the pan. Test for salt, then top with a few drops of sesame oil.

Eight Treasures "Meatballs"

"Eight Treasures" denotes an elaborate combination of prized ingredients—not necessarily eight, sometimes six, or seven, or more than eight. Eight Treasures Rice Pudding (see Chapter 8) and the Shanghainese Eight Treasures stuffed duck are two examples. The little "meatballs" here are both soft and crunchy, a tasty combination of seven minced ingredients. The soy-pickled cucumber (in cans or jars) and marinated gingerroot (in jars) are sold in Chinese stores. Since the preparation involves several steps, including lots of mincing, I suggest you devise a menu in which everything else is prepared in advance—a crisp cabbage relish, a soup for steaming (such as Velvet Turnip Soup), and maybe Eggplant with Fried Gluten or Chestnuts, which can be served at room temperature or reheated quickly just before serving. These little deep-fried balls are good with rice, but they are also fitting company for rice wine (Chinese usually don't serve rice when

14 ounces (393 g) regular or firm tofu

1 tablespoon (15 ml) each, minced: black (or shiitake) mushrooms, water chestnuts, toasted pine nuts or sunflower seeds, soy-pickled cucumber

1½ teaspoons (8 ml) marinated gingerroot, minced

1 tablespoon (15 ml) salted-dried bamboo shoot tips, presoaked and minced (optional) (see Note)

½ cup (125 ml) bamboo shoot, finely chopped

¾ teaspoon (4 ml) salt

2 + tablespoons (30 ml) flour

Vegetable oil for deep-frying

1½ teaspoons (8 ml) vegetable oil

1 tablespoon (15 ml) rice wine

1 tablespoon (15 ml) soy sauce

½ teaspoon (3 ml) sugar

½ teaspoon (3 ml) sesame oil

they are having wine), heated and served in a pottery decanter with little cups or glasses.

Note: See On Salted-dried Bamboo Shoot Tips in Chapter 5 for more information. These can be omitted if unavailable.

See On Readying Tofu, earlier in this chapter. Mash the tofu. You should have about 1⅓ cups. Combine it with the minced ingredients, chopped bamboo shoot, ¾ teaspoon salt, and 2 tablespoons flour. Form into balls, using 1 tablespoon mixture for each. Roll lightly in flour.

Prepare oil for deep-frying. Deep-fry the balls to a golden brown (medium-high to high heat). Drain on paper towels.

Heat a skillet over medium heat. Add in succession: 1½ teaspoons vegetable oil, the tofu balls, 1 tablespoon rice wine (around the edge of the pan), 1 tablespoon soy sauce, and ½ teaspoon sugar; stir-fry gently until the pan is dry (1 minute). Top with ½ teaspoon sesame oil.

Variation: When not using salted-dried bamboo shoot tips, you can add 2 teaspoons Madras curry powder to the mixture for heightened spiciness.

Meaty Stuffed Cucumber

Cucumber sections are filled with a tofu mixture and braised until tender. When planning a menu, you might want to keep in mind that these are a bit like stuffed green peppers. They're especially good with rice and an asparagus and mushroom soup, either plain or spicy. Do not try to use the hothouse (English) or Oriental cucumber, whose seed sections are so small that there would be no room for the filling.

2 large cucumbers

7 ounces (197 g) regular or firm tofu

½ teaspoon (3 ml) salt

1 tablespoon (15 ml) (heaping) each, presoaked and minced: black (or shiitake) mushrooms, tree ear (or green pepper), and salted-dried bamboo shoot tips (see Note)

3 tablespoons (45 ml) vegetable oil

½ cup (125 ml) water

1 tablespoon (15 ml) soy sauce

½ teaspoon (3 ml) sugar

1 teaspoon (5 ml) sesame oil (optional)

Note: See On Salted-dried Bamboo Shoot Tips in Chapter 5 for more information. These can be omitted if unavailable.

Pare the cucumbers and cut crosswise into 1-inch lengths. Poke or scoop out the seeds. Discard the end pieces.

See On Readying Tofu, earlier in this chapter. Mash the tofu. You should have about ⅔ cup. Combine tofu with salt and the minced ingredients. Stuff the cucumber sections with this mixture. Pat the cucumber dry with paper toweling.

Heat a skillet over high; add 3 tablespoons oil. When oil is hot, reduce heat to medium and put in the cucumber sections. Brown them on both sides (about 2 minutes each side). Spoon or pour out excess oil, leaving the pan with a light coating only. Return the pan with cucumbers to medium-high heat; add ½ cup water and 1 tablespoon soy sauce; cover and cook at a fast simmer, turning two or three times. After 8 minutes, or when only about 2 tablespoons liquid remain in the pan, sprinkle on ½ teaspoon sugar and (if desired) 1 teaspoon sesame oil. Turn once again, then serve.

Stuffed Eggplant Ambrosia

For Stuffed Eggplant Ambrosia, ½-inch-thick slices of eggplant are cut into quarters; then each

Triangular "sandwiches" of eggplant, stuffed with a meatlike mixture of tofu and mushrooms, are browned, then cooked until tender in mushroom

wedge is cut inward from the point end, leaving the other end connected, forming a pocket for a tofu-mushroom stuffing.

4 ounces (112 g) regular or firm tofu

1½ tablespoons (22.5 ml) each, minced: fresh mushrooms, presoaked black (or shiitake) mushrooms, and presoaked salted-dried bamboo shoot tips (see Note)

¼ teaspoon (1.5 ml) salt

1 medium to large eggplant

5 tablespoons (75 ml) vegetable oil

¼ cup (60 ml) soaking liquid from black mushrooms and dried bamboo shoot tips

2 teaspoons (10 ml) soy sauce

¼ teaspoon (1.5 ml) sugar

liquid and soy. You'll want large slices of eggplant, so do not use the Oriental varieties. Portions of the eggplant go unused; with these you could make up an additional recipe of Eggplant with Fried Gluten or Chestnuts (Chapter 6), which will keep in the refrigerator. Since eggplant soaks up a lot of oil, combine this selection with refreshing relishes— Szechuan Style Cabbage Relish is a good choice— and a steamed dish, say, Fava or Lima Beans in Mustard Sauce. These can be made ahead. If you include a steamed soup as well, your pre-serving time can be devoted to this recipe.

Note: See On Salted-dried Bamboo Shoot Tips in Chapter 5 for more information. These can be omitted if unavailable.

See On Readying Tofu, earlier in this chapter. Mash the tofu. You should have about ⅓ cup. To make the filling, combine tofu with the minced ingredients and salt.

Pare the eggplant. Cut it lengthwise into slices ½ inch thick. For this recipe, use only two large slices. Lay them flat on a board and cut each into quarters (pie-slice wedges). Then, with knife blade parallel to the table, begin at the pointed end of each wedge and slice into a sandwich shape, stopping short of the bottom so that the two halves remain connected. Stuff with about 1 tablespoon of the tofu mixture, making a sort of sandwich. Smooth the filling to conform with the edges of the eggplant. You should have eight of these.

Heat a skillet over high; add 5 tablespoons oil. When oil is hot, reduce the heat to medium-high and put in the sandwiches; first stand them up to brown the filling sides (they will not fall over if you have smoothed the filling flat), then flat-side down to brown top and bottom (eggplant sides). Remove the pan from the burner and spoon off excess oil, if any. Return pan to medium-high heat; add ¼ cup soaking liquid; sprinkle on 2 teaspoons soy sauce and ¼ teaspoon sugar. Cook, turning once, until the pan is nearly dry—1 to 2 minutes. (If your original eggplant slices are more than ½ inch thick, you will need more than ¼ cup liquid or the eggplant will not be tender.)

Boiled Pot-stickers *(Shwei Jow)*

For Boiled Pot-stickers, the edge of a 3-inch-diameter wrapper is pressed together around the filling, with four or five tiny flush pleats helping to form a tight seal.

With their scalloped edges, these ravioli-like *"shwei jow"* make an elegant and inviting appearance on the platter. They are especially popular among the Northern Chinese, who are likely to order twenty, thirty, or even more for an individual lunch or dinner. (Rice is not eaten with these.) Boiled pot-stickers are the most common, but they are also steamed and fried. Chinese restaurants that specialize in them often make their own wrappers on the spot, but in the United States, commercial wrappers are the rule. You can make your own by following the simple directions below. The less ambitious may want to buy the special round wrappers sold in most Oriental markets. These are packaged under such names as pot-sticker skins, *suey gow* skins, and *gyoza* wraps—*suey gow* is the Cantonese for boiled pot-stickers; *gyoza* is the Japanese for the fried version. Or you can substitute wonton wrappers. Before using any of these, test one to make sure they can be sealed: moisten the perimeter of one side with water, fold in half to join, and press tightly around the edge. If it does not seal, you had better make your own wrappers, as they will not hold together in the boiling.

To entertain three or four persons to a noontime repast, serve these with Szechuan Style Cabbage Relish or Snappy Cucumber Relish and a soup (Hot-and-Sour Soup is a popular accompaniment). For dinner you'd want to add another relish or entree and perhaps double this recipe as well. A big eater could easily consume the whole batch all alone! You can mix the dip in saucers ahead of time, or provide the makings—cruets of soy sauce, vinegar, sesame oil, chile oil—for each person to mix individually at the table.

Boiled pot-stickers can be a bit slippery, so if you are using chopsticks, with less than perfect mastery, I suggest that you also provide a porcelain Chinese soup spoon for each person. Pick up a dumpling, holding the spoon under it in case of slippage; bring it to the mouth this way, where the spoon will be handy in case you bite only half instead of consuming it whole. Some people find a pot-sticker hard to pick up at all; they can easily nudge it into the spoon and use chopsticks to direct it into the mouth. This is not an uncommon way of eating fried rice and in fact can be very graceful. In any case, pot-stickers should not be pierced, as with a fork, for you lose any juice that may be inside. And this is one test of a good pot-sticker: a seal that allows no juice to escape and no water to enter.

Since these are obviously time-consuming to prepare, Chinese sometimes make the meal a social effort, with everyone pitching in—even guests if it is an informal affair with close friends. You might prefer to make these ahead and freeze them.

This recipe makes 2 dozen.

Filling:

8 ounces (224 g) regular or firm tofu

2 tablespoons (30 ml) each, presoaked and minced: black (or shiitake) mushrooms and tree ear

1 tablespoon (15 ml) dried lily buds, presoaked and minced (see Chinese Ingredients)

1 tablespoon (15 ml) green onion, minced

½ teaspoon (3 ml) salt

2¼ teaspoons (11.5 ml) soy sauce

2¼ teaspoons (11.5 ml) sesame oil

Wrappers:

1 cup (250 ml) all-purpose flour

¼ cup (60 ml) water

Dipping Sauce:

Soy sauce

Vinegar

Water or soaking liquid from black mushrooms

Sesame oil (optional)

Chile oil (optional)

See On Readying Tofu, earlier in this chapter. Mash the tofu to yield about ¾ cup.

To make the filling, combine mashed tofu with the minced ingredients, salt, soy sauce, and sesame oil.

To make the wrappers, mix flour and water by hand, kneading just enough to make a ball of dough. Cover and let rest at least an hour.

Knead the dough 2 minutes or so. With the palms of your hands, roll it into a long, cylindrical shape, 12 inches long, 1 inch in diameter. Cut crosswise into ½-inch pieces; you will have 24. If your climate is dry, keep the dough covered. Shape these, cut-side up, into a round shape. Flatten them with the palm or heel of your hand on a flour-dusted board. With a pastry roller, small rolling pin, piece of dowel, or even an empty jar—all of these should be wielded under the palm of one hand—roll each into a round wrapper, 3 inches in diameter, thicker in the center, thinner toward the edge. This is easily done by rolling the pastry roller from the edge of the piece of dough to the center, and back again, turning the dough counterclockwise a little with your left hand after each roll. Continue all the way around several times, also turning the dough over once or twice, until you have a thin, 3-inch wrapper.

To assemble, place 1½ teaspoons filling (or as much as the wrapper will hold) in an elongated mound in the center of each wrapper; fold the dough over the filling so that the edges meet. Press the edges together for a tight seal, at the same time making four or five tiny pleats, pinched tightly flush with the edge (see illustration). Be sure that it is completely sealed to keep the water out and the filling in. (With commercial wrappers, it may be necessary to moisten half of the inside edge first to get a seal.)

Bring 4 cups water to the boil in a pot. Immerse eight dumplings at a time for 3 minutes (add an extra minute if frozen—do not defrost them first). Lest they break open, add a little water to slow the boil whenever it becomes too rapid. Stir occasionally in case some of them stick to the bottom (true to their name). After 3 minutes, remove the dumplings with a slotted spoon. Cook the remaining two batches in the same way.

Serve hot, accompanied by small dipping saucers of soy sauce and vinegar (cider or Chinese dark), mixed in roughly equal proportions, or to taste, and thinned with water or mushroom liquid if too strong; add perhaps a drop of sesame and/or chile oil. Some people like to add a little crushed garlic, minced green onion, and/or gingerroot.

Advance preparation: These can be assembled ahead and frozen. Do not defrost before cooking.

Open-face Steamed Dumplings *(Shao Mai)*

Open-face Steamed Dumplings (Shao Mai) *are a popular dim sum treat and attractive luncheon dish.*

These little open-faced steamed dumplings, a popular item in dim sum teahouses, are a special treat, for you seldom see a vegetarian version. With their flowerlike appearance and savory filling, they are an attractive luncheon dish. You can use the ready-made wrappers, sold in refrigerated or frozen sections of some markets ("*shu mai* skins"). "*Suey gow* skins" or "*gyoza* wrappers" are too thick and will dry out during steaming. Wonton wrappers can be substituted, but trim off the pointed corners. Better yet, prepare your own wrappers according to the directions below.

This recipe makes 15 bite-sized small dumplings, for a serving of three or four per person. If you steam them in a bamboo basket, transfer the basket directly from stove to table (with a plate under it). You can do the serving or let individuals help themselves. Have the saucers of dip already set out, along with one or two colorful, crunchy relishes to snack on—Sweet-and-Sour Relish Sticks, or even Green Peas or Soybeans in the Pod if you're being informal. Because of the flour wrappers, you probably won't want rice with these, but a substantial soup can fill out the menu for lunch very well. Try one of the potages in Chapter 7—Spinach and Tofu, or Tomato and Tofu. These call for last-minute attention, which you can be giving while the *shao mai* are steaming.

Wrappers:

⅔ cup (170 ml) all-purpose flour

2 tablespoons (30 ml) and 2 teaspoons (10 ml) hot water

Filling A:

5 ounces (140 g) regular or firm tofu, mashed to yield ½ cup

1½ teaspoons (8 ml) (packed) Tientsin preserved cabbage minced (see Chinese Ingredients)

1 tablespoon (15 ml) each, presoaked and minced: tree ear and lily buds

3 tablespoons (45 ml) black (or shiitake) mushrooms, presoaked and minced

1½ teaspoons (8 ml) green onion, minced

1 teaspoon (5 ml) sesame oil

1 teaspoon (5 ml) vegetable oil

⅛ teaspoon (.5 ml) salt

2 teaspoons (10 ml) soy sauce

To prepare wrappers, combine flour and hot water. Knead a couple of minutes into a smooth dough; cover and let rest at least 1 hour. Place on a lightly floured board and follow directions in Boiled Potstickers (preceding recipe) for making wrappers, but make the roll only 7½ inches long; cutting at ½-inch intervals, yield will be 15 wrappers. Roll these out to a diameter of 3½ inches or so.

Prepare Filling A or B by combining the ingredients. Place approximately 1 tablespoon filling on the center of each wrapper. Holding the wrapper on your left fingers, encircle it from below with your right thumb and index finger, gathering the wrapper up around the filling. Squeeze gently around the middle to make a kind of neck; some of the filling should emerge at the top. (See illustration.) The bundle should hold together securely or it will collapse during steaming. Pat the bottom with your left hand to make a flat base. If the skin is not too floppy, you can also turn the edge slightly outward (like an open flower), pinching it if necessary to make it secure.

Place a layer of damp cloth in a bamboo steaming basket or on a flat, perforated rack (you can use a heatproof plate if you have neither of these, but circulation of steam is somewhat impaired this way). Arrange the *shao mai* on it. With the rack well above the boiling water in a steamer, steam for 10 minutes (if frozen, do not defrost first). They will stick to the cloth, but if you wash and reuse the same cloth each time, they will not stick as much.

Filling B:

3 tablespoons (45 ml) each,
minced: water chestnuts;
presoaked black (or
shiitake) mushrooms;
bamboo shoots; carrot

2 teaspoons (10 ml) green
onion, minced

½ teaspoon (3 ml) gingerroot,
minced

1 tablespoon (15 ml) soy
sauce

¼ teaspoon (1.5 ml) sugar

1 teaspoon (5 ml) cornstarch

1½ teaspoons (8 ml) sesame oil

Dipping sauce:

Soy sauce

Mushroom soaking liquid

Sesame oil

Serve while still hot, before the skin hardens—as is, or with small dipping saucers of soy sauce and mushroom liquid (from the black mushrooms), mixed in equal proportions. Add a few drops of sesame oil.

Advance preparation: These can be assembled in advance, frozen, and steamed just prior to serving.

Chewy Stuffed Dumplings, Fried

These dumplings have the thinnest of crispy brown outer crusts with a soft and incomparably chewy inside that only glutinous rice flour dough can give. Add to that a savory filling, and you have a very special treat. You need to buy the "sweet" rice flour sold in many supermarkets. It is also packaged under different brands as "glutinous rice flour." Just be sure not to use regular rice flour.

A delightful lunch could include a clear steamed soup (any of those in Chapter 7 with mushrooms) and a clean-tasting relish ("Crystal Icicles" Relish or Sweet-and-Sour Relish Sticks). For dinner, choose an entrée that can be started ahead, like Braised Chinese Cabbage with Delicacies. Because of the rice flour, rice would be redundant in the same meal. This recipe makes ten small dumplings; a serving of two or three per person is about right.

Filling:

   3 ounces (84 g) regular or
   firm tofu

1½ teaspoons (8 ml) each:
   black (or shiitake)
   mushroom and tree ear,
   presoaked and minced;
   green onion, minced

   1 teaspoon (5 ml) (scant)
   sesame oil

   1 teaspoon (5 ml) vegetable
   oil

   ¼ teaspoon (1.5 ml) (scant)
   salt

   1 teaspoon (5 ml) soy sauce

Dough:

   1 cup (250 ml) glutinous
   ("sweet") rice flour

   1 teaspoon (5 ml) vegetable
   shortening (Crisco)

   ⅓ cup + 1 tablespoon (85 +
   15 ml) hot water

   3 tablespoons (45 ml)
   vegetable oil for frying

See On Readying Tofu, earlier in this chapter. Mash the tofu to yield ¼ cup.

To make the filling, combine mashed tofu with minced ingredients, sesame oil, 1 teaspoon vegetable oil, salt, and soy sauce.

To make dough: Combine the glutinous rice flour, shortening, and hot water in a mixing bowl; work into a smooth ball by pressing and squeezing. This flour is easy to work with if you keep in mind that it tends to crumble. Just moisten with a little more water if it seems too dry; if too sticky, dust with a little more flour. Cover dough and let rest 10 minutes. Knead briefly—less than a minute. Roll into a cylindrical shape 10 inches long. Cut into ten equal pieces (1-inch lengths). Turn these cut-end up and form into a round shape. On a lightly floured board, flatten them gently with the palm of your hand. Dust each side lightly with flour. Pick up each round between your fingers and thumbs and gently work it into a round wrapper by pressing and pinching, until it is 3 inches in diameter—preferably thicker in the center.

It is a good idea to fill each wrapper as soon as you finish forming it, for they do not stack well without sticking. The dough also dries quickly, so keep it and the filled dumplings covered with plastic wrap. Place at least 1½ teaspoons filling in the center of each wrapper; carefully gather wrapper up around the filling and press-pinch lightly so that the filling is completely enclosed. Gently roll between your palms into a ball shape. If a break occurs, ease the dough back together with a little pinching pressure.

Heat a skillet over high. Add 3 tablespoons oil; when oil is hot, reduce heat to medium and put in the dumplings one by one. Keep them separated or they will stick together. With a Chinese spatula or pancake turner, gradually flatten them just a bit into a patty shape (go easy lest they break open). Brown them lightly on both sides. This should take about 4 minutes, as you want the inside to get done. Then turn heat to high and give them a golden browning (about 1 minute on each side). Toward the end they will puff up slightly. Serve hot.

4

More "Meat Without Bones" −Pressed Tofu

"Meat without bones" is a popular phrase used by Chinese to describe tofu. Americans are already well acquainted with the soft, regular, and firm types of tofu—bone-free, of course, tender, and protein-rich. But, for all its wonders, to hear such a custardy substance equated with meat seems to smack of poetic license.

In fact, there is a form of tofu that is much closer to meat in every way —dense, firm, chewy, and with a more concentrated flavor. It is pressed or "dry" tofu, regular tofu from which most of the moisture has been forced out. The consistency is also much like a firm cheese, although it holds together better and is not crumbly like some cheeses.

This is a familiar item in the markets, restaurants, and street stalls of China. It is the "meaty" ingredient in many a Chinese vegetarian dish —including, in this chapter, "meat shreds," "pork," and "kidneys." Even in nonvegetarian cooking it frequently appears in soups or with meat and fish, slow-cooked so as to become porous and juicy. Chopped and shredded, it is used in fillings (Spring Rolls). The dense cakes are fermented to become tofu "cheese" (see Chapter 1) as well as "stinking" tofu. The people of Nanking are especially fond of pressed tofu, producing it in different shapes, sizes, and varieties, including smoked.

The most widespread and favorite way of eating it also happens to be the easiest to fix: just slice it thinly and add a dash of soy sauce and sesame oil (see Spiced Pressed Tofu with Peanuts). The two most common forms of pressed tofu are the plain and the "five-spiced." You can prepare these yourself at home from regular tofu, and the result will be more tender and much more flavorful than store products. Easy directions follow, along with recipes for cold and hot dishes.

Anyone living near Chinese specialty markets in the United States has a good chance of purchasing both flavors right off the refrigerated shelves. In San Francisco, for example, plain pressed tofu is sold in 7-ounce packages labeled "Firm Pressed Tofu." The spiced variety also comes in 7-ounce packets (with four to five patties each). One brand is called "Flavored Soy Bean Cake." Other brands have names that do not necessarily indicate "spiced," so check the list of ingredients to see if spices are included (in some of these, the "spice" flavor is very light).

To shred pressed tofu, place cakes flat on the cutting board. With blade parallel to the board, slice each square into several thin layers. Stack these, cut vertically into thin strips, and cut strips into shorter lengths.

The recipes in this chapter will serve three or four persons if you add one or two additional entrees as well as soup and rice. Most of them are also excellent one-dish meals for a single person, with rice (see Suggested Menus for some choices).

Plain Pressed Tofu—Basic Recipe

Buy regular or firm tofu at your grocery store—any amount you like, although it is suggested that you start with a pound or so for this first batch. (This will yield approximately 10 ounces after pressing.)

After rinsing, cut your block of tofu vertically into slices, about ¾ to 1 inch thick. Wrap the slices individually and tightly in small (8-inch) squares of muslin or similar thin cloth. Place these on a flat surface. If the surface allows drainage, such as outside or on kitchen drainboard (flat, not grooved), so much the better. However, drainage is not essential, and you can just as well use a cookie sheet, etc. Arrange the wrapped tofu on it, leaving a couple of inches or so between the pieces. Cover them with a cutting board or similiar flat object. Place heavy weights, such as bricks, on top of the board. Increase the weight gradually rather than all at once. Thus, you could start with two bricks, side by side, then add a couple more after a few minutes, and so on. I find that two columns of bricks, eight or nine bricks in each, for a total of 80 pounds, is about right to press four squares of tofu. Let sit two to three hours. Don't worry if the tofu sits in the extracted liquid during this period.

When the tofu is flattened to a thickness of ½ or ⅜ inch, unwrap it; pat dry or set aside for a few minutes to let excess moisture evaporate. If you started with a pound of tofu, divided into four squares, each should now weigh 2 to 2¼ ounces. Store, wrapped tightly in plastic, in the refrigerator, where they will keep a week or so. Do *not* store in water.

Spiced Pressed Tofu—Basic Recipe

It is possible to purchase this item ready-made; some brands are bland, some are quite good. But you should treat yourself to the far more tender and flavorful homemade delicacy. It takes only a few hours to prepare, and you can make enough to use in several of the following recipes. It will keep for a week or so in the refrigerator.

To start with, you need patties of *plain pressed* tofu. Home-pressed tofu will be more tender, but you can also use the commercial plain pressed (one brand is labeled "Firm Pressed Tofu," in 7-ounce packages, refrigerated in Chinese markets, often side-by-side with the spiced variety).

Then make one of the following marinades. The first is a more traditional concoction. For those who can't easily procure the Chinese spices (see Chinese Ingredients for more information), the second uses items available in any market and reproduces nearly the same flavor.

4–8 squares plain pressed tofu (up to 20 ounces [562 g])

Marinade I:

2 star anise

2 teaspoons (10 ml) whole cloves

2 pieces (1-inch [25 mm] squares) dried tangerine or orange peel (see Note)

1 stick cinnamon (2¼ inches [57 mm])

2 teaspoons (10 ml) whole Szechuan peppercorns

4 cups (1000 ml) water

½ cup (125 ml) soy sauce

Marinade II:

2 teaspoons (10 ml) whole cloves

1 stick cinnamon (2½ inches [63 mm])

2 teaspoons (10 ml) fennel seed + 2 teaspoons (10 ml) anise seed; or 4 teaspoons (20 ml) fennel seed

1 piece fresh lemon peel (1-inch [25 mm] square)

4 cups (1000 ml) water

½ cup (125 ml) soy sauce

Note: Dried tangerine (or orange) peel is sold packaged in Chinese markets.

First make the marinade by placing all ingredients except tofu and soy sauce in a pot. Bring to the simmer, reduce heat to low, and maintain the *barest* simmer, covered or partially covered, for 1½ hours. Turn off the heat, cover completely, and let stand another hour or so. Strain out the spices and measure the liquid. You should have about 3½ cups. Add ½ cup soy sauce (or ¼ cup per 1¾ cups liquid) to the pot with liquid.

Now immerse squares of plain pressed tofu in the marinade. This amount will accommodate eight squares comfortably. Steep over very low heat, uncovered, for 2 hours, turning once. (If the pot is covered, you will get an uncharacteristic—but not necessarily unpleasant—porous texture.) The squares can be used at once. Or pat dry, let cool, wrap tightly in plastic, and store in the refrigerator, where they will keep for many days. (Do *not* store them in water.)

Although the marinade can be refrigerated, tightly covered in a jar, and reused, I prefer to make it fresh, especially when more than a week elapses between batches.

See introduction above on how to shred spiced pressed tofu.

Spiced Pressed Tofu with Peanuts

At many small restaurants and street stalls in China, pressed tofu is often ordered as a side dish with something like noodles or as a snack with wine. A variety of other cold appetizers would be available, too—Szechuan Style Cabbage Relish, green soybeans in the pod, as well as cold cuts and tea eggs in nonvegetarian restaurants. When eaten with peanuts, the spiced pressed tofu is supposed to taste like Chinese ham. With or without peanuts, it is highly enjoyable. If you like, serve the nuts in a separate dish. This makes an excellent "meat" entree in a cold supper or with hot vegetable dishes. Since it can be fixed well in advance, make this an occasion for preparing something more complicated, such as Boiled Pot-stickers or Fried Noodles with Garden Vegetables.

7–8 ounces (197–224 g) spiced pressed tofu (4–5 squares)

1 tablespoon (15 ml) (generous) soy sauce

½ teaspoon (3 ml) sugar

1½ teaspoons (8 ml) sesame oil

¼ cup (60 ml) roasted peanuts (optional)

Unless it has just been made, freshen spiced pressed tofu by dunking or rinsing in hot water for a few seconds, then pat dry.

Slice vertically into strips. Or carve off thin, bite-sized slices of irregular shape by holding the knife at a slight angle to the board. Place strips or slices in a small serving bowl and toss with the other ingredients. Let sit at least half an hour before serving, stirring several times in the interim.

Piquant Pressed Tofu Patties

Like the preceding recipe, this is a good appetizer. It can be enjoyed either hot or at room temperature. Plain pressed tofu is first soaked in pickle brine to give it a faint and lingering savor. You can vary the taste by using different brines each time—from dill pickles, sauerkraut, preserved snow cabbage (see Chinese Ingredients), etc. Some Chinese use the solution in which amaranth stems or bamboo shoots have fermented for a number of days. The stems are steamed with rice as a flavoring.

Make this in amounts as large or small as you like, and soak as long as you like, but allow at least a day. On the day of serving, brown the patties and serve them plain or dressed with seasonings. Don't count this as an entree, but rather as a little side dish to add pleasing variety. On the other hand, if all you want is a light supper, whether early evening or around midnight, a plate of this with congee and a relish can go down very well.

8 ounces (224 g) plain pressed tofu (4–5 squares)

¾ cup (180 ml) pickle brine, or enough to cover tofu

2 tablespoons (30 ml) vegetable oil

1 teaspoon (5 ml) soy sauce (optional)

½ teaspoon (3 ml) sesame oil (optional)

Pack the pressed tofu into a small bowl or jar. Pour in brine to cover. Store, covered, in the refrigerator for at least one day.

Remove the pressed tofu from the soaking solution and pat dry. Brown it till golden on both sides over medium or medium-high heat in 2 tablespoons oil. Remove from the pan to a chopping board and cut into small (1- or 1½-inch) squares. Serve hot or cold in a small bowl or on a plate, either plain or tossed with a little soy sauce and sesame oil.

Gingery "Meat Shreds"

As a light "meat" entree or side dish, this is zesty and quick with no cooking oil or extra main ingredients. For this reason it suits rich or filling dishes like Chinese Pumpkin or Yellow Squash with Pine Nuts, or Eggplant Sautéed with Garlic. Be sure to include a crunchy, refreshing relish, such as "Crystal Icicles." This does not have to be served piping hot, so you can have it ready well in advance of mealtime. The yield is 3 or 4 very small portions, so double the recipe if you want heftier servings.

4 ounces (112 g) spiced pressed tofu (2–3 squares)

2 tablespoons (30 ml) water, or soaking liquid from black mushrooms (see Note)

1½ teaspoons (8 ml) rice wine

2–3 teaspoons (10–15 ml) soy sauce

¼ teaspoon (1.5 ml) sugar

½ teaspoon (3 ml) (scant) gingerroot, grated or finely minced

1½ teaspoons (8 ml) sesame oil

Note: Use soaking liquid from several black mushrooms, and save the mushrooms for another recipe.

Unless it has just been made, freshen the tofu by dunking or rinsing in hot water, then rinse and pat dry. Shred tofu to yield 1 heaping cup, loosely packed.

Put the pressed tofu into a pan with 2 tablespoons water or mushroom liquid; place over high heat. When this boils, add 1½ teaspoons rice wine. Stir in 2 to 3 teaspoons soy sauce, depending on how salty the tofu is (if mild, as in the homemade version, use 3 teaspoons; the commercial product may need only 2 teaspoons). Sprinkle on ¼ teaspoon sugar, and stir-fry 30 seconds or until the pan is nearly dry. Remove from the heat. Stir in gingerroot and sesame oil.

Celery and "Meat Shreds"

Tantalizing with their aroma and flavor of spices, the "meat shreds" are moist and tender, while the celery, also shredded, contributes a pleasant crunchiness. An excellent one-dish meal for a single person, with plain steamed rice, or as a co-entree with something lightly seasoned (Taro, Yuca Root, Mountain Yam, or Potato Temptation) or mildly hot (Hearty Bean and Black Mushroom Soup).

½ pound (225 g) celery

4 ounces (112 g) spiced pressed tofu (2–3 squares)

2 tablespoons (30 ml) vegetable oil

1 tablespoon (15 ml) soy sauce

Dash salt

½ teaspoon (3 ml) (scant) sugar

½ teaspoon (3 ml) sesame oil

String the celery if necessary and split it lengthwise into strips ¼ or ⅓ inch wide. Pound or press with the flat side of a cleaver or broad knife to break the celery open. Cut into 1¼-inch lengths. You should have about 2 cups, loose.

Shred tofu to yield 1 cup, loosely packed.

Heat a pan over high; add 2 tablespoons oil; when oil is hot, put in the celery and stir-fry 1 minute. Add the tofu; reduce heat to medium and stir-fry 1 minute. Stir in 1 tablespoon soy sauce, a dash or pinch of salt, and a scant ½ teaspoon sugar; stir-fry 30 seconds. Remove from the heat, top with sesame oil, and serve.

Crunchy Green Pepper and "Meat Shreds" with Green Soybeans or Peas

This trio of green pepper slivers, flavorful "meat shreds," and crunchy green soybeans (or tender peas) could be a whole meal, with just plain rice and perhaps a soup (try Gingery Fried Gluten Soup or Clear Mushroom Soup). Green soybeans are very flavorful and lend good textural appeal to many Chinese dishes and soups. Unlike many other beans, they are best while still firm yet tender. The fresh ones are nearly impossible to scare up here, but Oriental markets often have them frozen (buy the shelled ones for this recipe). Peas are a good substitute but, of course, not as chewy.

1 medium green bell pepper

4 ounces (112 g) spiced
pressed tofu (2–3 squares)

½ cup (125 ml) green soybeans
or peas (fresh or frozen)

2 tablespoons (30 ml)
vegetable oil

1 tablespoon (15 ml) (scant)
soy sauce

Dash salt (if needed)

½ teaspoon (3 ml) sesame oil

Seed the pepper. Slice very thinly lengthwise (top to bottom), then cut into approximately 1½-inch lengths. Yield is 1 cup, loosely packed.

Shred tofu to yield 1 cup, loosely packed.

Frozen soybeans and peas should be defrosted only enough to separate them. Fresh ones should be parboiled until almost tender.

Heat a pan over high; add 2 tablespoons oil; when oil is hot, reduce heat to medium-high. Put in the green pepper; stir-fry 1½ to 2 minutes. Add the soybeans or peas; stir-fry 30 seconds. Add the spiced pressed tofu and stir-fry 30 seconds. Add 1 scant tablespoon soy sauce and, if needed, a dash of salt (commercial brands of pressed tofu probably need no salt); stir-fry 30 seconds more. Before serving, add ½ teaspoon sesame oil.

Pressed Tofu and Mashed Tofu with Bamboo Shoots

The Chinese title is more arresting: "Vegetarian Kidneys and Brains." Whether or not you find this name appetizing, the combination of pressed tofu, regular tofu, and bamboo shoots is as delicious as it is wholesome. This is a mild-flavored dish, so team it up with some contrasting flavors. Zesty Chinese Cabbage Stems (either gingery, garlicky, hot, or all three) is a good relish choice, and Curried Broccoli Stems or Asparagus is a flavorful vegetable accompaniment.

4 ounces (112 g) plain
  pressed tofu (2–3 squares)

12 ounces (337 g) regular or
  firm tofu

⅔ cup (170 ml) bamboo
  shoot, sliced

2½ tablespoons (37.5 ml)
  vegetable oil

1½ teaspoons (8 ml) rice wine

2 tablespoons (30 ml) soy
  sauce

½ teaspoon (3 ml) sugar

1 teaspoon (5 ml) cornstarch
  dissolved in 1 teaspoon (5
  ml) cold water

2 teaspoons (10 ml) toasted
  sesame seeds

½ teaspoon (3 ml) sesame oil

With a knife, score one face of the pressed tofu in a fine, criss-cross grid pattern, cutting halfway down. Cut each square into smaller (1- or 1½-inch) squares, then cut each square in half diagonally to make small triangles.

To prepare the regular tofu, see On Readying Tofu, Chapter 3. Mash the tofu, or stir to break it up.

Slice bamboo shoot thinly, lengthwise.

Heat a pan over high; add 2½ tablespoons oil; when oil is hot, reduce heat to medium-high. Put in the pressed tofu, mashed tofu, and bamboo shoot; stir-fry 1½ minutes. Add 1½ teaspoons rice wine around the edge of the pan. Sprinkle on 2 table-spoons soy sauce, ½ teaspoon sugar, and cornstarch mixture. Stir-fry until well mixed and the pan is nearly dry (under 1 minute). Remove from the heat and stir in 2 teaspoons sesame seeds and ½ tea-spoon sesame oil.

Hot Pepper Tofu with "Pork"

This recalls the famous dish that originated in the roadside eateries at the north gate of the capital of Szechuan. Economical yet delicious, it was an attraction to all. A certain Widow Chen's was regarded as the best. Since she was pockmarked, the dish became known as "Old Lady Pockmark's Tofu." In this recipe, crumbled spiced pressed tofu replaces the meat. If you do not like hot seasonings, just go easy on the red pepper or chile oil or omit it altogether. Be sure to have a relish to go with this (I suggest Snappy Cucumber Relish) or, for a change, a bowl of cool and refreshing Litchi Gelatin (Chapter 8).

1 pound (450 g) regular or firm tofu

3 ounces (84 g) spiced pressed tofu (1½ squares)

2 tablespoons (30 ml) Chinese bean sauce or dark miso (see Note)

¼ teaspoon (1.5 ml) red pepper or chile oil

2½ tablespoons (37.5 ml) vegetable oil

1 teaspoon (5 ml) (heaping) garlic, minced

1 teaspoon (5 ml) (packed) gingerroot, minced or grated

1 tablespoon (15 ml) (heaping) green onion

1 tablespoon (15 ml) soy sauce

¼ cup (60 ml) water

1 teaspoon (5 ml) rice wine

½ teaspoon (3 ml) (scant) sugar

½ teaspoon (3 ml) sesame oil

Note: Use either regular or ground bean sauce, sold in Chinese markets. Miso is available in Japanese groceries and health food stores. In this recipe use the dark kind, which is saltier.

See On Readying Tofu, Chapter 3. Cut tofu into ½-inch cubes.

Crumble the spiced pressed tofu coarsely to yield ¾ cup, loose.

In a small bowl, combine bean sauce or miso and red pepper or chile oil (if you are using miso, also blend with 2 tablespoons water).

Into a preheated pan over high heat, put 2½ table-spoons oil. When oil is hot, reduce heat to medium-high, add garlic, gingerroot and green onion; stir-fry till the aroma rises. Add pressed tofu, bean sauce or miso mixture, tofu, 1 tablespoon soy sauce, ¼ cup water, 1 teaspoon wine, and a scant ½ teaspoon sugar. Stir-fry gently until well mixed and the pan is nearly dry. Remove from the heat, test for salt, add ½ teaspoon sesame oil, and serve.

Peking Style Noodles with Bean Sauce and Mixed Garnish

This dish seems to please everybody, for it is a standard in noodle shops. It owes its savory taste to Chinese bean sauce, which is like miso (you can use miso in its place). Both consist of fermented soybeans, but rice is added to miso, and Chinese bean sauce is sometimes made from fava beans. In this recipe you can use either the ground or the regular bean sauce (see Chinese Ingredients). There is a hint of garlic in this dish, and meaty substance is provided by tender pressed tofu. The garnish—a combination of green soybeans, diced bamboo shoot, and cucumber—comprises almost a meal in itself. For one or even two persons, this is all you need for a lunch or dinner, unless you want to add a light soup, such as Three Delicacies Soup or Clear Mushroom Soup.

Use your choice of any Chinese flour noodle. I suggest a flat type. There is time enough while the noodles are cooking to prepare the sauce, but if you would rather take things one at a time, cook the sauce first, then give it a quick reheating before serving. The green soybeans and bamboo shoot (but not cucumber) can be heated with the sauce, too, if you want everything as hot as possible. Add them just before removing sauce from the stove. (You can cook the noodles first; in this case, I like to add them to the sauce for a quick reheating, too.)

Bring this to the table on a plate or in a bowl and toss to combine the garnishes before serving.

8 ounces (224 g) noodles (3–4 cups after cooking)

6 ounces (170 g) plain pressed tofu (4–5 squares)

½ cup (125 ml) green soybeans, frozen or fresh, or 2 ounces (56 g) baby corn spears

½ cup (125 ml) bamboo shoot, diced finely

2 ounces (56 g) cucumber

1 teaspoon (5 ml) garlic, minced

3 tablespoons (45 ml) Chinese bean sauce or 4 tablespoons (60 ml) dark miso

3 tablespoons (45 ml) vegetable oil

1½ cups (375 ml) water

1–1½ tablespoons (15–22.5 ml) soy sauce

½ teaspoon (3 ml) sugar

2½ tablespoons (37.5 ml) cornstarch dissolved in 3 tablespoons (45 ml) water

½ teaspoon (3 ml) sesame oil

If you are cooking the noodles first, drain them, remove to a bowl or serving platter, and toss with ½ tablespoon sesame oil to prevent sticking (do not rinse in cold water as this reduces flavor).

Crumble the pressed tofu coarsely to yield 1½ cups.

Parboil green soybeans till almost tender yet still firm (10 minutes for frozen). If using fresh baby corn spears, steam or parboil till tender; if canned, rinse with boiling water. Rinse green soybeans or corn in cold water and chop finely. You should have about ½ cup baby corn.

It is not necessary to peel or seed the hothouse (English) or Oriental cucumber. Regular cucumber should be pared and seeded, but leave a few narrow strips of skin for color and texture. Julienne finely to yield ½ cup.

If you are using miso, dissolve it in ¼ cup warm water.

Put 3 tablespoons oil into a preheated pan over high. When the oil is hot, reduce heat to medium-high. Add garlic and stir-fry a few seconds to release aroma. Add pressed tofu and bean sauce or miso. Stir-fry briefly to mix. Add 1½ cups water, 1 table-spoon soy sauce, and ½ teaspoon sugar. Cook, stirring occasionally, until the boil is reached. Gradually stir in cornstarch mixture and cook, stirring, another minute or so until the consistency is like a light gravy, not too thick. Test for salt, and add an extra ½ tablespoon soy sauce if needed. (At this point, if you like, you can heat noodles and/or green soybeans, baby corn, and bamboo shoot by combining with the sauce until just mixed.) Add ½ teaspoon sesame oil. Remove from the stove. Pour sauce over noodles, and top with garnish in separate arrangements (garnish with just the cucumber if you have added soybeans or baby corn and bamboo shoot to the sauce). Toss before serving.

Spring Rolls

Americans commonly call these "egg rolls," a mis-
nomer actually, since eggs do not play a role in any
version, vegetarian or not. (In fact, there *is* a Chinese egg roll, the skin of which is a sort of paper-thin
omelet.) For this recipe, the "egg roll wrappers"
found in supermarkets can be used. However, if you
can obtain the *paper-thin, round* (8-inch diameter)
skin, sold refrigerated or frozen in some Chinese
markets, the result will be less doughy and more
crispy. This type of skin is the product of an exacting
technique that requires a light and deft hand. A
thick iron grill is heated to the appropriate temperature. Then a ball of dough, held by hand, is touched
to the hot surface in one lightning-swift, twisting
motion so that only the thinnest of round films of
dough is applied. A Japanese chef who had studied
cooking styles around the world once commented
that this was the hardest technique he ever tried to
master.

This recipe makes six rolls. Serve these as appetizers with any crisp, tart relish (Sweet-and-Sour Relish
Sticks is good since it contains no oil).

2 ounces (56 g) spiced pressed tofu (1–2 squares)

2 tablespoons (30 ml) black (or shiitake) mushrooms, presoaked and shredded

1 cup (250 ml) (heaping, packed) Chinese cabbage, shredded

2 tablespoons (30 ml) bamboo shoot, chopped or shredded

1 tablespoon (15 ml) vegetable oil

Pinch salt

1½ teaspoons (8 ml) soy sauce

6 spring roll skins or "egg roll wrappers"

Flour paste (4½ [67.5 ml] tablespoons flour + 1 tablespoon [15 ml] cold water)

6 tablespoons (90 ml) vegetable oil

Dipping sauce (optional):

Soy sauce

Mushroom soaking liquid

Unless it has just been made, freshen the spiced pressed tofu by dunking or rinsing in scalding hot water, then pat dry. Shred to yield ½ cup, loosely packed.

To prepare the filling, heat a pan over high. Add 1 tablespoon oil. When oil is hot, put in the mushrooms and stir-fry a few seconds. Add the Chinese cabbage and stir-fry 1 minute or until wilted. Reduce heat to medium-high. Put in the spiced pressed tofu and bamboo shoot; stir-fry 1 minute. Add a pinch of salt and 1½ teaspoons soy sauce; stir-fry 1 minute. Remove from the heat.

You can assemble the rolls now or wait until the filling has cooled. On a wrapper or skin, place about 2 tablespoons filling in a finger-shaped row below center (with square skin, this is usually done diagonally). Fold the bottom up over the filling and roll upward a half-turn. Spread some flour-and-water paste over the side flaps; fold them in toward the center, envelope style. Spread paste over the top flap; roll up all the way.

Put 6 tablespoons oil in a preheated skillet (high heat). When the oil is hot, put in the spring rolls, seam-side down. Reduce heat to medium-high. Fry to a deep golden brown on *all* sides by turning frequently. Reduce heat further if they seem to be browning too rapidly. Drain on paper towels. Leave whole or cut in half.

Serve with or without a dip, as you like. Suggested mixture is one part soy sauce to four parts mushroom liquid (from the black mushrooms), in small individual dipping saucers.

5

"Duck," "Chicken," and Other Specialties

Devising fanciful names for food is a time-honored and cultivated practice in China. Vegetarian and nonvegetarian menus are replete with elegant, imaginative allusions to phoenixes, dragons, gods and fairies, gems, jades, gold, and silver, all the better to enhance the appeal of the edibles in their culinary transformation. On occasion, these titles are whimsically descriptive. Where else would one find large meatballs known as "lions' heads"? Or a combination of ground pork and bean threads called "Ants Climbing a Tree"? The most common of fare can be made to sound enticing and worthy even of an emperor's delectation. A story is told of the Ch'ien Lung emperor who, while staying with an eminent scholar on a visit to southern China, was served a simple vegetarian dish of spinach and browned tofu. The scholar had grown up in humble circumstances and knew such dishes well, but it was a marvelous new delicacy to the emperor's jaded and pampered palate. He inquired its name. Replied the scholar, inventing a suitably exalted one on the spot: "Red-beaked Green Parrots with Gilded Tablets of White Jade" (red beaks referring to the red-tinged root ends of the spinach).

Many Chinese vegetarian recipes, in temples and restaurants alike, are called by a nonvegetarian name and indeed may have been created in a deliberate attempt to duplicate a popular meat dish—either in taste or appearance or both. Sometimes, although the result might be quite delicious, the resemblance is in name only, serving but to whet the appetite. But there are cases, too, in which the original model is surpassed. Vegetarian "chicken," for example, (made from bean curd sheet and/or bean curd skin) can not only taste and look like the real thing, but is melt-in-the-mouth tender.

These duplications certainly provide an avenue for culinary inventiveness, in which otherwise plain ingredients are given wondrous new guises and character. However, the point is not to replace chicken, ham, or whatever the namesake might be, or even to be a substitute for them. More aptly, these are delicious, different, and nourishing offerings that can stand on their own merits. If the titles only augment their appeal, then everyone comes out ahead, including the chicken and duck populations.

By now you are familiar with tofu, pressed tofu, bamboo shoots, and black mushrooms and how they are accorded distinct favor by this school of cooking. There are other specialty ingredients that appear frequently—some almost exclusively—in vegetarian cuisine and contribute to its uniqueness. Salted-dried bamboo shoot tips, bean curd sheet, and bean curd skin are three outstanding ones. (The term "bean curd" is used here instead of tofu since these products currently are being packaged under those names.)

These ingredients are featured in this chapter. You may have to search a little to find them, and a few more steps are required in the preparation. But the rewards are some very unusual and satisfying eating, seldom to be enjoyed in this country, even at restaurants.

In some instances the entire dish can be assembled in advance to be steamed just before serving. In any case, the "viand" part of it can usually be made ahead of time.

Unless otherwise stated, these recipes yield three or four servings. Serve them as entrees, just as you would any other meat.

On Salted-dried Bamboo Shoot Tips

Salted-dried bamboo shoot tips, 2 to 3 inches long, have a gray, gnarled, dusty appearance; they are imported from mainland China in bamboo leaf baskets.

Bien jien swun, as they are called in Chinese, are admired for their piquant, salty flavor and tender yet chewy texture. They are used by Cantonese, Shanghainese, and vegetarian chefs. Thin, tender shoots (the very tips and the base portions are not used) are salted and dried. They become dun colored, with a gnarled, dusted appearance, usually several inches in length and ¼ inch wide.

In Chinese markets here, they may be sold in small plastic bags labeled "Salted Bamboo Tips" or in a basketlike container weighing over 2 pounds, imported from mainland China. Those from Hangchow are considered superior. Remember, it is essential that you use the *salted* and dried type. An unsalted product labeled "Dried Bamboo Shoot Tips" is often seen, but will not provide the necessary flavor.

Dried bamboo shoot tips must be soaked before use. You will need three to four strands to yield 1 tablespoon, shredded, after soaking. Without rinsing (which would wash away some of the flavor), cover them with cool water for 3 to 4 hours or until soft. Reserve the soaking liquid for use in the same recipe if liquid is required; if not, save it for inclusion in soups. This solution is very salty, so always test before adding salt or soy sauce to the dish.

To shred the softened tips, squeeze liquid back into the soaking vessel. Sliver them very finely lengthwise or at a slight angle, then cut into ½- or 1-inch lengths.

On Bean Curd Sheet

*W*hereas tofu results from pressing soybean custard in a mold, bean curd sheet is obtained from pressing the custard in thin layers between cloth, then steaming. Each sheet comes out resembling a square of thick cloth, flexible and with the weave of the cloth imprinted faintly on it. (If you remember that this ingredient looks like a small square of thick yellow *sheet*ing, or even canvas, you won't confuse it with bean curd *skin*—see section immediately following.) It is possible to make this at home, but it is not the easiest of procedures. Custard must be of the right consistency and pressure evenly applied to produce a sheet of consistent thinness.

In these recipes, the sheets are often steamed in a roll to become the tender, solid, "fleshy" part of a vegetarian "duck" or "chicken" dish. They are also cut into strips and tossed or stir-fried, much like noodles.

Frozen bean curd sheets are available in certain Chinese markets. Look for labels saying "Bean Curd Sheet" or "Bean Curd in Sheets," but there is also the occasional oddity: "Fresh Bean Curd (Heavy)." (Chinese names include *bai yeh, chien jang,* and *chien tsung.*) An 8-ounce package contains 15 to 25 sheets. Usually they are 5 to 6 inches square, which is the size you want for these recipes. If larger (11 × 11), cut them into 5½-inch squares after defrosting. Fresh or frozen, these must be steeped in a baking soda solution before use, in order to soften them. (Unfortunately, bean curd *skin* is also sometimes labeled "sheet" in English, so keep the description of the product in mind when shopping, and it is helpful to ask for assistance, using the Shopping List with Chinese names at the end of the book. Also, please see Note at the end of the next section, On Bean Curd Skin.)

To steep fresh or frozen bean curd sheets: When using only a few from a package, defrost just enough to allow peeling off the required number of sheets. Refreeze the remainder. Or if you intend to use the sheets within a couple of days, they can be kept in the refrigerator. In a pot, bring 3 cups water to the boil; remove from the stove and add from 1½ teaspoons to 3 tablespoons baking soda (guidelines on the amount follow below). Put in the sheets, one by one, and steep over low or medium-low heat until they soften and become creamy white—15 to 20 minutes, or longer if extra thick. Do not layer the sheets in the pot; they do not have to lie flat. Tip or agitate the pot frequently, or gently swish the sheets a bit, so that all are evenly soaked. Keep the solution quite hot but do not let it simmer. Since the sheets are used whole in most recipes, you do not want them so soft that they will tear during handling. *When they are starting to feel silken to the touch and losing their yellow-brown hue,* they are probably ready. The consistency should resemble that of a tender noodle; in other words, not tough.

Thickness, quality, and condition are all variable, so it is impossible to specify exactly how much baking soda or soaking time will be required. You can use two approaches: either start with a minimum, 1½ teaspoons baking soda, increasing the amount if you see no results after 10 or 15 minutes. Or you can start with what is probably the maximum you'll ever need, 3 tablespoons baking soda (for 3 cups water). If this works too fast—that is, if the sheets become too soft almost immediately—you'll know you can lessen the amount of soda next time. (You can probably still use these sheets—just drain and rinse them right away.) Try testing one sheet first. Generally speaking, once you arrive at the optimum proportions, you can use the same amount next time. The length of steeping time will probably remain fairly constant, too, if you stick with the same brand of sheets.

After steeping, run cool tap water into the pot to rinse the sheets, drain carefully, and repeat another two or three times. Carefully pick up each sheet separately (it is helpful to have water in the pot so the sheets don't mass or stick together). Lay each sheet on paper toweling and gently pat dry.

The sheets are then usually stacked in twos or threes and rolled up (occasionally, but not usually, with a filling). The bottom layer must be untorn. A few sheets will tear during handling, but don't worry. Pick one that is thick and in one piece for this bottom position. Torn sheets can be pieced together on top of it. If your sheets tear too easily, you probably steeped them too long or used too much baking soda, or both.

These rolls are then usually wrapped or rolled up in bean curd skin, which helps hold everything together.

On Bean Curd Skin

While bean curd sheets serve as the viand "flesh," a wrapping of "skin" is often provided by bean curd skin. Remarkably, this may also provide a skinlike flavor. The skin, which is the film formed on soybean "milk," is said to be almost 100 percent protein. I've been taught to make it, but it is a tricky process, requiring soybean milk of the proper consistency and temperature. Of course it is very tender. At places where good quality soybean milk is available for breakfast, a thick skin forms on top and some people like to ask for this to wrap around a long, crispy deep-fried cruller. Fresh skin is sold at markets in China, commonly called "vegetarian chicken." But of course the dried form is quite different, for it has been lifted off the heated soybean milk with a thin stick, then hung up to dry in a flat layer.

For these recipes, there are two types of bean curd skin available, frozen and dried. The frozen is preferred since it is easier to handle and more flavorful.

Frozen: This type is folded and sold in small packages, or in bulk, at select Chinese markets. It is usually unmarked, or marked in Chinese *(dofu pi, fu pi, dofu yi,* or *syan fu ju).* The large, round skins are about 22 inches in diameter, slick and pliable, a golden yellow in color. When a recipe calls for "1 bean curd skin," you will want a whole 22-inch circle. It will then usually be cut into quarters or sixths, divided like a pie into roughly triangular shapes. This type of skin keeps indefinitely in the freezer, and it defrosts *immediately.* Air quickly turns it brittle, so keep it in a plastic bag when not actively working with it, both before and after cutting. If drying occurs, soften between damp paper towels. No extra preparatory steps are needed.

Dried: This is surely the most fragile food product in the world. Thin as paper and brittle as autumn leaves, it must be stored very carefully. The fact that it can be shipped at all from as far away as Hong Kong, and arrive intact, is no less than a phenomenon, especially as the packaging is merely thin paper and a plastic bag. To protect them from the general jostle, most Chinese markets hang these large, flat sacks high on the wall. They will probably escape your notice, so—as with the frozen skin— you should ask if they are in stock. The label on the bag will read "Bean Curd in Sheets."

These dried skins come in *half* circles, 18 or 19 inches in diameter. In a recipe calling for "1 bean curd skin," use two of these half circles. For "½ bean curd skin," use only one of the half circles. Although fragile, it is very easy to handle once you've completed the first step, as follows:

Dampen a two-panel length of paper toweling and squeeze it dry. Spread this out on a table. Lay a dried skin on top. Then place another dampened and squeezed paper towel on top of the skin. Begin patting very gently. As you feel the skin softening, apply a little more pressure. When it feels soft and pliable, you can remove the towel and begin working with the skin. It is important that the towels be just barely damp—if they are too wet, the skin all but dissolves. Like the frozen type, it turns brittle again very quickly, so keep it covered with the dampened paper toweling while not working with it, and after rolling things up in it.

Frozen and dried skins usually have a narrow, thick edge, which you can cut off. Freeze these and use in a recipe of Chinese "Ham" or Feast of Delicacies.

Other types of skin: There is a very papery thin, flexible, dried skin that is not brittle and comes in similarly large, round half circles, of somewhat darkish color. This is called *dofu yi,* or bean curd "wrap," but it is not usually found in stores here.

Note: One San Francisco firm packages the above frozen product as bean curd "sheets" instead of skin; so when in doubt, show the shopkeeper the Chinese name (see Shopping List), and make it clear you want the kind used for wrapping. Do *not* use a dried product called *"san bien fu ju"* for these recipes requiring skin. It comes in oblong yellowish sheets, in packages variously labeled "Beancurd Dried," "Dried Bean Curd," and, confusingly, even

"Beancurd Sheet." Derived from soybean milk of a different consistency, it is thicker, altogether less flavorful, and less tender than the above frozen and dried skins. It is not considered a skin at all and is used in stir-fried vegetarian dishes.

Bean Curd Sheet Noodles

Steeping bean curd sheet is quite easy once you learn to recognize the right moment for removing it from the hot solution. This takes beginner's luck, or one or two practice sessions. Here is a good recipe to start out with, for once the sheet (here cut into strips) is ready, all you have to do is toss it with flavorings. For warm-weather enjoyment, this is a light and tasty side dish or lunch.

8 bean curd sheets

½–3 tablespoons (7.5–45 ml) baking soda dissolved in 3 cups (750 ml) boiling water

1 teaspoon (5 ml) salt

1 tablespoon (15 ml) soy sauce

⅔ teaspoon (3.5 ml) sugar

1 tablespoon (15 ml) sesame oil

Defrost frozen bean curd sheets. Cut into narrow (¼-inch) strips. Steep and rinse these according to directions earlier in this chapter, On Bean Curd Sheet.

Sprinkle the bean curd sheet with 1 teaspoon salt and toss carefully by hand for a minute. Rinse two or three times. Squeeze out excess water from a handful of the strips at a time (do not be afraid of mashing them; use the same manner of squeezing as with relishes, described in Chapter 1).

Toss the strips with soy sauce, sugar, and sesame oil. The noodles can be served immediately.

Advance preparation: Prepare the noodles in advance, then refrigerate or not, but keep them covered. Toss them with the remaining ingredients shortly before serving, at room temperature.

Greens and Bean Curd Sheet Noodles

This is like a cold pasta salad, but the "noodles" are actually thin layers of tofu, in strips. They have an incomparably light and tender texture and a subtle flavor. Serve this as an attractive salad or cold course. With spinach it is delicate and slightly sweet in taste; with celery, crunchy and, if you like, spicy.

¾ pound (340 g) spinach or 6 ounces (170 g) celery hearts

½ + 1 teaspoon (3 + 5 ml) salt

8 bean curd sheets

½–3 tablespoons (7.5–45 ml) baking soda dissolved in 3 cups (750 ml) boiling water

½ teaspoon (3 ml) sugar

1 tablespoon (15 ml) sesame oil

¼–¾ teaspoon (1.5–4 ml) chile oil, if using celery (optional)

Dash salt, to taste

To prepare spinach, separate the leaves, leaving stems (also keep the red root ends if desired, or simply eat them alone, tossed with a little soy sauce and sesame oil).

To prepare celery, string if necessary and make narrow, ¼-inch strips by cutting it lengthwise. Pound or press with a heavy object, such as the side of a cleaver, to break celery open. Cut into 1-inch lengths. You should have about 1½ cups.

Steam spinach or celery in a vegetable basket to wilt —1½ minutes for spinach, stirring once; 3 minutes for celery. (Or, instead of steaming, immerse in a pot of boiling water—30 seconds for spinach, till second hard boil for celery.) Cool in cold water to halt cooking and hold the color. Divide into several handfuls and squeeze firmly to remove liquid. Chop spinach coarsely.

Place spinach or regular celery in a mixing bowl, and sprinkle with ½ teaspoon salt (omit this step with Chinese celery). Mix-massage by hand for a minute; let stand 5 minutes for spinach, ½ hour for celery. Do not rinse spinach; rinse celery five times in cold water. Divide spinach or celery into several handfuls and *firmly* squeeze out liquid (see introduction to Chapter 1 for efficient squeezing method). Place in a medium-sized serving bowl.

Defrost frozen bean curd sheets. Cut into narrow (¼-inch) strips. Steep and rinse these according to directions earlier in this chapter, On Bean Curd Sheet. Then toss gently by hand with 1 teaspoon salt. Again rinse two or three times, drain, and squeeze firmly to rid of excess moisture.

Using chopsticks, gently toss spinach or celery and bean curd sheet strips with sugar and sesame oil. With celery, if desired, add chile oil to taste. Test for salt and add a dash or more if needed. Can be served immediately.

Advance preparation: Both the greens and bean curd sheet strips can be readied in advance. Refrigerate them separately, covered. Shortly before serving time, toss together with the remaining ingredients, and serve at room temperature.

Bean Curd Sheet Noodles with Garlic Chives or Leek

A dish of special delicacy, in which marvelously tender strips of bean curd sheet are sautéed with a generous portion of garlic chives or shredded leek. Garlic chives are the flat-leaved variety, also called Chinese chives.

8 bean curd sheets

½–3 tablespoons (7.5–45 ml) baking soda dissolved in 3 cups (750 ml) boiling water

5 ounces (140 g) garlic chives or leek

3 tablespoons (45 ml) vegetable oil

¼ teaspoon (1.5 ml) salt

1 teaspoon (5 ml) (scant) rice wine

2–4 tablespoons (30–60 ml) water (if needed)

Defrost frozen bean curd sheets. Cut into strips, ¼ inch wide. Soak according to directions earlier in this chapter, On Bean Curd Sheet. For this dish the strips should be *almost* but not quite tender, for they will be cooked a bit more, and if they are too soft they will break up excessively during frying (expect some breakage anyway). Rinse and drain according to basic directions.

Garlic chives: Cut into 1-inch lengths. Yield is 2 cups, packed. Leek: Cut lengthwise into fine shreds, 1 or 1½ inches long. Yield is about 1½ cups, loosely packed.

Heat a pan over high; add 3 tablespoons oil and half the salt (⅛ teaspoon). When the oil is hot, put in the chives or leek; reduce heat to medium-high; stir-fry 30 seconds (1 minute for leek). Swirl 1 scant teaspoon wine around the edge. Add the bean curd sheet and a little water if the pan is dry (about 4 tablespoons water with leek, 2 tablespoons or none with garlic chives); stir-fry 1 minute. Before removing from the heat, stir in remaining salt (⅛ teaspoon).

Crispy Fried "Duck"

This tender "duck meat" is basically a very simple creation: bean curd sheets are spread with a flavorful sauce, stacked together, rolled up, and fried to a crispy brown on the outside.

10 bean curd sheets

½–3 tablespoons (7.5–45 ml) baking soda dissolved in 3 cups (750 ml) boiling water

1 tablespoon (15 ml) soy sauce

1 tablespoon (15 ml) brown sugar

1 tablespoon (15 ml) sesame oil

1 teaspoon (5 ml) Szechuan peppercorns

3 tablespoon vegetable oil

Defrost frozen bean curd sheets. Soak and rinse according to directions earlier in this chapter, On Bean Curd Sheet. They should be as tender as possible and still permit handling without tearing. Drain on paper towels and pat dry.

Prepare a sauce by heating over medium heat the soy sauce, brown sugar, sesame oil, and Szechuan peppercorns until the sugar dissolves and the aroma rises. Strain to remove the peppercorns.

Stack the bean curd sheets one atop the other, spreading a little sauce (about 1 teaspoon) over each before adding the next. The bottom sheet must be whole and untorn. Do not spread sauce on the top sheet. Roll up tightly. Tie securely with string, making several passes around the roll from one end to the other. Hold the roll up vertically and squeeze with the gentlest of pressure, allowing excess liquid to drain out.

Heat a large, heavy pot (the sides will guard against spattering) over high heat; add 3 tablespoons oil. When oil is hot, put in the "duck," reduce heat to medium, and keep turning the roll until it is a golden brown all over and getting crispy. This should take at least 4 minutes, as you want it to heat all the way through. Remove to a plate, let cool slightly before removing the string, then slice slantwise. If any of the sauce is left, it can be reheated and spread over the "duck" slices.

Juicy Rice "Duck" Casserole

Ginkgo nuts ("white nuts") are too bitter to eat raw but after cooking become soft, chewy, and mellow. Shelled and blanched, they are available in cans and small jars. You can also gather them fresh if a tree grows near you. Resembling pistachios, fresh nuts in the shell are often sold by Chinese grocers.

A mouth-watering casserole-type dish consisting of a soft and chewy glutinous rice pancake topped with ginkgo nuts and a delectable tofu mixture. Ginkgo nuts have a tender yet dense texture. Buy them in cans (sometimes labeled Boiled White Nuts) or use fresh nuts, sold in bulk in Chinese markets. In the shell they look much like a pistachio. This is a superb steamed entree for lunch or dinner.

20 ginkgo nuts

½ cup (125 ml) glutinous rice (also called "sweet" rice)

⅓ cup (85 ml) water

3 tablespoons (45 ml) vegetable oil

7 ounces (197 g) regular or firm tofu

3 tablespoons (45 ml) (packed) each, minced: black (or shiitake) mushrooms, salted-dried bamboo shoot tips (both presoaked), and bamboo shoot (preferably winter)

⅔ cup (170 ml) soaking liquid from mushrooms and dried bamboo shoot tips, mixed to taste

1 tablespoon (15 ml) soy sauce, to taste

1 teaspoon (5 ml) sesame oil

If the ginkgo nuts are canned, use them as is. If they are in the shell, see parboiling directions in Chinese Ingredients.

Place ½ cup glutinous ("sweet") rice in a greased, heatproof bowl with ⅓ cup water. Place in a steamer and steam 30 minutes (follow directions in On Steaming Soups, Chapter 7).

Stir the rice. Heat a skillet over high; add 1 tablespoon oil; when oil is hot, reduce heat to medium. Put in the rice and stir-fry 2 to 3 minutes; also keep "cutting" it with the edge of a spatula or pancake turner, since it sticks together. After 2 or 3 minutes, start pressing the rice flat and forming it into a pancake shape, 5 to 6 inches in diameter. Keep turning and pressing for about 5 minutes, then turn the heat to high and give it a light golden browning on both sides—another 3 minutes. Transfer the pancake to a small casserole or fairly flat-bottomed heatproof bowl.

Dice the tofu finely to yield 1 cup. Heat a pan over high; add 2 tablespoons oil; stir-fry the minced ingredients (mushroom, dried bamboo shoot tips, and bamboo shoot) till their aromas rise, about 30 seconds. Add the diced tofu; stir just enough to combine the ingredients, then remove from the heat.

Spread the tofu mixture on top of the rice cake. Press the ginkgo nuts into it (or the nuts may be placed between the rice cake and tofu). Pour in ⅔ cup soaking liquid to barely cover. Add 1 tablespoon soy sauce. Place in a steamer and steam 20 minutes. Top with a little sesame oil, and serve in bowls.

Marvelous "Chicken"

(A)

(B)

For Marvelous "Chicken," a row of bamboo shoot strips and two rows of black mushroom strips are placed near bottom of a double thickness of bean curd sheet (A); sheets are then rolled up tightly. Each filled roll is then placed on a quarter of a bean curd skin (B) and rolled up inside it.

A most unusual "chicken," with tasty skin, light and dark meat, and a crunchy, edible "bone." It is actually bean curd skin, bean curd sheet, black mushroom, and bamboo shoot. This can be as good as, or better than, the real thing.

8 bean curd sheets

½–3 tablespoons (7.5–45 ml) baking soda dissolved in 3 cups (750 ml) boiling water

1 winter bamboo shoot (small)

10 black (or shiitake) mushrooms, presoaked

1 bean curd skin

Cornstarch paste (2 teaspoons [10 ml] cornstarch + 1 teaspoon [5 ml] cold water)

3 tablespoons (45 ml) vegetable oil

¼ cup (60 ml) mushroom soaking liquid

1 tablespoon (15 ml) soy sauce

Pinch salt

½ teaspoon (3 ml) sugar

½ teaspoon (3 ml) sesame oil

Defrost frozen bean curd sheets. Soak, rinse, and drain according to directions earlier in this chapter, On Bean Curd Sheet.

Cut the bamboo shoot into strips, ⅓ inch wide and ⅓ inch thick, 2½ to 3 inches long. You should have 12 or 15 strips.

Cut the black mushrooms into strips ½ inch wide.

Stack the bean curd sheets together in pairs; the bottom sheets should be untorn. Place a row of bamboo shoot and a double row of mushroom together toward the bottom (see illustration A). Roll up tightly. You will have four rolls.

Cut the bean curd skin into quarters (dried skin should be dampened lightly first; see On Bean Curd Skin, earlier in this chapter). Place a bean curd sheet roll on a piece of bean curd skin (parallel with a straight side) and roll up (see illustration B); seal with cornstarch-and-water paste. With a knife, trim the ends, which will be open. Repeat three more times. Place the rolls on a greased perforated rack (or greased heatproof plate) in a steamer and steam 10 minutes.

Remove the "chicken" from the steamer and brown it on all sides in 3 tablespoons oil in a skillet over medium or medium-high heat. Drain on paper towels. Cut into 1½-inch pieces.

Remove all but a light coating of oil from the skillet. Return the "chicken" to the pan along with ¼ cup mushroom soaking liquid, 1 tablespoon soy sauce, a pinch of salt, and ½ teaspoon sugar. Cook over medium or medium-high until the pan is dry, turning the rolls once. Before serving, add a few drops of sesame oil.

Sliced "Chicken Breast" with Tree Ear and Mushrooms

I have casually served this with no introduction or fanfare and everyone just assumed it was chicken! This has a light but richly seasoned gravy over the slices of tender "white meat," with tree ear and mushrooms.

8 bean curd sheets

½–3 tablespoons (7.5–45 ml) baking soda dissolved in 3 cups (750 ml) boiling water

2 tablespoons (30 ml) (packed) salted-dried bamboo shoot tips, presoaked (see Note)

2–3 tree ears, presoaked

8 black (or shiitake) mushrooms, presoaked

2 tablespoons (30 ml) vegetable oil

¾ cup (180 ml) soaking liquids from mushrooms and dried bamboo shoot tips

1 tablespoon (15 ml) soy sauce (to taste)

1 teaspoon (5 ml) sugar

1 teaspoon (5 ml) cornstarch dissolved in 1 teaspoon (5 ml) water

½ teaspoon (3 ml) sesame oil

Note: See On Salted-dried Bamboo Shoot Tips, earlier in this chapter, for more on this ingredient.

First make the "chicken" as follows: Defrost frozen bean curd sheets. Steep, rinse, and drain them according to directions earlier in this chapter, On Bean Curd Sheet. After draining on paper towels, stack four sheets together (make sure the bottom sheet is whole and untorn); roll up tightly. You will have two rolls. Roll up each of them in a piece of damp cloth about 10 inches wide; fold the sides in before rolling all the way up so that the bean curd sheet is completely enclosed. Steam 15 to 20 minutes on a rack in a steamer. Let cool slightly before unwrapping; if sticking occurs, use a knife to scrape the "chicken" from the cloth. Slice the rolls into bite-sized pieces ⅓ inch thick, wielding the knife slantwise at an angle to the table.

Shred the dried bamboo shoot tips; cut into 1-inch lengths.

Tear the tree ear into small pieces. Yield: about ½ cup, loose.

Cut larger mushrooms to bite-size.

Heat a pan over high; add 2 tablespoons oil. When oil is hot, reduce heat to medium-high and put in the mushrooms and dried bamboo shoot tips; stir-fry 30 seconds. Add the tree ear. Carefully fold in the "chicken" slices. Pour in ¾ cup soaking liquid; cook 1 minute. Add soy sauce to taste (1 tablespoon, more or less) and 1 teaspoon sugar; cook until the liquid is reduced to ⅓ cup—1 to 2 minutes. Blend in the cornstarch mixture. When the sauce is thick, remove from the heat and add a few drops of sesame oil.

Chestnut "Chicken"

Chestnut chicken as prepared by Shanghainese chefs has always been high on my list of favorites. This version is an entree well worth the extra trouble: rolls of bean curd sheet, bean curd sticks, and bean curd skin are browned, then simmered with fresh mushrooms and chestnuts in a little mushroom liquid and soy sauce. Bean curd sticks are most often found in stir-fried vegetarian dishes. They have a very chewy texture. Many Chinese markets have them in cellophane packages. They must be soaked in water several hours. When preparing this dish, cook up an extra portion of chestnuts, not only to snack on, but perhaps also to use in Eggplant with Chestnuts (Chapter 6). If you cook them without removing or piercing the shells, they will steam inside and be moist and tender.

½ cup (125 ml) chestnuts, fresh or canned

4 bean curd sheets

½–3 tablespoons (7.5–45 ml) baking soda dissolved in 3 cups (750 ml) boiling water

1 bean curd stick (12-inch [300 mm]), presoaked

½ bean curd skin, cut in half

Cornstarch paste (2 teaspoons [10 ml] cornstarch + 1 teaspoon [5 ml] cold water)

3 tablespoons (45 ml) vegetable oil

12 fresh mushrooms

¾ cup (180 ml) mushroom soaking liquid (see Note)

1½ tablespoons (22.5 ml) soy sauce

½ teaspoon (3 ml) sugar

2 teaspoons (10 ml) cornstarch dissolved in 1 tablespoon (15 ml) water

Note: Use soaking liquid from several black (or shiitake) mushrooms; save mushrooms for another recipe.

Fresh chestnuts: Cook in the shell in water to cover until tender—15 to 30 minutes, depending on size. *While still hot,* remove the shells and the reddish inner skin, including that in the grooves of the meat (a toothpick may help here). Unless you do this very quickly after removing chestnuts from the water, the skin will stick to the meat. The chestnuts should be tender but not crumbly; if necessary, cook them a little longer. Break large ones into smaller pieces. Yield after skinning should be ½ cup.

Canned chestnuts: Pick over them and remove any skins. If large, break into smaller pieces.

If bean curd skin is dried, dampen it before cutting according to directions earlier in this chapter, On Bean Curd Skin.

Defrost frozen bean curd sheets. Soak, rinse, and drain them according to directions earlier in this chapter, On Bean Curd Sheet. Stack them together in pairs. Cut presoaked bean curd stick to conform with width of the sheets. Place a length of stick near the bottom of each sheet and roll up tightly. Then place each roll on ¼ piece bean curd skin parallel with a straight side, and again roll up tightly, sealing with a little cornstarch-and-water paste. The ends of each roll (you will have two) will be open; trim them neatly with a knife.

Heat a skillet over high; add 2 tablespoons oil. When the oil is hot, reduce heat to medium and put in the rolls; brown them seam-side first, then keep turning to brown on all sides. Remove from the pan and cut each roll in half.

Return the skillet to medium heat with 1 tablespoon oil; stir-fry the fresh mushrooms 1 minute. Add ¾ cup mushroom soaking liquid, 1½ tablespoons soy sauce, ½ teaspoon sugar, chestnuts, and the "chicken" pieces. Stir gently to mix the ingredients, then cover and cook 5 minutes, stirring once or twice, until about ⅓ cup liquid remains. Thicken by stirring in the cornstarch solution; combine gently until the sauce is gravylike, not runny.

Potato "Goose"

This "goose" is composed of potato or, better yet, mountain yam—that is, yuca root or *naga imo*. The former, stocked by some Chinese grocers, has a rich firmness. *Naga imo*, sold in Japanese markets, is smooth and subtle. If neither of these is available, use potatoes. The tuber is wrapped in bean curd skin with an accompaniment of marinated gingerroot and soy-pickled cucumber (see Chinese Ingredients). This rich-tasting delicacy is served in chunks. To complete the meal, I suggest a simple green vegetable, one or two relishes (perhaps Pungent Bean Sprouts), and Clear Mushroom Soup. Rice would not be necessary, since you already have potato.

1 pound (450 g) potatoes; or yuca root or *naga imo*

1 bean curd skin

3 tablespoons (45 ml) soy-pickled cucumber, julienned

3 tablespoons (45 ml) marinated gingerroot, julienned

Cornstarch paste (2 teaspoons [10 ml] cornstarch + 1 teaspoon [5 ml] cold water)

4–5 tablespoons (60–75 ml) vegetable oil

1 tablespoon (15 ml) rice wine

2 tablespoons (30 ml) water

½ teaspoon (3 ml) sugar

½ teaspoon (3 ml) sesame oil

Potato may be left with skin intact; *naga imo* or yuca root must be peeled. Boil or steam until fork-tender. Cut into inch-thick strips.

Cut bean curd skin into quarters. If dried, dampen lightly before cutting, according to directions earlier in this chapter, On Bean Curd Skin.

Lay the bean curd skin out flat with a straight side toward you. Arrange an inch-thick row of potato from left to right and well below center. Place a row each of cucumber and gingerroot alongside the potato. Roll up tightly and seal with a little cornstarch-and-water paste. You will have four rolls. Trim ends (which will be open) and cut each roll in half.

Heat 4 tablespoons oil in a preheated skillet. When the oil is hot, reduce heat to medium-high or medium and put in the rolls, seam-side down. Brown them for a few seconds on this side, then keep turning to brown evenly on all sides. If the oil gets too hot and begins to smoke, reduce heat further or lift pan above the burner. Swirl 1 tablespoon rice wine around the edge of the pan, sprinkle on 2 tablespoons water and ½ teaspoon sugar. Keep turning the rolls for a minute or less, until the pan is all but dry. Remove from the pan, cut into 1½- or 2-inch pieces, and serve topped with a few drops of sesame oil.

Chinese "Ham"

This really tastes like ham, although the color and texture are different. Slice it hot as an entree, or serve it as an appetizer for starting a special meal, perhaps on a cold platter with cashews, black mushrooms, and young corn spears (see Succulent Black Mushrooms and Cashews, Chapter 1). This also makes a good cold supper, with hot congee.

1 frozen bean curd skin, or 6 pieces dried bean curd skin

1 green onion

1 tablespoon (15 ml) sesame oil

1 slice gingerroot

¼ cup (60 ml) water

1 tablespoon (15 ml) soy sauce

Pinch salt

½ teaspoon (3 ml) sugar

Cut the frozen bean curd skin in half (or use six half-circles of dried skin; they should be dampened lightly first—see On Bean Curd Skin, earlier in this chapter).

Stack the halves of skin and roll up tightly. Slice the roll crosswise thinly (¼ inch or less). Place the rolled strips in a mixing bowl and toss lightly to loosen and mix. Set aside.

Cut green onion into 1-inch lengths.

Heat sesame oil, green onion, and gingerroot in a pan or small pot over medium heat. When the aroma rises, remove from the heat. Discard onion and gingerroot. Add water, soy sauce, salt, and sugar; stir to mix. Gradually dribble this mixture over the bean curd sheet strips, tossing at the same time to mix evenly.

Divide the tossed skin into two portions, placing each on the center of a 12-inch square of thin cloth (or you can make one roll only, but it will require 2-3 hours steaming). Before rolling up, shape each mound into a roll about 8 inches in length. Fold the bottom flap of cloth over this, fold in the sides, then roll up as tightly as possible. Tie securely with a string, making several passes around each roll from one end to the other.

Place on a perforated rack in a steamer and steam 1 hour (or 2-3 hours for one large roll), turning once. Remove and unwrap. To serve, make ¼-inch slices with knife held at an angle to the table.

Advance preparation: This can be made ahead and stored in the refrigerator, wrapped in plastic. Before serving, slice and serve cold or reheat by steaming briefly.

Savory Steamed Casserole

This small casserole dish is steamed and has a meaty-rich flavor with delightfully chewy texture. The topping of bean curd skin can be omitted without altering the flavor significantly, but it is a nutritious addition.

½ bean curd skin (optional)

Vegetable oil for deep-frying bean curd skin

12 ounces (337 g) regular or firm tofu

2 tablespoons (30 ml) (packed) salted-dried bamboo shoot tips, presoaked and minced (see Note)

3 tablespoons (45 ml) black (or shiitake) mushrooms, presoaked and minced

2–3 tablespoons (30–45 ml) bamboo shoot (preferably winter), minced

1 tablespoon (15 ml) green onion, minced

1½ tablespoons (22.5 ml) soy sauce

1 tablespoon (15 ml) vegetable oil

½ teaspoon (3 ml) sesame oil

Note: See On Salted-dried Bamboo Shoot Tips, earlier in this chapter, for more on this ingredient.

If the bean curd sheet is dried, it is not necessary to dampen it before frying. Heat oil for deep-frying; it should not be too hot. Fold the skin in half to fit the pot. Fry the skin only a second or two on each side; remove it as soon as it is light brown, and drain on paper toweling. It will be limp while frying but turns crisp afterwards.

See On Readying Tofu, Chapter 3. Mash the tofu and combine with minced ingredients, soy sauce, and 1 tablespoon vegetable oil. Pack this mixture into a small heatproof bowl or casserole and top with the fried bean curd skin, broken into pieces. Place the bowl in a steamer and steam 15 to 20 minutes. Before serving, dribble ½ teaspoon sesame oil over the top.

Shredded Black Mushroom "Eel"

Those who might not be enticed by the name can be assured that this is merely shreds of black mushroom dusted with flour and deep-fried, then paired with julienned bamboo shoot and served up in a rich sauce. It's much easier to prepare than real eel, which requires meticulous deboning.

15 black (or shiitake) mushrooms

1 tablespoon (15 ml) flour

¼ teaspoon (1.5 ml) (scant) salt

Vegetable oil for deep-frying

1 tablespoon (15 ml) vegetable oil

½ cup (125 ml) bamboo shoot, julienned

⅓ cup (85 ml) soaking liquid from black mushrooms

1 tablespoon (15 ml) soy sauce

¼ teaspoon (1.5 ml) sugar

1 teaspoon (5 ml) cornstarch dissolved in 2 teaspoons (10 ml) water

½ teaspoon (3 ml) sesame oil (optional)

Cut the mushrooms into thin strips. You should have about 1 cup. Combine flour and salt; add mushroom strips and toss until evenly coated.

Heat vegetable oil for deep-frying. Deep-fry the mushrooms, small portions at a time, separating the strips and spreading them out evenly over the oil. Keep heat between medium-high and high. When browned, remove and drain on paper toweling.

Heat a pan over high; add 1 tablespoon oil. When oil is hot, put in the bamboo shoot and deep-fried mushrooms; reduce heat to medium and stir-fry 30 seconds. Add ⅓ cup mushroom soaking liquid and 1 tablespoon soy sauce; cook 1 minute. Stir in ¼ teaspoon sugar, then half the cornstarch mixture. Add the remainder only if necessary to make a slightly thick, but not pasty, coating. Add ½ teaspoon sesame oil, and serve.

Winter and Summer Bamboo Shoots

This crunchy vegetable dish has a likable piquant flavor, with two kinds of julienned bamboo shoots. The salted-dried tips are from a summer bamboo shoot. Winter shoots are liked for their crispness and perfumed fragrance (see Chinese Ingredients for details).

2 tablespoons (30 ml)
vegetable oil

1 cup (250 ml) bamboo shoot
(preferably winter), julienned

2 tablespoons (30 ml)
salted-dried bamboo shoot
tips, presoaked and
shredded (see Note)

2 tablespoons (30 ml) black
(or shiitake) mushrooms,
presoaked and minced

1 tablespoon (15 ml) soy sauce

¼ cup (60 ml) soaking liquid
from dried bamboo shoot
tips

½ teaspoon (3 ml) sugar

1 teaspoon (5 ml) sesame oil

Note: See On Salted-dried Bamboo Shoot Tips, earlier in this chapter, for more on this ingredient.

Heat a pan over high; add 2 tablespoons oil. When oil is hot, put in the bamboo shoot; stir-fry 30 seconds. Reduce heat to medium-high; add the dried bamboo shoot tips and mushrooms; stir-fry 1 minute. Sprinkle on 1 tablespoon soy sauce; add ¼ cup bamboo soaking liquid; reduce heat to medium; cook 1 minute or until the pan is almost dry, stirring two or three times. Before removing from the stove, stir in ½ teaspoon sugar and 1 teaspoon sesame oil.

Feast of Delicacies

There are many vegetarian and nonvegetarian versions of this dish, all a bountiful matching of ten main ingredients, more or less. It often plays a part in lunar New Year's festivities, for it can be made in large quantities and reheated. Traditionally, no knives are used during the first five days of the New Year (this taboo has been extended more rigorously by some people to the first 15 days and even into the second month), therefore all the kitchen chopping and much of the cooking must be done ahead of time. Preparations might begin in earnest a month in advance for special holiday fare. Markets, restaurants, and street stalls close over the holiday, too, so each household has to be well prepared. One of my teachers used to bring me a large supply of this dish to last the duration, and it was delicious even cold. A lot of variation exists with the components, so feel free to substitute, and omit or add, as convenience dictates.

12 pieces fried gluten

¾ cup (180 ml) fresh mushrooms, sliced

12 black (or shiitake) mushrooms, presoaked

3 tablespoons (45 ml) (packed) salted-dried bamboo shoot tips, presoaked and shredded (optional)

10 ginkgo nuts

¼ cup (60 ml) green soybeans or peas, fresh or frozen

½ bean curd skin; and/or 1 (12-inch [300 mm]) bean curd stick

½ cup (125 ml) bamboo shoot, sliced

⅓ cup (85 ml) dried lily buds, presoaked; and/or julienned carrot

4 + 2 tablespoons (60 + 30 ml) vegetable oil

2 tablespoons (30 ml) soy sauce

⅔ cup (170 ml) soaking liquids from mushrooms and dried bamboo shoot tips, mixed to taste

½ teaspoon (3 ml) sugar

Salt to taste

1 teaspoon (5 ml) sesame oil

See introduction and Basic Recipe, Chapter 6, for information on fried gluten.

Slice the black mushrooms.

See Chinese Ingredients for information on ginkgo nuts.

Do not defrost frozen soybeans or peas. Fresh green soybeans and very large fresh peas will have to be parboiled until almost tender.

If bean curd skin is dried, dampen it lightly first, according to directions earlier in this chapter, On Bean Curd Skin. Frozen skin needs only to be defrosted. Cut into narrow (¼-inch) strips.

See Chinese Ingredients for information on bean curd sticks. Cut presoaked and squeezed stick into 1-inch lengths.

See Chinese Ingredients for information on dried lily buds. Tie them in pairs.

Heat a pan over high; add 4 tablespoons oil. When oil is hot, put in the bean curd skin strips; fry on both sides for a few seconds. They will stick together, so remove them as soon as they are browned (have a plate or board handy), and chop them coarsely. Add 2 tablespoons more oil to the pan, along with bean curd skin, and all the remaining vegetables.

If not using bean curd skin, start with 3 tablespoons oil. Add all the vegetables. Reduce heat to medium-high and stir-fry 2 minutes. Sprinkle on 2 tablespoons soy sauce; pour in ⅔ cup soaking liquid. When this boils, add ½ teaspoon sugar; cook at a fast simmer, stirring frequently, for 3 minutes. Test the liquid for salt. Turn heat to high and stir-fry until the pan is nearly dry. Top with 1 teaspoon sesame oil, and serve.

Advance preparation: This recipe can be made ahead, kept in the refrigerator, and reheated or served at room temperature.

Bean Curd Skin Rolls

These are similar to Spring Rolls, but the wrapper is the very thin, nutritious bean curd skin. A choice of fillings is given. After frying, the rolls are seasoned with soy and combined with an optional vegetable (bamboo shoot, greens, or broccoli). Or they can be deep-fried and served like Spring Rolls (see Variation).

1½ bean curd skins

　　Choice of fillings A, B, or C below

　　Cornstarch paste (2 tablespoons [30 ml] cornstarch + 1 tablespoon [15 ml] cold water)

½ cup (125 ml) sliced bamboo shoot, or 4–5 ounces (112–140g) greens or broccoli flowerets (optional)

3½–4 tablespoons (52.5–60 ml) vegetable oil

½ teaspoon (3 ml) (scant) sugar

1½–2 tablespoons (22.5–30 ml) soy sauce

2–4 tablespoons (30–60 ml) water, or soaking liquid from black mushrooms

½ teaspoon (3 ml) sesame oil

Prepare one of the fillings by combining the ingredients.

Cut the bean curd skin into sixths (pie-slice shape); 1½ skins will yield nine pieces. To avoid drying, keep it in a plastic bag before and after wrapping the filling. If skin is the dried type, dampen it first according to directions earlier in this chapter, On Bean Curd Skin.

Wrap 1½ or 2 tablespoons filling in each piece of skin, as follows: With pointed end toward you, place a 3-inch row of filling below center (but not all the way to the sides). Fold the bottom flap of skin over the filling; roll once. Apply a little cornstarch-and-water paste over the two sides of the skin; fold these over envelope-fashion, keeping right angles. Then spread paste over the top flap and roll up tightly all the way.

Optional vegetable: Scald greens until just wilted, then rinse under cool water. Broccoli flowerets, cut into small pieces, should be steamed or parboiled until almost done, then cooled in water. Set aside.

Heat a skillet over high; add 3½ to 4 tablespoons oil. When oil is hot, reduce heat to medium; put in the rolls seam-side down. Brown them on this side, then keep turning to brown on all sides. Do only a few at a time if the pan seems too crowded.

Filling A:

> 7 ounces (197 g) regular or firm tofu (mash to yield ⅔ cup [170 ml])

> 4 tablespoons (60 ml) black (or shiitake) mushroom, presoaked and minced

> 2 tablespoons (30 ml) tree ear, presoaked and minced

> ½ teaspoon (3 ml) salt

Filling B:

> 7 ounces (197 g) regular or firm tofu (dice to yield 1 cup [250 ml])

> 2 tablespoons (30 ml) each, presoaked and minced: black (or shiitake) mushrooms, salted-dried bamboo shoot tips

> 2 tablespoons (30 ml) winter bamboo shoot, minced

> 1 tablespoon (15 ml) soy sauce

If you are including bamboo shoots, greens, or broccoli, remove the rolls from the pan and stir-fry the vegetable 1 minute in 1 tablespoon oil (there may be enough oil left in the pan for this), medium heat. Return the rolls to the pan with the vegetable.

Even if you are not including a vegetable, return the rolls to the pan. Sprinkle ⅓ teaspoon sugar over the top, then 1½ tablespoons soy sauce and 2 tablespoons water or mushroom soaking liquid (with a vegetable, use 2 tablespoons soy sauce and 3 to 4 tablespoons water). Turn heat to medium-high or high and cook 1 to 2 minutes, or until the pan is dry, turning the rolls once. Remove from the heat, add ½ teaspoon sesame oil. Serve whole, or cut into smaller pieces.

Variation: Bean curd skin rolls can be deep-fried; hold them with tongs or chopsticks during the first few seconds, as the skin puffs up and is apt to unroll. Then turn until they are a uniform golden brown, remove, and drain on paper towels. Serve whole or cut into sections.

Filling C:

½ cup (125 ml) green
vegetable, chopped
(Chinese cabbage, baby
mustard cabbage, etc.);
mix with ½ teaspoon (3
ml) salt, let stand 10
minutes, squeeze dry

½ cup (125 ml) spiced
pressed tofu, shredded
finely (see Chapter 4)

½ cup (125 ml) bamboo
shoot, minced

⅔ teaspoon (3.5 ml) salt

"Chicken" and Tofu Ball Soup

A sumptuous steamed soup laden with good things
—tofu balls, dried bamboo shoot tips, shiitake
mushrooms, and pieces of "chicken" (steamed bean
curd sheet and skin).

7 ounces (197 g) regular or firm tofu

1½ teaspoons (8 ml) green onion (or 1 tablespoon [15 ml] cedar buds), minced

½ teaspoon (3 ml) (scant) salt

2 tablespoons (30 ml) flour

3 tablespoons (45 ml) vegetable oil

6 bean curd sheets

½–3 tablespoons (7.5–45 ml) baking soda dissolved in 3 cups (750 ml) boiling water

½ bean curd skin, cut in half

Cornstarch paste (2 teaspoons [10 ml]) cornstarch + 1 teaspoon [5 ml] cold water)

12 black (or shiitake) mushrooms

2 tablespoons (30 ml) (packed) salted-dried bamboo shoot tips, presoaked and shredded (see Note)

3 cups (750 ml) liquid (soaking liquids from mushrooms and dried bamboo shoot tips + water)

1 tablespoon (15 ml) soy sauce

⅛ teaspoon (.5 ml) salt

½ teaspoon (3 ml) sesame oil

Note: See On Salted-dried Bamboo Shoot Tips, earlier in this chapter, for more information on this ingredient.

See On Readying Tofu, Chapter 3. Mash the tofu to yield ⅔ cup. Combine mashed tofu with green onion (or cedar buds), salt, and flour. Form into small balls, 1 tablespoon each. Stir-fry these in 3 tablespoons hot oil over medium-high heat until browned. Drain on paper towels and set aside.

Defrost frozen bean curd sheets. Soak, rinse, and drain according to directions earlier in this chapter, On Bean Curd Sheet. Stack the sheets together in threes, and roll up; you will have two rolls. Then roll up each of them in ¼ bean curd skin (if dried, dampen it first according to directions earlier in this chapter, On Bean Curd Skin). Seal with a little cornstarch-and-water paste; trim the ends (which will be open). Place the two "chicken" rolls on a greased perforated rack or greased heatproof plate and steam 3 minutes. The rack should be well above the boiling water. After they are steamed, let the rolls cool slightly, then cut into 1¼-inch lengths.

Slice the mushrooms.

In a heatproof bowl, place mushrooms, dried bamboo shoot tips, tofu balls, and "chicken" pieces. Pour in 2 cups liquid; reserve 1 cup to add after steaming (the "chicken" holds together better while steaming if liquid is kept at a minimum). Season with 1 tablespoon soy sauce and ⅛ teaspoon salt. Steam 15 minutes. Pour in 1 additional cup hot liquid, top with ½ teaspoon sesame oil for aroma, and serve. Or, for best results, let sit in the steamer over very low heat, covered, another 15 minutes or longer.

Advance preparation: This can be reheated by steaming.

6

"Meat from Wheat"
—Fried Gluten

Gluten is probably one of the most untapped sources of protein we have.

Most anyone familiar with bread making knows that gluten is what gives elasticity to a flour dough. Some know that it constitutes the protein content and that the rest of the dough is starch. But not everyone knows that you can wash this starch out and retain just the gluten, a nutritious, delicious protein substance used in many vegetarian dishes. The Chinese call it "flour muscle."

Various forms of gluten are used in vegetarian cooking, ranging from solid and chewy, to spongy, to puffy and light. This chapter will concentrate on fried gluten (actually deep-fried) since it is available canned and can also be made at home. From start to finish, the process is fascinating, even entertaining. Under running tap water you literally wash the starch from a ball of dough. This leaves the sticky gluten, which expands dramatically into puffs when deep-fried. The puffs deflate soon after frying (unless glutinous rice flour or yeast has been added). But that is not important, for after deep-frying, the balls are softened in hot water to become chewy, tender, and ready for use in a variety of preparations—stir-fried, braised, steamed, and soups. They contribute variety, nutrition, and richness, besides absorbing the juices and flavorings of the dish.

The canned product needs no preparation at all. Several brands are available in Chinese markets. The best include Chin Yeh, Hsin Tung

Yang, and Wei-Chuan. These are all in small cans (5.5, 4.23, or 6 ounces). Companion brand's "Chai Pow Yu (Braised Gluten)" comes in a 10-ounce size.

Add these, or your homemade gluten, directly to Chinese dishes and just about any vegetable you might cook—frozen peas, canned soup, fresh greens. Fried gluten is also delicious simply heated and eaten by itself. The canned product is of excellent quality and already deliciously seasoned. The following Basic Recipe tells you how to season your own homemade puffs for use in the recipes in this chapter.

Even if fried gluten is unavailable and you lack the time to make it at home, you can prepare the following recipes without it. Simply omit it, or use the alternate ingredient.

Like most of the other recipes in this book, these serve three or four persons in a menu of three or four dishes.

Fried Gluten Puffs—Basic Recipe

In the following recipes—all of which call for fried gluten as a desirable but not required ingredient— use either this homemade version or canned fried gluten (see introduction to this chapter for more information). Some Chinese markets also sell large fresh fried gluten balls. This recipe makes approximately 20 small puffs with semolina flour (enough for use in two dishes), or 60-70 puffs with gluten flour. You can also include them in soups (Gingery Fried Gluten Soup, Deep-fried Tofu or Fried Gluten Soup with Bean Threads, Three Delicacies Soup, all in Chapter 7) and other recipes, such as Feast of Delicacies.

The flours used in this recipe are available in many supermarkets and health food stores. Semolina (pasta flour) is also sold in Italian markets. It is possible to use all-purpose flour only, but the result will be tougher and grayish in color. Although the procedure for making these puffs may sound involved, once you get into the swing and know what to expect, it actually takes just about an hour and a half of working time. After deep-frying, these puffs will keep in the refrigerator, in a plastic bag, for several weeks. Before using, soften and freshen them in hot water, according to the directions below, and toss with seasonings.

⅔ cup (170 ml) semolina (durum wheat) flour or gluten flour

⅔ cup (170 ml) all-purpose flour

½ teaspoon (3 ml) salt

½ cup (125 ml) water

Vegetable oil for deep-frying

Seasoning: (for 20 puffs)

½ teaspoon (3 ml) soy sauce

¼ teaspoon (1.5 ml) (heaping) sugar

Dash salt

2 teaspoons (10 ml) sesame oil

In a mixing bowl, toss ⅔ cup durum wheat or gluten flour with ⅔ cup all-purpose flour and ½ teaspoon salt. Gradually add ½ cup water, and mix by hand into a dough. Knead on a lightly floured board, working in more flour or water if necessary, for about 5 minutes until smooth and elastic. Cover and let rest 1 hour.

Hold the ball of dough loosely between your hands under a trickle of lukewarm tap water. During the first couple of minutes, just gently roll the ball around between your palms. You will note the cloudy color of the water as the starch washes out. Gradually you can begin to gently press and flatten the ball, and soon begin to squeeze it with your fingers, alternating hands—*but keep rolling it back into a round shape* (this will prevent dropping any solid bits of dough). You can get a rhythm going: squeeze, squeeze, roll; squeeze, squeeze, roll. After several minutes you will be able to really dig in with your fingers for the squeeze.

Little by little, the ball will get smaller and begin to take on a ragged appearance. At this time (after 8 to 10 minutes), you can work it with more vigor and even begin a "scrubbing" action *between both palms.* Remember to keep rolling back into a cohesive ball shape, for this is when solid bits can easily be lost. After 15 minutes, the ball will have an almost rubbery elasticity and you can scrub quite aggressively. It will have an appearance resembling cauliflower. When the water runs fairly clear, after about 15 to 20 minutes, set the ball on a cutting board to drain (it is as sticky as chewing gum, so don't drain on paper towels). It will be only about one-third the size of your original dough.

To deep-fry the gluten, pull off small pieces and roll into marble-sized balls. Heat oil for deep-frying. I use a small pot and keep the heat around medium. Deep-fry only a few at a time; the oil should bubble gently, not froth, around them. Start with one ball. It will stick to the bottom of the pot; but allow it to puff up before scraping it loose with a spoon or fork.

It will then rise to the surface. Press it against the side of the pot *firmly* with fork or spoon (it helps to have another fork or spoon in your other hand to keep it from escaping). Keep pressing and turning the ball for a minute or so—this will help it puff up all the more. When it feels fully inflated and the surface starts to harden, you can stop pressing, but leave it in the oil another minute or so, turning frequently, to lightly brown.

You can get a sequence going in which three balls are in the pot at one time: while a new ball is puffing up, a second ball is being pressed, and a third is browning. Don't let them touch, as they stick together. A little gluten will stick to your utensil as well; a bit won't matter, and use your other utensil to scrape off extra build-up. Don't expect the balls to brown too much. A light coloring is enough. Drain them on paper towels. They will deflate soon after removing from the oil.

Store them in a plastic bag in the refrigerator.

Before using them or the commercial balls, sold fresh in some Chinese markets, they must be softened in hot water, which also removes oiliness. Warm a small pot of water till very hot (but not simmering). Put in the balls, and keep submerging them with a spoon, or weigh them down with a small plate. When they have absorbed water to become spongy (a couple of minutes), remove, rinse under cold tap water, and squeeze dry.

Toss the softened fried gluten with seasonings: for 20 small puffs, use ½ teaspoon soy sauce, ¼ teaspoon (heaping) sugar, dash salt, and 2 teaspoons sesame oil. Now the fried gluten is ready to use. When a recipe calls for "10" or "15 pieces fried gluten," use 10 or 15 of these. (If you are using fresh, large commercial balls, cut them into bite-sized pieces or slices to total 10 or 15.)

Eggplant with Fried Gluten or Chestnuts

(A)

(C)

(B)

Chinese eggplant (A) is 7 to 12 inches long, thin, and violet in color. Black eggplant or Japanese eggplant (B), ranging from a few inches to a foot in length, is purple-black with firm, heavier flesh. Baby eggplant (C) is a small variety of black eggplant.

What is often called Chinese eggplant is slender and tubular, anywhere from seven inches to a foot long, and a vivid violet in color. It is lightweight with soft flesh that cooks quickly. The purple-black, more gourd-shaped variety is called black eggplant in Chinese (or Japanese eggplant in Japanese groceries). It ranges from "baby" size (like a thumb) to as much as a pound in weight. This type has a firmer, heavier flesh. There are, in addition, white-skinned versions of both these types. All these are mild in flavor with none of the bite that the larger "regular" eggplant can have. The skins, too, are usually thin and edible. Any of these eggplants are good in this recipe.

Fried gluten or chestnuts (see Variation) add regal richness to this dish, but the steamed or boiled eggplant can also stand alone, tossed with the sauce. You have your choice of two sauces. Spices for Sauce II are found in most Oriental and some natural food stores (see Chinese Ingredients). You need only 2½ tablespoons of sauce for this eggplant dish, but the recipe allows you to make a plentiful supply, which can be stored in a jar in the refrigerator and used as a dip. It will keep indefinitely. If you want to make a smaller amount, use only one or two sections of a star anise and reduce other ingredients proportionately.

Since this recipe is steamed or boiled and can be made in advance, keep it in mind when you need something to go with one of the stir-fried dishes. It can be served at room temperature or quickly reheated just before serving. It will also keep overnight in the refrigerator. I especially like it with congee.

¾ pound (340 g) eggplant (see Note)

10–15 pieces fried gluten

Sauce I:

   2 tablespoons (30 ml) soy sauce

   1½ teaspoons (8 ml) sesame oil

Sauce II:

   1 cup (250 ml) soy sauce

   1 star anise

   1½ teaspoons (8 ml) Szechuan peppercorns

   ½ cup (125 ml) sugar

Note: When using regular eggplant, purchase about 14 ounces, since it must be pared.

When using the Oriental varieties of eggplant, immerse them unskinned in a pot of boiling water and cook, covered, over medium heat until fork-tender. Drain. If desired, you can also steam them.

Regular eggplant should be pared, then cut into thick slices. To help remove any sharp taste in the larger specimens, scrape off some of the seeded portion and soak the slices in cold water 15 minutes. Drain, then steam in a steaming basket until very soft and fork-tender.

If using canned fried gluten, no advance preparation is required. If fresh, soften the balls in hot water over low heat (according to preceding Basic Recipe), rinse, squeeze dry, and cut into smaller pieces if large.

Meanwhile, if you are using Sauce II, prepare it as follows: Heat 1 cup soy sauce, 1 star anise, 1½ teaspoons Szechuan peppercorns, and ½ cup sugar in a pot over medium heat, stirring constantly. When the sugar dissolves and the aroma rises, remove it from the heat. Strain out the spices.

When the cooked eggplant is cool enough to handle, use your fingers to "peel" the flesh into long strips. Discard skins of the Oriental eggplants only if tough. Place in a serving bowl, add fried gluten, and toss with ingredients of Sauce I or 2½ tablespoons of Sauce II. Or, if you prefer, serve Sauce II in dipping bowls.

Variation: Add ½ cup cooked chestnuts, broken into pieces, in place of fried gluten (see Chestnut "Chicken," Chapter 5, for directions on preparing chestnuts).

Eggplant Sautéed with Fried Gluten or Garlic

This is a rich dish well suited for cold-weather dining, especially if prepared with fried gluten. Use any of the varieties of eggplant described in the previous recipe. Since the eggplant soaks up a lot of oil, serve this with steamed, baked, or broiled dishes and soups. Any of the mushroom soups (see Chapter 7) go well with this.

¾ pound (340 g) eggplant (see Note 1)

10–15 pieces fried gluten; or 3 large cloves garlic

6 tablespoons (90 ml) vegetable oil

1 tablespoon (15 ml) soy sauce

½ cup (125 ml) water or mushroom soaking liquid (see Note 2)

½ teaspoon (3 ml) (scant) salt

2 slices gingerroot (1-inch [25 mm] diameter)

½ teaspoon (3 ml) sugar

1 teaspoon (5 ml) rice wine (if using garlic)

Note 1: When using regular eggplant, purchase about 14 ounces, since it must be pared.

Note 2: Use soaking liquid from several black (or shiitake) mushrooms. Save the mushrooms for another recipe.

To prepare regular eggplant, pare, cut lengthwise into quarters or eighths, then cut crosswise into bite-sized wedges, ⅜ to ½ inch thick.

To prepare Oriental varieties of eggplant, halve lengthwise without paring, then make diagonal or crosswise slices—¼ inch thick for black ("Japanese") eggplant, ½ inch thick for the long, violet, softer "Chinese" type.

If using canned fried gluten, no advance procedure is required. If fresh, soften and season the balls according to the Basic Recipe earlier in this chapter. Cut into smaller pieces if large.

If you decide to use garlic, do not include fried gluten, as the flavors are not complementary. Crush the garlic.

Put 6 tablespoons oil and garlic in a preheated pan (high). Stir-fry garlic until browned, then remove and discard. Put in the eggplant and stir-fry 4–5 minutes until tender; after the first minute of frying, reduce heat to medium-high. After this 4- to 5-minute period, add in succession, stirring after each addition: 1 tablespoon soy sauce, ½ cup water or mushroom soaking liquid, a scant ½ teaspoon salt, 2 slices gingerroot, fried gluten, ½ teaspoon sugar (¼ teaspoon if fried gluten is canned), and—if using garlic—1 teaspoon rice wine. Stir-fry until the pan is nearly dry—1–2 minutes. Test for salt.

Before serving, remove the gingerroot slices.

Chinese Cabbage with Fried Gluten Nuggets or Bean Threads

An elegant way to embellish Chinese (Napa) cabbage—with succulent black mushrooms, tender nuggets of fried gluten, and bamboo shoots. A variation is to use bean threads ("cellophane noodles," now in the Chinese section of many supermarkets) in place of the fried gluten. Either way, this is one of my favorite recipes. It is also one that does not get overcooked easily, so you can do the first stage of cooking in advance—say, shortly before guests arrive. Many of the tofu recipes are very successful with this, including cold-tossed Tofu Dressed with Gingerroot and Green Onion, or Hot Pepper Tofu with "Pork." For a relish, choose something tart: Sweet-and-Sour Relish Sticks or Tangy-rich Carrot Relish. These also add color.

1 pound (450 g) Chinese cabbage (see Note)

15 pieces fried gluten

8 black (or shiitake) mushrooms, presoaked

½ cup (125 ml) bamboo shoot, sliced

3 tablespoons (45 ml) vegetable oil

2–3 tablespoons (30–45 ml) soaking liquid from black mushrooms

1 tablespoon (15 ml) soy sauce

¼ teaspoon (1.5 ml) salt

½ teaspoon (3 ml) sugar

½ teaspoon (3 ml) sesame oil

Note: You should buy a 1¼-pound head of Chinese cabbage in order to have 1 pound after trimming.

Tear the Chinese cabbage into bite-sized pieces.

If you are using canned fried gluten, no advance preparation is necessary. If fresh, soften and season the balls according to the Basic Recipe earlier in this chapter; cut into small pieces if extra large.

Cut large black mushrooms into halves or thirds; leave small ones whole.

Heat a wok or skillet over high; add 3 tablespoons oil. When oil is hot, put in the cabbage; reduce heat to medium-high, and stir-fry 1½ minutes. Add black mushrooms and bamboo shoot; stir-fry 2 minutes. Sprinkle on 2–3 tablespoons mushroom liquid; cover, reduce heat to medium, and cook until the cabbage is tender (4 minutes), stirring two or three times. The cabbage exudes moisture of its own, but if the pan seems too dry during this period, add extra mushroom soaking liquid or water, perhaps 2 or 3 tablespoons. (If you are preparing this in advance, instead of cooking 4 minutes, turn off the heat, cover, and let stand until shortly before you want to serve it; then proceed as below.)

Add fried gluten. Sprinkle on 1 tablespoon soy sauce, ¼ teaspoon salt, and ½ teaspoon sugar. Turn heat to high and stir-fry 2 to 3 minutes until the cabbage is very tender and hardly any liquid remains. Test for salt. Sesame oil (½ teaspoon) is added last.

Variation: Use 2 ounces bean threads instead of fried gluten. Cover them with cold water and let sit 3 to 4 hours (or if time is short, pour boiling water over them and let stand 15 to 30 minutes). Rinse in cold water, drain, and snip into 2-inch lengths (otherwise they mass together during frying). Proceed as above, but after adding the bean threads, pour in ¼ cup + 3 tablespoons mushroom soaking liquid, and use 2 tablespoons soy sauce, ¼ teaspoon salt, and 1 teaspoon sugar. Add a little more liquid if the pan becomes too dry.

Asparagus, Black Mushrooms, and Fried Gluten or Sweet Basil

Another delicious blend for nippy days, with a light, thickened sauce. Or instead of fried gluten, include some fresh sweet basil. Most people here do not associate basil with Chinese cooking, but my experience was just the opposite. After enjoying it in several Chinese dishes in the Far East, I dried some to bring back with me, thinking it unavailable in this country! You can also have gratifying success with this dish using just asparagus and black mushrooms, especially in the spring when fresh asparagus comes into season. When fresh is not available, I'd take frozen over canned. This recipe yields three small portions, so you may want to double it when serving four or more persons, or add a side dish of something like Tofu "Cheese." Zesty Chinese Cabbage Stems, gingery and/or hot, is a good choice of relish for this.

1–1½ cup (250-375 ml) (heaping) fresh asparagus, or ½–1 cup (125-250 ml) frozen or canned asparagus

10–12 black (or shiitake) mushrooms, presoaked

15 pieces fried gluten or 1 ounce (28 g) fresh sweet basil

2½ tablespoons (37.5 ml) vegetable oil

½ cup (125 ml) soaking liquid from black mushrooms

2 teaspoons (10 ml) soy sauce

½ teaspoon (3 ml) (scant) sugar

1 teaspoon (5 ml) cornstarch dissolved in 2 teaspoons (10 ml) cold water

½ teaspoon (3 ml) sesame oil

To prepare fresh asparagus, discard tough base portion. Slice diagonally, ¼ inch thick and 2 inches long. You should have about 1 heaping cup when using fried gluten and an extra half cup with sweet basil.

To prepare frozen asparagus, defrost completely, then squeeze gently to remove excess liquid; cut crosswise into 1¼-inch lengths. Use ½ to ¾ cup with fried gluten; 1 cup with basil.

To prepare canned asparagus, drain, squeeze gently, and cut crosswise into 1¼-inch lengths. Use ½ to ¾ cup with fried gluten; 1 cup with basil.

Slice the mushrooms into narrow strips.

Slice canned fried gluten into strips. Soften and season fresh fried gluten according to Basic Recipe earlier in this chapter. Use as many balls as needed to yield fifteen narrow slices.

If using sweet basil, cut the leaves crosswise into narrow strips. You should have about ½ cup, loosely packed.

Heat 2½ tablespoons oil in a preheated pan over high. When oil is hot, reduce heat to medium-high. Stir-fry *fresh* asparagus 2 minutes. Then add mushroom and fried gluten; stir-fry 30 seconds. (If asparagus is frozen or canned, put mushroom strips into the hot oil first, then asparagus and fried gluten; stir-fry 1 minute.) Stir in sweet basil. Pour in ½ cup mushroom soaking liquid, 2 teaspoons soy sauce, and a scant ½ teaspoon sugar; cook, stirring once or twice, until the liquid is reduced by half—1 to 2 minutes (with fresh fried gluten, which is more absorbent than canned, 2 to 4 tablespoons more liquid may be needed). Add the cornstarch mixture, combining for a minute or less. Test for salt before serving, and top with a dash of sesame oil.

Tofu "Meatballs" with Delicacies

A main course dish, complete with tender "meat-balls" and an array of vegetables, including bright green broccoli flowerets. Fried gluten is a further enrichment but can be omitted if unavailable or you are too busy to make some. I suggest this elegant dish for an occasion when you are serving warmed Chinese rice wine. Immerse small serving jugs or flagons of wine in a pot with a couple of inches of hot water, and warm them over medium heat till the aroma rises. For wine cups, use tiny Chinese or saké cups, shot glasses, or other small glasses. Toast everyone collectively as well as individually. In Chinese custom, you would never take a sip alone, but would continue the toasting with special wishes and "bottoms-up" throughout the meal.

Other dishes that could complete a delightful menu include Eggplant with Chestnuts, Spicy Green Beans, any of the relishes, and Spicy Asparagus and Mushroom Soup.

10–12 ounces (281–337 g) regular or firm tofu

¼ teaspoon (1.5 ml) salt

1 tablespoon (15 ml) (heaping) tree ear, presoaked and minced; or green pepper, minced

2 + tablespoons (30 ml) flour

Vegetable oil for deep-frying

6 black (or shiitake) mushrooms, presoaked

½ cup (125 ml) bamboo shoot, sliced

¾ cup (180 ml) broccoli flowerets

10–15 pieces fried gluten

1½ tablespoons (22.5 ml) vegetable oil

½ cup (125 ml) soaking liquid from black mushrooms

1 tablespoon (15 ml) soy sauce

½ teaspoon (3 ml) sugar

½ teaspoon (3 ml) sesame oil

See On Readying Tofu, Chapter 3. Mash the tofu to yield 1 cup. Combine tofu with salt, tree ear (or green pepper), and 2 tablespoons flour. Form into small balls, 1 inch in diameter. Roll lightly in flour.

Heat oil for deep-frying. Do not crowd the tofu balls in the pot; move them about till they are just lightly browned—1 to 2 minutes should be enough. Remove and drain on paper towels.

Cut the larger mushrooms into halves or thirds.

Cut the broccoli flowerets into small pieces; parboil or steam till almost tender, then rinse in cold water.

No preparation is needed for canned fried gluten. Soften and season fresh fried gluten according to the Basic Recipe earlier in this chapter; if they are the large size, cut into smaller pieces. Use as many balls as needed to yield 10 to 15 pieces.

Heat 1½ tablespoons oil in a preheated pan over high. Add in succession the mushrooms, bamboo shoot, broccoli, fried gluten, and tofu balls. Pour in ½ cup mushroom soaking liquid, 1 tablespoon soy sauce, and ½ teaspoon sugar. Reduce heat to medium-high; cook 3 to 4 minutes, stir-frying gently. When only 1 tablespoon liquid remains in the pan, add ½ teaspoon sesame oil and remove from the heat.

7

Soups for All
Seasons

A pot of tea with meals is by no means the general rule at restaurants in China, nor is it the practice at home. A soup is much more common, served along with the other dishes. Even during the summer, when the weather is hotter than any soup, it continues to appear for lunch and dinner both.

On reflection this shouldn't seem so strange. How many of us give up our steaming morning coffee when summer arrives? Furthermore, a hot beverage is always considered by the Chinese to be more beneficial to one's system than something cold, no matter what the surrounding temperature might be; and in a typical Chinese meal, the soup serves as a beverage.

Different each day, with seasonal vegetables and fresh stock, a soup adds variety and interest to meals. It serves as palate-cleanser and thirst-quencher all at once. Therefore the consistency (but not the character) is usually thin enough for sipping and washing things down. The selections in this chapter are also full of nourishing ingredients, so you can actually consider them another "dish."

Most of them make an excellent light lunch with a relish and perhaps something like Spring Rolls or fried noodles.

Many Chinese even have a soup for breakfast. En route to Taiwan, crossing the Pacific in a Chinese freighter, I started each day with a hearty bowl of noodles in soup, complete with shreds of Chinese cabbage and meat, all capped with a fried egg. I still think of this as the ultimate in breakfasts for a sea voyage—and even occasionally on land. The Northern Chinese especially like hot soup on cold mornings. In such places as Yangchow, you might go out for a bowl of beef broth, with a round of heavy bread, specially made for dunking. The Pekingese like a thick chowder containing liver, tree ear, and variety meats. In Shanhsi the morning soup is an invigorating combination of lamb, lotus root, mountain yam, wine, medicinal herbs, and other ingredients, called "eight jewels soup." Throughout the country, soybean milk is eaten hot like a soup, sweetened or with piquant seasonings, sometimes even with slices of lamb.

I learned quickly that I was a soup fan. My happiest meals in Taipei, bar none, were in company with the king of them all, the soup that can go on for hours, called *hwo gwo,* or firepot. In the center of the table a pot of stock sits on a sunken charcoal brazier or on a gas hot plate. Surrounding it are platters of chrysanthemum greens, Chinese cabbage, cubes of tofu, and bean threads. For nonvegetarians, there are plates of sliced meats, frozen before slicing to enable a paper-thin cut that cooks quickly. As the pot bubbles gently away, each person adds whatever he likes, then retrieves it (no matter if the contributions get intermingled), to dip it into a bowl of *sha-cha* sauce. Thick and spicy (of Malaysian origins), this sauce is often mixed with a beaten raw egg. Naturally, with the successive infusion of ingredients, the firepot stock gets better and better. Wine and beer are usually consumed throughout, while a picnic spirit of lively conviviality and good cheer prevails. From late fall to early spring, whole restaurants as well as open-air stands are given over to this wonderful repast.

You could easily put on a firepot meal at home, using an electric hot plate. The *sha-cha* paste is sold in jars or cans at Chinese markets.

There is also a Northern Chinese style firepot, called swishing lamb, which employs a different set up. The cooker is a self-contained unit, often copper-plated, consisting of a miniature charcoal stove with chimney encircled by a round trough for the soup. Lamb, other meats, tofu, and greens are swished in the hot broth by each diner and dipped into a variety of sauces.

Obviously these are complete feasts unto themselves; no other dishes are needed or wanted. If you are a soup lover, you might decide that some of the soups in this chapter, too, are all you need for a whole meal, especially for one or two persons (see Suggested Menus for some appropriate choices). Many include one or more vegetables along with tofu and/or beans. Fresh ingredients, of course, play a part, but so do dried and preserved foodstuffs, such as dried black mushrooms, tree ear, and Szechuan pickle. Fresh bean sprout stock is often used, though not required, for in many cases black mushrooms contribute flavor to the broth.

Choose these ingredients with discrimination, especially black mushrooms (or shiitake) and bamboo shoots. For best results use the thicker black mushrooms with crackled surface. And remember always to include the soaking water as part of the 3 cups liquid. (The recipes uniformly call for 3 cups liquid.) After soaking black mushrooms, you will usually have ½ to ¾ cup liquid. Measure this amount (after soaking and squeezing the mushrooms), then make up the difference with water—or sometimes water and stock—to total 3 cups.

Bamboo shoots are another common ingredient in Chinese vegetarian soups. For more details, especially on how to slice them for maximum crispness, see On Bamboo Shoots, in the Chinese Ingredients section. Some of the canned varieties, such as the "giant" *(mao swun)* and its large "tips," or the "green," may be acceptable in fried dishes but can adversely affect the flavor of a soup. Winter bamboo shoots are more desirable, for their crispness, flavor, and delightful fragrance.

This section gives you a good opportunity to use soft, or "silken" tofu, with its smooth, luxurious texture. But you can also use regular or firm.

In a few instances, you will find green soybeans included. See Chinese Ingredients for more information. These are obtainable fresh in China. In the United States, some Oriental stores stock them frozen. Buy a bag of the shucked beans to store in your freezer. It will see you through many soups, since the amount called for each time is no more than a handful. This seems negligible, but the idea is simply to munch on an occasional sweet, crunchy bean, not to be overwhelmed by them. Peas are an adequate substitute, but the textural appeal is missing. (Green soybeans in the pod are also sold frozen, for a different use— see Green Peas or Soybeans in the Pod, Chapter 1.)

Steaming is the best way to prepare many of these soups, for it is gentler than boiling and results in a more fully developed flavor, with pristine clarity. The procedure, which is really very simple, is described below. However, if your time is short, instead of steaming you can bring the soup to the boil in a pot, then simmer for a few minutes, and serve.

The final step, just before serving, is to top the soup with a few drops of aromatic sesame oil, which can help enrich the taste as well. Once again, a reminder that this must be Chinese or Japanese style sesame oil, not the colorless type.

As part of a lunch or dinner, serve the soup with the other dishes. If you want to follow Chinese custom, set a tureen (or the steaming bowl) on the table and let each person ladle out as much as he or she wants into an individual soup bowl. These are usually somewhat smaller than a rice bowl. Small porcelain spoons are used, though in very informal circumstances some people may sip from their bowl. If there are guests, the host or hostess may do the serving. A round table with a lazy Susan in the center makes this, as well as self-service, very convenient in large parties. No hand passing is needed for any dishes. But lacking this arrangement, you may find it more practical to serve up individual portions of soup in the kitchen.

There is no reason you couldn't serve these soups with an American meal as a separate first course, if preferred. Soups do come separately in multi-course Chinese banquets, but are interspersed between other dishes.

Each recipe is enough for three or four people in a menu of two or three other dishes, with rice. The proportions can be doubled easily to serve six to eight persons, and halved for one person. Most of these soups can be reheated the next day if any is left over.

On Steaming Soups

Although most everyday Chinese soups are boiled, some are steamed in order to obtain a beautifully clear and particularly flavorful result. It is a welcome method if you have no kitchen help, for it frees you from pot watching for 20 to 30 minutes—ample time to put the finishing touches on everything else.

Some soups are never steamed, mainly those in which an ingredient requires short—or closely watched—cooking, such as bean threads, or with a cornstarch thickener (which would not be clear in any case).

But when the ingredients are only improved by gentler and longer cooking, allowing individual flavors to commingle, steaming is an ideal method. Soups with black mushrooms and bamboo shoots are prime examples of this kind.

The only equipment you need is a heatproof bowl (a ceramic or glass mixing bowl) and a covered pot big enough to hold it (corn or stock pot). To keep the bowl from wobbling, and off the heat, it is helpful to have a rack. A round "broil and cake rack," as one manufacturer calls it, is available in cookware stores and suits the purpose admirably, but this is not required. The ideal piece of cookware is a Chinese stewing and steaming pot or casserole *(dwun joong)*. This is a deep ceramic pot with cover. Some of them come fitted snugly in a metal framework, having legs for a stand and handles for lifting. They may be handsomely glazed in brown and come in several sizes. I find the medium size most convenient, with a capacity of 5 to 6 cups (the largest is too tall to fit into a regular corn pot). These can be ordered from Tai Yick Trading Co., 1400 Powell St., San Francisco, CA 94133; telephone (415) 986-0961.

Whatever equipment you use, the procedure is basically the same. First place all the soup ingredients, except sesame oil, in the bowl. This can be assembled ahead of time, if you wish. If you refrigerate the bowl, however, bring it back to room temperature before steaming.

Put ½ to 1 inch of water in the outer pot, along with optional rack. Bring the water to a boil, then put in the soup bowl (or Chinese casserole, with lid), and cover the pot. Now begin timing—usually for 20 minutes. Medium-high heat should be about right; you want to maintain a good but not furious boil.

If you wish to keep condensed steam out of the bowl and help hold in flavor, the bowl itself also can be covered. With a Chinese steaming pot, always use the lid. With a bowl, use a heatproof plate, or better yet, plastic wrap secured with a rubber band—or both. Of course, be sure to cover the pot, too.

Stock—Basic Recipe

This stock is not strong, since many of the ingredients that go into the soup selections are delicate in flavor and easily overpowered. Use either mung bean sprouts or soybean sprouts. Mung bean sprouts are those sold in most markets, and the stock they make is comparatively light. Soybean sprouts are available in some Oriental groceries; they are similar in appearance but larger, with the sprout emerging from a smallish bean. Their stock is richer, and they are the kind normally used in vegetarian cooking.

I find this fresh sprout stock preferable, but chefs also make a stock with dry soybeans. (Soak ¾ cup beans overnight, rinse well, and cook gently with 7 cups water, covered or partially covered, 1½ hours. Discard beans and add a little rock sugar to the stock.)

These stocks will keep in the refrigerator for about a week, or they can be frozen.

1 pound (450 g) mung bean sprouts, or ½ pound (225 g) soybean sprouts

8 cups (2000 ml) water

Put sprouts in a pot with 8 cups water. Bring to the simmer; reduce heat to low, cover partially or completely, and maintain a *bare* simmer for a half hour. Turn off heat, cover completely, and let sit a half hour. Strain to remove the bean sprouts (they will be sodden and flavorless by this time, so discard them). You should have about 7 cups stock. This recipe can be halved if you want only 3½ cups, and doubled for 14 cups.

Clear Mushroom Soup

For this classically simple and savory soup, which can accompany almost any meal, you can use either fresh or black mushrooms. A very agreeable lacing of wine complements the full mushroom flavor. To retain as much of the goodness and aroma as possible, cover the bowl tightly during steaming. The Variation, below, combines fresh or black mushrooms with tree ear or ginkgo nuts. These are delicacies that lend elegance but do not flavor the broth.

2 cups (500 ml) fresh mushrooms, sliced; or 12 black (or shiitake) mushrooms, presoaked

3 cups (750 ml) liquid (water + soaking liquid from black mushrooms)

1 tablespoon (15 ml) rice wine

¾ teaspoon (4 ml) salt

½ teaspoon (3 ml) sesame oil

Fresh mushrooms: Slice them very thinly; you should have 2 cups. Place mushrooms, 3 cups water, wine, and salt in a heatproof bowl. Cover the bowl tightly with plastic wrap secured with a rubber band and/or lid or plate. Place in a steamer and steam 20 to 30 minutes, or until the mushrooms are tender. Before serving, test for salt and top with sesame oil.

Black mushrooms: Be sure to use the *best*, thickest mushrooms for this recipe. Arrange them in a heatproof bowl; sprinkle with rice wine. Pour in 3 cups liquid (including mushroom soaking liquid). Add salt. Cover the bowl as above and steam 20 to 30 minutes. Afterwards, test for salt, and add a few drops of sesame oil.

Variation: For variety when using fresh mushrooms, add one to two tree ears, presoaked and torn into very small pieces to yield ⅓ cup, loose. With black mushrooms, include 12 precooked ginkgo nuts (see Chinese Ingredients).

Asparagus and Mushroom Soup

This has a highly flavorsome broth, sweet and bright with fresh or frozen asparagus. Chinese often favor the canned white asparagus in dishes like this, since it is peeled. With either color, the result will be pleasantly rich-tasting.

1 cup (250 ml) (heaping) fresh asparagus, sliced; or 1 cup (250 ml) frozen or canned asparagus, cut

1 cup (250 ml) (heaping) fresh mushrooms, sliced

6 black (or shiitake) mushrooms, presoaked

3 cups (750 ml) liquid (mushroom soaking liquid + water + optional 1½ cups [375 ml] stock)

1 tablespoon (15 ml) soy sauce

⅛ teaspoon (.5 ml) salt

½ teaspoon (3 ml) sesame oil

To prepare fresh asparagus, discard fibrous base. If the diameter is no more than ¼ inch, cut into 1-inch lengths; if thicker, cut diagonally into thin (¼-inch) slices, 1¼ inches long.

To prepare frozen asparagus, defrost just enough to allow cutting into 1-inch lengths to yield 1 cup.

To prepare canned asparagus, cut into 1-inch lengths; use ¾ to 1 cup.

Slice fresh mushrooms ¼ inch thick, yielding 1 heaping cup.

Slice the black mushrooms.

You can either steam or boil the soup. I recommend steaming, especially when not using stock, in order to get maximum flavor from your ingredients. To steam the soup, if asparagus and mushrooms are fresh, first simmer them 5 minutes in the liquid; then put all ingredients (except sesame oil) into a heatproof bowl and steam 15 minutes. To boil, place all ingredients (except sesame oil) in a pot, bring to the boil, reduce heat, and simmer until asparagus and mushrooms are tender (5 minutes if they are fresh).

Before serving, test for salt; you can add up to an extra 1 teaspoon soy sauce or an extra ⅛ teaspoon salt. Top with ½ teaspoon sesame oil.

Spicy Asparagus and Mushroom Soup

Sweetened with fresh ingredients, the broth owes its additional vegetable flavor to the lusty and peppery Szechuan pickle. Since you want the pickle shreds to be crunchy, this soup is not steamed. Those who dislike hot foods should use only 1 tablespoon (or less) of this spicy condiment. If you have fire insurance, you can try an extra tablespoon or two.

1 cup (250 ml) fresh asparagus, sliced; or 1 cup (250 ml) frozen or canned asparagus, cut

1 cup (250 ml) fresh mushrooms, sliced

2 tablespoons (30 ml) (packed) Szechuan pickle, shredded

3 cups (750 ml) liquid (all water; or half stock and half water)

1½ teaspoons (8 ml) soy sauce

¼ teaspoon (1.5 ml) salt

½ teaspoon (3 ml) sesame oil

To prepare fresh asparagus, slice it diagonally no more than ¼ inch thick and about 1½ inches long. Discard the base if fibrous and tough.

To prepare frozen or canned asparagus, cut crosswise into 1-inch lengths. Defrost frozen asparagus just enough to permit cutting.

Slice the fresh mushrooms ¼ inch thick, yielding 1 cup.

Shred the Szechuan pickle by slicing very thinly, then cutting into 1-inch shreds.

Simmer fresh or frozen asparagus and mushrooms in the liquid several minutes until tender. Add the Szechuan pickle, canned asparagus, soy sauce, and salt. Turn up the heat. When the boil is reached, remove from the stove. Add sesame oil.

Young Luffa Gourd Soup

Young luffa gourd, 1 to 2 feet long, has ribbed, thick, rough green skin but tasty, lush flesh.

Lush and light-tasting, this soup is easy to prepare. (For more information on luffa gourd, see Chapter 2, Young Luffa Gourd with Gingerroot.) The vegetable is first stir-fried briefly in a little oil. Some people like the enrichment this gives, and the result is not really oily; but if you prefer a "cleaner" soup, transfer the vegetable to a pot after stir-frying.

10 ounces (281 g) young luffa gourd (see Note)

2 tablespoons (30 ml) green soybeans or peas, frozen or fresh

4 black (or shiitake) mushrooms, presoaked

2 tablespoons (30 ml) vegetable oil

1½ teaspoons (8 ml) gingerroot, minced or grated

½ cup (125 ml) bamboo shoot, sliced

3 cups (750 ml) liquid (soaking liquid from black mushrooms + 1½ cups [375 ml] stock + water)

¾ teaspoon (4 ml) salt

Note: To obtain 10 ounces trimmed luffa gourd, purchase 1 to 1¼ pounds, or two firm, medium-sized young gourds.

Skin the luffa. Cut in half lengthwise, then slice diagonally—or crosswise, if large—to make thin (¼-inch), bite-sized pieces. Yield is 2½ to 3 cups.

Do not defrost frozen peas or green soybeans. If fresh, they should be parboiled until just tender.

Slice the black mushrooms.

In a preheated pan, heat 2 tablespoons oil until very hot. Add luffa, reduce heat to medium-high, and stir-fry 3 to 4 minutes until soft. Transfer vegetable to a pot or leave in the pan. Add gingerroot, green soybeans or peas, bamboo shoot, black mushrooms, liquid, and salt. Bring to the boil; if necessary, simmer a minute longer until the vegetable is quite tender.

Deep-fried Tofu or Fried Gluten Soup with Bean Threads

A delicious soup for any meal. In fact, it is a very satisfying lunch in itself for one or two persons without being too filling. The bean threads, also called "cellophane noodles," can often be found in supermarkets. Chinese cooks usually leave these threads long in soups; they are raised high above the tureen and allowed to slip into the individual soup bowls. You may want to cut them in half or even shorter lengths after soaking, but they are elusive even this way, so try eating the soup as the Chinese do, with chopsticks in one hand and perhaps a soup spoon in the other to catch and hold the slippery strands. In any case, be sure not to overcook them or let this soup sit too long, for the noodles continue to swell and can even dissolve if simmered too long.

2 ounces (56 g) bean
threads

10 pieces deep-fried tofu, or
15 pieces fried gluten
(see Note)

2 tablespoons (30 ml)
green soybeans or peas,
fresh or frozen

6 black (or shiitake)
mushrooms, presoaked

½ cup (125 ml) bamboo
shoot, diced or sliced; or
1 cup (250 ml) bok
choy, sliced

3 cups (750 ml) liquid
(mushroom liquid +
optional 1½ cups [375
ml] stock + water)

2 tablespoons (30 ml) soy
sauce

½ teaspoon (3 ml) (scant)
salt

¼–½ teaspoon (1.5–3 ml)
(scant) sugar

½ teaspoon (3 ml) sesame
oil

Note: See Chapter 3, On Deep-frying Tofu, for recipe; or Chapter 6 for Fried Gluten Puffs Basic Recipe. Or use the commercial products.

Soak the bean threads in cold water 3 to 4 hours;
or, to shorten the soaking period, pour boiling water
over them, let sit 15 to 30 minutes. Rinse and drain.
Cut them into 2-inch lengths.

To prepare deep-fried tofu, unless it has just been
made, freshen it by plunging into scalding hot water
for a few seconds, rinse, and squeeze dry. Use
ten small cubes or triangles; slice larger pieces to
bite-size.

To prepare fried gluten, soften and season fresh
balls according to Basic Recipe in Chapter 6. Cut
into smaller pieces if necessary. Canned fried gluten
needs no advance preparation.

It is not necessary to defrost frozen peas or green
soybeans. Fresh ones will have to be parboiled until
almost tender.

Place deep-fried tofu or gluten in a pot with mushrooms, bamboo shoot or sliced bok choy, 3 cups
liquid, soy sauce, salt, and sugar (with canned fried
gluten, ¼ teaspoon sugar is enough); bring to the
boil. Add green soybeans or peas, and bean threads.
Bring to a second boil; reduce heat, simmer 2 minutes. Test for salt, top with sesame oil, and serve
right away.

Garden Vegetable Soup with Bean Threads

Baby mustard cabbage is about 6 inches high. It is sometimes called baby bok choy but the stem part is actually thin and light green, fanning out into dark green leaves.

The broth is very light, making this a good selection for savoring the fresh vegetable flavors. It is enjoyable by itself, or with a simple side dish of Tofu "Cheese," or Fava or Lima Beans in Mustard Sauce. Also it complements stronger-tasting vegetables, such as Curried Broccoli Stems or Asparagus. Crisp baby mustard cabbage is ideal in this soup, not only for its delightful, lively taste but for its attractive color and crispness, providing good contrast for the silky bean threads (see Chinese Ingredients for information on these ingredients). You can also use bok choy.

2 ounces (56 g) bean threads (cellophane noodles)

4 black (or shiitake) mushrooms, presoaked

1 medium carrot (2½ ounces [84 g])

4 ounces (112 g) baby mustard cabbage, or bok choy

¼ cup (60 ml) (heaping) green onion, chopped (¼ inch)

3 cups (750 ml) liquid (soaking liquid from black mushrooms + stock)

¾ teaspoon (4 ml) salt

¼ teaspoon (1.5 ml) sugar

½ teaspoon (3 ml) sesame oil

Soak the bean threads 3 to 4 hours in cold water; or, to shorten the period, pour boiling water over them and let sit 15 to 30 minutes.

Cut larger mushrooms into pieces.

Slice the carrot, cut into bite-sized pieces to yield ½ cup, and steam in a steaming basket 2 minutes or until almost tender (or simmer carrot in the 3 cups liquid for 5 minutes).

Slice cabbage or bok choy diagonally at half-inch intervals to make bite-sized pieces.

Place all ingredients except sesame oil in a pot, bring to the boil, and remove from the heat. Test to see if the bean threads are tender; if necessary simmer a little longer, but do not overcook them. Test for seasoning, add ½ teaspoon sesame oil, and serve immediately.

Spicy Three Shreds Soup

For adding spark to a meal, a popular choice in many restaurants is a soup of Szechuan pickle and meat shreds. This vegetarian soup is similarly full of crunchy and tender shreds. Remember that a little Szechuan pickle goes a long way. Small amounts blend with the bamboo shoot and black mushrooms to produce a very smooth-tasting broth. Used more generously, it can spike this soup with fiery hotness. I would say 3 tablespoons is close to the maximum. Or decrease the amount to 1 tablespoon, according to your taste. If you have some salted-dried bamboo shoot tips (see Chapter 5), try the Variation. These meaty shreds are a special delicacy.

1–3 tablespoons (15–45 ml) (packed) Szechuan pickle, shredded

½ cup (125 ml) bamboo shoot (preferably winter), julienned or diced finely

6 black (or shiitake) mushrooms, presoaked

3 cups (750 ml) liquid (soaking liquid from black mushrooms + water)

1½ teaspoons (8 ml) soy sauce

½ teaspoon (3 ml) sesame oil

Slice the pickle very thinly, then cut into shreds.

Slice the mushrooms into julienne strips or shreds.

Place all ingredients except sesame oil in a pot. Bring just to the boil, then reduce heat and simmer a minute. To retain crispness, do not overcook the Szechuan pickle. Add sesame oil before serving.

Variation: Include 1 tablespoon (packed) salted-dried bamboo shoot tips, presoaked and shredded. Use bamboo soaking liquid as part of the 3 cups liquid. Omit soy sauce and test for salt before serving.

Black Mushroom and "Meatball" Soup

Tasty balls of tofu, flecked with bits of Szechuan pickle and other ingredients, are cooked just briefly in a mushroom broth. With a relish, this is a good lunchtime soup. Or have it for dinner with a simple dish of Garland Chrysanthemum or Spinach with Wine and Soy Sauce, and perhaps Noodles with Sesame Sauce, or Taro, Yuca Root, Mountain Yam, or Potato Temptation.

10–12 ounces (281–337 g)
regular or firm tofu

1 tablespoon (15 ml) green
onion, minced; or 2
tablespoons (30 ml)
fresh cedar buds (see
Chinese Ingredients)

1 tablespoon (15 ml) tree
ear, presoaked, or green
pepper, minced

1 tablespoon (15 ml)
(packed) Szechuan
pickle, minced

2 tablespoons (30 ml) flour

½ teaspoon (3 ml) sesame oil

6 black (or shiitake)
mushrooms, presoaked

3 cups (750 ml) liquid
(soaking liquid from
black mushrooms +
optional 1½ cups [375
ml] stock + water; see
Note)

1 tablespoon (15 ml) soy
sauce

¼ teaspoon (1.5 ml) salt

Note: If your mushrooms are of good, thick quality, it is not necessary to include stock.

See on Readying Tofu, Chapter 3. Mash the tofu to yield 1 cup. Combine mashed tofu, minced ingredients, flour, and sesame oil. Form into bite-sized balls, using 2 teaspoons of mixture for each.

Cut larger mushrooms into halves or thirds.

Place the balls and mushrooms in a pot with 3 cups liquid. Bring just to the simmer; do not allow to boil or the balls will break up. Reduce heat. Season with soy sauce and salt; simmer gently 2 minutes.

Variation: Dust the tofu balls with flour and deep-fry to a light brown before adding them to the liquid with mushrooms, soy sauce, and salt; simmer 2 minutes, and serve.

Hot-and-Sour Soup

This very popular cold-weather soup, both tangy and peppery, is especially good with pot-stickers and noodles. It's lightly thickened and offers a mouthful of textures. Tomato, optional bean curd skin, tofu, and tree ear are the ingredients, rivaling with great success the traditional nonvegetarian counterparts —usually chicken's blood, egg, and meat shreds. The diced tomato provides vivid, appetizing color. If fresh tomatoes are not ripe, red, and juicy, it is preferable to use a good canned product, labeled "whole peeled." Vinegar gives this soup its tang, which combines agreeably with the spicy flavorings. If you want a mild version, omit the Szechuan pickle and use only a couple of pinches of pepper.

6 ounces (170 g) fresh or canned tomato (1 small)

4 ounces (112 g) regular or firm tofu

½ bean curd skin, optional (see Chapter 5, On Bean Curd Skin)

3 cups (750 ml) stock

½ cup (125 ml) (loose) tree ear, presoaked and shredded

½ cup (125 ml) bamboo shoot, julienned or sliced

1 tablespoon (15 ml) (packed) Szechuan pickle, shredded (optional)

½ teaspoon (3 ml) (packed) gingerroot, minced or grated

1 tablespoon (15 ml) soy sauce

½ teaspoon (3 ml) salt

2–4 pinches (large) fine-ground black pepper (1/16–1/8 teaspoon [.25–.5 ml])

2 teaspoons (10 ml) cider vinegar or Chinese dark vinegar

2 tablespoons (30 ml) cornstarch dissolved in 2 tablespoons cold water

1½ teaspoons (8 ml) green onion, chopped

½ teaspoon (3 ml) sesame oil

Cilantro garnish (optional)

Skin fresh tomatoes by plunging into boiling water for a few seconds, then peeling. Dice fresh or canned tomatoes to yield ¾ cup.

Cut the tofu into 2½-inch strips, ¼ inch thick.

Cut the bean curd skin into thin strips (if dried, dampen before cutting).

Place stock, tomatoes, tree ear, bamboo shoot, tofu, Szechuan pickle, gingerroot, soy sauce, salt, and pepper into a pot. Bring to the boil. Add bean curd skin and vinegar. Slowly dribble in the cornstarch mixture, stirring constantly. Cook for another 30 seconds or so, stirring frequently. Remove from heat, stir in green onion, top with sesame oil and an optional sprinkling of cilantro leaves.

Velvet Turnip Soup

The turnips are velvet-smooth and so is the flavor of this sublime soup, with sliced bamboo shoots and black mushrooms.

10 ounces (281 g) turnips

1 teaspoon (5 ml) salt

2 tablespoons (30 ml) vegetable oil

6 black (or shiitake) mushrooms, presoaked

½ cup (125 ml) bamboo shoot, sliced

3 cups (750 ml) liquid (soaking liquid from black mushrooms + water)

1 tablespoon (15 ml) soy sauce

½ teaspoon (3 ml) sesame oil

Pare the turnips. Halve or quarter lengthwise, slice thinly, and place in a medium-sized ceramic bowl. Mix-massage (as described in Chapter 1) with 1 teaspoon salt; let stand a half hour. Rinse well and squeeze out the liquid. Brown the slices lightly in 2 tablespoons oil. Remove to a heatproof bowl.

Slice mushrooms and bamboo shoot. Add them to the bowl, along with liquid and soy sauce. Steam 20 minutes or until the vegetable is quite tender. Add sesame oil, and serve.

Spinach and Tofu Potage with Black Bean Sauce

A warming, thickish soup tinged with a hearty bean sauce. Black bean sauce is sold in jars at Chinese groceries. (Beware—for this recipe, anyway—of additives like garlic or chile in the sauce. Also do not use loose, salted black beans.) If this sauce is not available, use regular Chinese bean sauce (see Chinese Ingredients) or Japanese miso. Soups thickened lightly with cornstarch, like this one, keep warm longer in cold weather, but they lose their silken quality rather quickly, so serve immediately.

6 ounces (170 g) spinach

4 ounces (112 g) soft, regular, or firm tofu

3 cups (750 ml) stock

½ teaspoon (3 ml) sugar

1 tablespoon (15 ml) black bean sauce, 2 tablespoons (30 ml) Chinese bean sauce, or 3 tablespoons (45 ml) dark or light miso

2 tablespoons (30 ml) cornstarch dissolved in 2 tablespoons (30 ml) water

Salt to taste

½–1 teaspoon (3–5 ml) sesame oil

Chop the spinach, including stems, finely to yield 2 cups, packed.

Dice the tofu (½ inch) to yield about ¾ cup.

Bring stock to the boil. Add tofu, spinach, sugar (omit sugar with light miso), and the bean flavoring (if you are using miso, dissolve it first in a small bowl with a little of the hot stock before adding it to the pot). When the simmer begins, gradually stir in the cornstarch mixture. Cook about 30 seconds longer, stirring frequently, before removing from the heat. Test for salt. Add sesame oil—1 teaspoon with black bean sauce, ½ teaspoon otherwise.

Variation: Substitute ½ cup shredded plain pressed tofu (see Chapter 4) for the tofu, and 1 tablespoon salted-dried bamboo shoot tips, presoaked and finely shredded (see Chapter 5), for the black bean sauce. Also include six black (or shiitake) mushrooms, presoaked and cut into pieces. For liquid use water or stock, plus soaking liquids from mushrooms and dried bamboo shoot tips, to make 3 cups. Bring this to the boil along with the dried bamboo shoot tips and mushrooms. Add pressed tofu, chopped spinach, and ¼ teaspoon sugar. When the simmer returns, gradually stir in the cornstarch mixture; cook briefly before removing from the heat. Test for salt; probably only ⅓ teaspoon will be necessary. Add 1 teaspoon sesame oil.

Chowder of Fava or Lima Beans

This chowder is not thickened, but it *is* thick with good things—crushed or pureed fava or lima beans, diced tofu and potato, bits of walnut, and sesame seeds. (For details on favas, see Chapter 2, Luscious Fava Beans with Bamboo Shoot. For an illustration, see page 35.) Canned fava beans are sold in some Middle Eastern markets. Use fresh or canned favas, or frozen or canned baby limas. For reasons of texture, the fresh or canned beans are mashed by squeezing in a cloth. Frozen limas are pureed in a blender to a smooth consistency. So depending on which bean you use, and its form, you'll have a slightly different result each time, all with a light and nutty flavor—and slightly spicy if you want to add curry powder. This makes a nourishing lunch, yet the effect is not at all heavy. You can assemble the soup ahead of time, then do the final cooking just before serving.

1½ cups (375 ml) fava or lima beans (see Note)

8 ounces (224 g) soft, regular, or firm tofu

4 ounces (112 g) potato (preferably new potato)

½ bean curd skin (optional) (see Chapter 5, On Bean Curd Skin)

5–6 fresh mushrooms

1 tablespoon (15 ml) white sesame seeds, toasted and crushed

1 tablespoon (15 ml) walnut bits, lightly toasted

3 cups (750 ml) liquid (2 cups [500 ml] stock + 1 cup [250 ml] water or canned bean liquid)

¼ teaspoon (1.5 ml) sugar

1 teaspoon (5 ml) Madras curry powder, or more to taste (optional)

⅓–1 teaspoon (1.6–5 ml) salt

Note: For fresh favas, you will need 5 to 6 cups raw beans to yield 1½ cups steamed and skinned. Steam them until *very* tender, rinse under cold water, then pinch them out of their skins to yield 1½ cups; discard skins. Or use one 17-ounce can fava or lima beans (reserve liquid), or 9 ounces frozen baby limas.

To prepare fresh or canned beans, place them in a clean cloth, about ½ cup at a time; squeeze firmly between your palms to mash. Crumble them into a small bowl and set aside.

To prepare frozen limas, after thawing, puree in a blender with 1 cup water. Then for liquid use 2 cups stock only.

Dice the tofu and potato (with skin, if you like) finely. The potato should be very finely diced, almost minced.

Cut the bean curd skin into very small squares (if dried, dampen it lightly before cutting).

Slice the fresh mushrooms (¼ inch).

Place potato in a pot with 2 cups stock. Bring to the boil. Reduce heat and cook a few minutes until potato is almost tender. (If you are preparing this in advance, remove from stove, add remaining ingredients, cover, and refrigerate. Then just before serving, bring to the boil and, if necessary, cook a little longer at a simmer until potato and mushrooms are done.) Add mushrooms and cook gently 1 to 2 minutes. Add crumbled or pureed beans, remaining 1 cup liquid, tofu, bean curd skin, sesame seeds, walnut bits, sugar, optional curry powder, and salt— about ⅓ teaspoon salt if using canned liquid, or ¾ to 1 teaspoon with fresh favas or frozen limas. Bring to the simmer over high heat, then reduce heat to medium and cook 2 minutes longer.

Gingery Fried Gluten Soup

This soup has a congenial richness with "zing." It's not heavy, yet has plenty of nourishment, and the light ginger spiciness can perk up a meal. Try it with any of the noodle or tofu dishes, including the "chicken" and "duck" viands in Chapter 5. Green vegetables are especially enhanced when served with this.

1 cup (250 ml) (loose) fried gluten (see Note 1)

4 black (or shiitake) mushrooms, presoaked

½ cup (125 ml) (loosely packed) tree ear, presoaked

1½ tablespoons (22.5 ml) (packed) gingerroot, shredded (½ ounce [14 g], see Note 2)

3 cups (750 ml) liquid (soaking liquid from black mushrooms + water)

¼ teaspoon (1.5 ml) salt

½ teaspoon (3 ml) sesame oil

1½ teaspoons (8 ml) green onion, chopped

Note 1: See Chapter 6 for information on fried gluten and Fried Gluten Puffs Basic Recipe. If using fresh fried gluten, soften and season the puffs according to Basic Recipe. If balls are very large, cut into ½-inch strips. You should have 1 cup, loose. Canned fried gluten needs no advance preparation.

Note 2: See Chinese Ingredients for information on gingerroot. Most commonly available is old gingerroot, but if you have young, double the proportions.

Leave fried gluten whole or cut into strips. Also cut mushrooms and tree ear into narrow strips.

Place all ingredients except sesame oil and green onion in a pot and bring to the boil. Test for seasonings, add sesame oil and green onion, and serve.

Tomato and Tofu Potage with Golden Needle Mushrooms or Bean Sprouts

This is one of the most attractive soups you could serve—bits of bright red tomato and white tofu, strands of light yellow mushrooms or bean sprouts, with a garnish of green cilantro. The taste is very smooth, while the crunchy mushrooms or bean sprouts contrast wonderfully with the tender ingredients. Golden needle mushrooms—a long, thin stem with tiny cap—are packaged fresh and sold in some Japanese and health food groceries, as well as in cans or jars in Oriental markets and some supermarkets. The label may read "enoki mushrooms" (the Japanese name). Don't expect much contribution by way of flavor, but their texture has a unique crunch, providing a very enjoyable eating experience. Try to obtain luscious, ripe, red tomatoes. Canned (whole, peeled) will do almost as well and are preferable to a flavorless, unripe, or grainy fresh product. As with the other potages, this is just slightly thickened and is well suited for fall, winter, and spring. It fits into menus with ease and is especially good with green vegetables, any of the relishes in Chapter 1, and Bean Thread Noodles.

2 cups (500 ml) fresh or canned tomato, diced

8 ounces (224 g) soft, regular, or firm tofu

2 tablespoons (30 ml) vegetable oil

½ teaspoon (3 ml) (packed) gingerroot, minced or grated

3 cups (750 ml) stock

¾ teaspoon (4 ml) salt

½ teaspoon (3 ml) sugar

2 ounces (56 g) golden needle mushrooms (½ cup [125 ml]) or ¼ pound (112 g) mung bean sprouts

2½ tablespoons (37.5 ml) cornstarch dissolved in 2½ tablespoons (37.5) cold water

1½ teaspoons (8 ml) green onion, chopped

¼ teaspoon (1.5 ml) sesame oil

Cilantro garnish or dash of black pepper (optional)

Skin fresh tomatoes by plunging into boiling hot water for a few seconds, then remove and peel. Dice fresh or canned tomatoes to yield 2 cups.

Dice tofu (½ inch) to yield 1 heaping cup.

Heat 2 tablespoons oil in a pan or heavy pot over high heat. Add the gingerroot and tomatoes; stir-fry a few seconds just to mix. Add stock, tofu, salt, and sugar. When the boil is reached, add mushrooms or bean sprouts. When the second boil begins, gradually stir in the cornstarch mixture; cook another 30 seconds to 1 minute, stirring frequently. Remove from the stove, stir in green onion, top with sesame oil and optional cilantro leaves or dash of black pepper.

Silken Tofu and Black Mushroom Soup

The smooth texture of soft or "silken" tofu is custardlike—in fact, it is preferable to use soybean custard in this recipe. I have occasionally seen it in markets here, packed in cartons like tofu. Even in China, you might have to go the neighborhood tofu factory for it. People begin showing up with small pails sometimes before midnight to bring some custard home for a late snack (they might also pick up soybean milk for breakfast the next day). Street vendors sell bowls of the custard, hot or chilled, perhaps sprinkled with boiled peanuts, in a sweet, thin syrup (just heat water and brown sugar; I also like to add gingerroot). Another popular way of enjoying it is to add a dash of soy sauce and sprinkle with pungent condiments—gingerroot, green onion, dried shrimp, pepper, chile sauce. If soybean custard or silken tofu is not available, you can also make this soup with regular or firm tofu; see Variation.

8 ounces (224 g) soft tofu or soybean custard (1 cup [250 ml])

7 black (or shiitake) mushrooms, presoaked

½ cup (125 ml) bamboo shoot, sliced

3 cups (750 ml) liquid (soaking liquid from black mushrooms + water + optional 1½ cups [375 ml] stock; see Note)

1 tablespoon (15 ml) (loose) Tientsin preserved cabbage or Szechuan pickle, minced (optional)

1½ tablespoons (22.5 ml) soy sauce

½ teaspoon (3 ml) (scant) salt

½ teaspoon (3 ml) sesame oil

Note: If your mushrooms are thick, flavorful ones, you can omit the bean sprout stock. But it will fill out the flavor in any case.

Carefully freshen soft tofu or custard by running cool water into the container. When adding it to the soup, below, use a soup ladle or large spoon to scoop off thick, bite-sized pieces.

Place all ingredients (except Szechuan pickle and sesame oil) in a heatproof bowl. If you put in the liquid first, before adding the scoops of tofu, they will hold together better. Steam for 15 minutes. If using Szechuan pickle, add it now and steam another 2 to 3 minutes. Top with ½ teaspoon sesame oil before serving.

Variation: Use one slice (3 to 4 ounces) regular or firm tofu, diced finely. Also dice the bamboo shoot, to yield ½ cup, and cut the black mushrooms into smaller pieces. Otherwise, ingredients and procedure are the same as above.

Hearty Bean and Black Mushroom Soup

A splendid steamed soup for wintry days, using a dry bean of your choice. Dried favas are sold in Chinese groceries. Soak them a full night and day, and remove skins. Pintos and kidneys will yield a heartier flavor than favas or limas. If you have Szechuan pickle on hand, add some for enrichment.

⅓ pound (150 g) dry beans— pinto, lima, kidney, or fava

12 black (or shiitake) mushrooms

3 cups (750 ml) liquid (soaking liquid from black mushrooms + water)

1–2 tablespoons (15–30 ml) soy sauce

2 tablespoons (30 ml) Szechuan pickle, minced (optional)

⅛ teaspoon (.5 ml) salt

½ teaspoon (3 ml) sesame oil

Soak the dry beans overnight, then rinse several times. Steam in a vegetable basket or cook in water until tender (this could take 1 to 1½ hours). You should have 2 cups cooked beans.

Cut the mushrooms into smaller pieces.

Put 2 cups precooked beans in a heatproof bowl with mushrooms, liquid, and soy sauce (if using Szechuan pickle, add only 1 tablespoon soy sauce; otherwise use 2 tablespoons). Steam 20 minutes. Add Szechuan pickle and steam another 2 to 3 minutes. Test for salt, adding ⅛ teaspoon or so if needed. Also add ½ teaspoon sesame oil.

Three Delicacies Soup

Three rather unusual ingredients combine to make an exquisite soup. Don't serve it in a meal that includes another dish with fried gluten, but otherwise it goes with just about anything. The bean curd skin and salted-dried bamboo shoot tips together produce a light, sometimes almost hamlike tang, while the fried gluten adds richness.

½ bean curd skin (see Chapter 5, On Bean Curd Skin)

10–15 pieces fried gluten

1 tablespoon (15 ml) (packed) salted-dried bamboo shoot tips, presoaked and shredded (see Chapter 5, On Salted-dried Bamboo Shoot Tips)

3 cups (750 ml) liquid (soaking liquid from dried bamboo shoot tips + water)

1–1½ tablespoons (15–22.5 ml) soy sauce

½ teaspoon (3 ml) sesame oil

Chop the bean curd skin into very small squares (if dried, dampen before cutting).

Use fried gluten right out of the can. If using fresh, soften the balls in hot water over low heat, rinse, squeeze dry, cut into small pieces if necessary, and season according to Basic Recipe in Chapter 6.

Place all ingredients except sesame oil (start with 1 tablespoon soy sauce) in a heatproof bowl. Steam 15 minutes. Or place ingredients in a pot, bring to the boil, reduce heat, and simmer 2 minutes. Add sesame oil. Test for saltiness; you may want to add an extra ½ tablespoon soy sauce, but take care not to oversalt.

Broth with Winter Melon

This is a simple consomme-like soup with the salty-rich flavor of salted-dried bamboo shoot tips (see Chapter 5 for information on these; allow about 3 hours for presoaking). Add some chunks of winter melon if available (see Chinese Ingredients and Juicy Winter Melon or Cucumber, Chapter 2). The broth and soft, delicate-flavored melon are a good match.

2 tablespoons (30 ml) (packed) salted-dried bamboo shoot tips, presoaked and shredded

10 ounces (281 g) winter melon (optional; see Note 1)

1 teaspoon (5 ml) Tientsin preserved cabbage, minced (optional; see Note 2)

3 cups (750 ml) liquid (soaking liquid from bamboo shoot tips + stock or water)

2 tablespoons (30 ml) green soybeans or peas, fresh or frozen

1 teaspoon (5 ml) soy sauce, to taste

½ teaspoon (3 ml) sesame oil

Note 1: Purchase 12 ounces winter melon in order to yield 10 ounces trimmed. Seed the melon, cut off rind, and slice into bite-sized pieces, about 1 inch square and ½ inch thick, to yield about 2 cups.

Note 2: If you are using water instead of stock, include a bit of Tientsin preserved cabbage (see Chinese Ingredients).

Place dried bamboo shoot shreds and optional winter melon in a pot with 3 cups liquid—including soaking liquid. Add Tientsin preserved cabbage if using water instead of stock. Add fresh peas (if they are extra large) or fresh green soybeans now, but wait until later for frozen ingredients or small fresh peas. Bring to the boil, then reduce heat to low and simmer gently 10 minutes, covered. Toward the end, put in the peas or green soybeans (allow about 2 minutes for unthawed frozen ingredients, longer for small fresh peas). Turn up the heat if necessary to maintain a simmer, and continue to cook until the peas (and melon) are done. Test for saltiness, adding about 1 teaspoon soy sauce, to taste. Top with a few drops of sesame oil before serving.

8

Fruit and Nut Desserts

Fresh fruit is the most common end to a lunch or dinner in China, leaving the body freshened rather than burdened. But this does not mean that the Chinese lack a sweet tooth. They simply save such indulgences for other occasions—at tea time with friends, during a shopping break, or an evening mah-jong game. And, I suspect, they savor these treats much more as a result!

True, a banquet or festive celebration will conclude with a sweet soup and puree-filled steamed bun. This is a gesture more than anything else —could anyone possibly have any room left? Some restaurants in China also offer a sort of syrup fondue with chunks of apple or banana, and a bowl of ice water to crystallize the coating. And, of course, there are the dim sum teahouses. Surely no one who enjoys this Cantonese version of brunch can pass up those delicious little custard tarts with their flaky crust, or some of the sweet buns, deep-fried sesame-covered balls, or pudding made with fresh water chestnuts. But now we're back in the realm of off-hours eating. The whole point of dim sum, after all, is the pursuit of pleasurable and sophisticated snacking. Dim sum, in Chinese, simply means any snack or dessert. Literally it means to touch the heart—in other words, "hit the spot"—which is, after all, every-one's aim in snacking. It could be something salty, something sweet, something meaty, something rich, whatever you might hanker after.

In the teahouses, carts laden with tidbits and such delicacies as *shao mai*, barbecued pork buns, steamed meatballs, and stuffed tofu cease-lessly trundle by, offering the small plates and steaming baskets. Each portion is small, allowing you to sample a great variety, as little or as much as you like, at one sitting. Chinese call this "having tea," and there is always a pot of tea at the table—jasmine, green, sometimes chrysanthemum.

Out in the streets of China, too, there are sweet treats to be enjoyed, at shops or stalls along the way, or from street-plying carts that stop at your doorstep. Many vendors specialize in little else but one or two offerings. To warm you on wintry days, there are thick sweet soups made with red beans, lotus seeds, peanuts. In the summer, plates of shaved ice are splashed with a light syrup and heaped with mixed sweetmeats of all kinds—tapioca pearls, tart dried fruits, candied peanuts, sweet beans.

Certain treats are associated with particular holidays, such as the moon cake of Mid-Autumn Festival, just after the harvest time when the moon is large and full. In the fourteenth century, when an underground revolt was brewing against the Mongol rulers, secret information was concealed inside these cakes, which were then passed on to spread to the word. Suchow, Peking, and Canton all have their different varieties. At Chinese bakeries in this country you might see the small, dense Cantonese kind—a rich, thin outer dough with a center of different sweet pastes or nuts, and sometimes meats. The lotus seed variety includes the yolk of a duck egg.

Come the fifteenth day of the New Year, everyone has *yuen syau*, sweet-filled glutinous rice-flour dumplings in a bowl of hot, sweet liquid. The soft, chewy balls may be filled with red bean paste, ground sesame seeds, cassia blossom flavoring.

In spring, for the Dragon Boat Festival, every family makes its own *dzongdz*, dumplinglike packets of glutinous rice steamed in a wrapping of bamboo leaf. This holiday commemorates a Chinese statesman who was forced to commit suicide by drowning in 250 B.C. when the rulers rejected his counsel. Originally these packets, leaf-wrapped to keep the fish from eating them, were thrown into the river as food offerings to the dead hero. Southern Chinese fill them with sweet bean paste or meats. Northerners often leave them plain, to appreciate the subtle bamboo flavor of the leaf-wrapped rice, or perhaps dip them in sugar or a rose syrup.

Since a "natural" fruit, nut, or bean is so often the primary ingredient of these desserts, merely enhanced with sweetener, the result is clean-tasting and not cloying. Rarely does something seem overly sweet or disastrously rich. The sweetening agent, too, is often rock sugar, which gives a fuller flavor and is thought to be more nutritious. A charming legend is told tracing the origin of sugar-making in China. A certain monk, who had apparently learned the process abroad, was living as a recluse in the hills of Szechuan. Whenever he needed supplies, he would send his white donkey into the village with a shopping list and the cash. Townsfolk would fill the order and send the donkey back up the mountain. The animal once stopped to munch on some sugarcane shoots. This displeased the farmer whose crop it was, and he complained to the monk. That worthy man provided recompense by revealing how to use the cane for making sugar.

Whatever your style for sweetening life may be—snacking or dessert-ing—the recipes in this chapter will help you celebrate it. They are lively, colorful combinations of tart and sweet, firm and runny, smooth and chewy, or crisp. The selection supplies something to complement any repast, light or heavy, whatever the season or time of day.

Sliced Pears and Water Chestnuts

A luscious, hot concoction to be prepared just before serving. The scented pear slices are in perfect contrast to the crisp, sweet water chestnuts, and the whole is coated in a light sauce. I prefer Anjou pears for their juiciness and fine, smooth quality, but you can experiment with other types. Select a couple of small pears, just ripe enough for eating and no more, otherwise they will almost liquefy in the cooking. You can use either canned or fresh water chestnuts. The fresh ones, which resemble little flower bulbs with dark brown skin (look for shiny skin and firmness) are often stocked by Chinese groceries. Peel these with a paring knife, working in a circular motion from top around to the bottom. They are delightfully crisp and as sweet as candy. In fact, in areas where they are grown, they are often eaten as a fruit, skewered on sticks. Some Chinese consider these fresh ones a cure for various illnesses, including the common cold.

This recipe makes four to five small servings.

1 cup (250 ml) fresh water chestnuts, peeled; or one 5-ounce (140 g) can

2 small pears

1 tablespoon (15 ml) corn or peanut oil (see Note)

1 tablespoon (15 ml) granulated sugar, or 1½ tablespoons (22.5 ml) finely crushed rock sugar

2 teaspoons (10 ml) cornstarch dissolved in 4 teaspoons (20 ml) water

Note: If you prefer, you can use butter or margarine instead of oil.

Thinly slice the water chestnuts.

Peel the pears if skin is thick. Quarter lengthwise and core. Slice crosswise rather thinly (⅓ to ¼ inch). You should have about 1½ cups.

Heat a pan over high; add 1 tablespoon oil. When oil is hot, reduce heat to medium; put in the water chestnut slices and stir-fry a few seconds. Add pears and sugar; stir-fry 30 seconds. Pour cornstarch mixture over the top and stir-fry another 30 seconds until all is well coated. Remove to a plate or small individual plates, and serve immediately.

Black Date–Pine Nut Cookies

Pine nuts and Chinese black dates give this crumbly cookie its intriguing taste. Prunes are a fine substitute but will not duplicate the distinctive smoky flavor of the black dates, available in Chinese stores (not to be confused with California or Chinese preserved dates, which are also used in this recipe). While shopping for the black dates, check also for black sesame seeds—or use white sesame seeds. Pine nuts are available in Italian, Chinese, or natural food stores. Be sure to sample one to make sure of freshness and taste. If unavailable, substitute sunflower seeds. Chinese use oil in their baking instead of butter, and since butter is not part of a strictly vegetarian diet, this recipe is offered with apologies to those who may frown at the departure.

This recipe makes two dozen cookies.

½ cup (125 ml) butter or
    margarine

¼ cup (60 ml) sugar

6 Chinese black dates or
    prunes

6 California dates or Chinese
    preserved "honey" dates

¼ cup (60 ml) almonds,
    toasted and chopped

¼ cup (60 ml) walnuts,
    toasted and chopped

1½ tablespoons (22.5 ml) pine
    nuts or sunflower seeds,
    toasted

1½ tablespoons (22.5 ml) black
    or white sesame seeds,
    toasted and crushed

¾ cup (180 ml) all-purpose
    flour

Cream ½ cup butter or margarine and ¼ cup sugar.

Pit and chop the dates. Toss dates, nuts, and sesame seeds with ¾ cup flour to coat the bits separately. Combine with the creamed sugar and butter. Using 1 tablespoon dough each, form into 1½-inch patties and arrange on a greased cookie sheet. Bake in a preheated, 350° F. oven 15 minutes or until just lightly browned (do not overbake or the dates will harden). When done, remove to a plate.

Tangerine Segments in Hot Juice

This ends the meal on a refreshing, tangy note. At formal banquets, a soup like this would likely appear with Steamed Sweet-Stuffed Buns or other sweet goodies. Tiny, fragrant flowers of the cinnamon cassia are sometimes obtainable refrigerated in Chinese specialty markets (or the preserved form, cassia blossom jam, *gwei hwa jiang*) to add an elusive yet faintly exotic aroma and enhancement. No substitutes can really compare, but this is just as delightful without the cassia flavoring. Serve in small bowls, the more attractive the better. You can do the serving in the kitchen or at table from a small tureen. For a special occasion, treat everyone as well to Black Date–Pine Nut Cookies or Steamed Sweet-Stuffed Buns—which you can assemble ahead and freeze.

This makes three to four small servings.

1½ cups (375 ml) fresh tangerine, tangelo, or mandarin orange segments, including juice (or one 11-ounce can mandarin orange segments, including syrup)

1–2 tablespoons (15–30 ml) sugar, to taste

1–1½ cups (250–375 ml) water

¼ teaspoon (1.5 ml) (heaping) cassia blossom flavoring (optional)

To prepare fresh fruit, cut in half and seed. Using a grapefruit spoon, remove as much of the fruit as conveniently possible without the membrane (it is not desirable to have the membrane in this soup, and this method is easier than peeling each segment), then squeeze to obtain remaining juice. You should have 1½ cups segments with juice. Place in a pot with 1½ cups water. Sweeten to taste—1 to 2 tablespoons sugar, depending on how tart the fruit is and how sweet you want the soup to be.

If using canned mandarin orange segments, place the segments and syrup in a pot with 2 teaspoons sugar and 1 cup water.

Bring to the boil. During heating, stir in optional cassia blossom flavoring. Serve hot.

Litchis in Hot Syrup

Litchis (sometimes spelled lychees) have a tough, reddish skin, which peels off easily to reveal the juicy, bite-sized globes of firm, white fruit. Very occasionally, the fresh fruit is available here, but the canned is just as good in this light, hot soup for ending a meal or as refreshment on a winter's afternoon. You can add a further note of fragrance and flavor with a few cassia blossoms or their jam (see Tangerine Segments in Hot Juice).

1 can (20-ounce [562 g]) litchis in syrup; or 1 cup (250 ml) fresh litchis, peeled and seeded

Water

1½ tablespoons (22.5 ml) sugar (if using fresh litchis)

¼ teaspoon (1.5 ml) (heaping) cassia blossom flavoring (optional)

Canned litchis: Put litchis and syrup into a pot; thin the syrup by adding water as needed—¾ to 1 cup for most brands. Bring to the boil. Add the cassia blossom flavoring, if you have it, while this is heating. Serve hot in small bowls.

Fresh litchis: Peel and seed the fruit to yield 1 cup. Place it in a pot with 1½ cups water and 1½ tablespoons sugar. Bring to the boil, reduce heat, and simmer 2 minutes, adding optional cassia flavoring. Serve hot in small bowls.

Lotus Seed Squares

This is a kind of gelatin dessert to be cut into squares and nibbled, or eaten with a small fork. If you use agar-agar the result will be somewhat firmer. Agar-agar is derived from a seaweed, but the product itself is colorless and featherlight. The Chinese type is usually in foot-long strands, which are sometimes included in cold-tossed dishes. The Japanese is in a bar shape. Check your Oriental foods supplier for either kind. Unlike gelatin, it does not require refrigeration in order to set. See Chinese Ingredients for information on lotus seeds. For a Western-style embellishment, you can also serve this with a hot sauce (see Variation).

This makes six to eight servings.

¾ cup (180 ml) (4 ounces [112 g]) dried white lotus seeds

2 envelopes unflavored gelatin, or ⅛ ounce (3.5 g) agar-agar

6 tablespoons (90 ml) rock sugar or 5 tablespoons (75 ml) honey

Soak the lotus seeds in water at least 8 hours. Rinse. Place them in a heavy pot with water to cover, bring to the boil, then drain. This step purges the seeds of an unpleasant odor. Cover generously with fresh water, cover the pot wholly or partially, and cook over medium or low heat 1½ to 2 hours, stirring occasionally, until tender (some of the seeds will stay crunchy, however).

Reserve the cooking liquid. Pick over the seeds and remove any green sprouts, which are bitter. Measure what remains of the cooking water; add fresh water if needed to make 2 cups total.

When using gelatin, toss the gelatin with sweetener in a bowl. (If rock sugar is in large lumps, you will have to crush it or heat it with the 2 cups liquid until dissolved.) Heat the 2 cups liquid. Pour it into the bowl and stir until the sugar and gelatin dissolve. Add the lotus seeds.

When using agar-agar, put the precooked lotus seeds, 2 cups liquid, agar-agar, sweetener in a pot; cook at a bare simmer, stirring occasionally, until the agar-agar is dissolved, perhaps 25 minutes.

Pour into a greased 8-inch cake pan; let cool, then place in the refrigerator to set. Using a sharp knife, cut into small squares or rectangles.

Variation: To make sauce, in a pot dissolve 1½ tablespoons cornstarch in 1 cup cold water. Add ¼ cup sugar and 2½ tablespoons butter or margarine. Bring to the boil over medium heat, stirring, and cook 1 minute. Remove from heat and stir in ½ teaspoons vanilla or 1½ teaspoon bourbon or rum. Top lotus seed squares with sauce and serve. It is not necessary to bring gelatin to room temperature.

Cranberry Jelly Fritters

Cranberry tartness suggests the original Chinese ingredient, a firm, gelatinous jelly flavored with the hawthorn berry (or *shan dza*, which in northern China is also pureed to make a deliciously tart, thick, cooling drink). Enclosed within a light, deep-fried batter, the strips of jelly become hot and soft or, in the case of cranberry, almost liquid. Buy the "jellied cranberry sauce," not the whole-berry type.

This recipe makes three to four small servings.

8 ounces (224 g) cranberry jelly, canned

5 tablespoons (75 ml) flour

½ teaspoon (3 ml) baking powder

½ teaspoon (3 ml) sugar

5 tablespoons (75 ml) water

Vegetable oil for deep-frying

Flour for dredging

Cut the jelly crosswise into three round slices, ½ inch thick. Cut each slice into three strips, approximately ½ × ½ × 2½ inches.

Prepare a batter by blending the flour, baking powder, sugar, and water.

Heat oil for deep-frying; after it is hot, keep the heat around medium-high. Dredge the cranberry jelly strips lightly in flour, making sure all sides, including the ends, are dusted. Then dip them in the batter to coat completely, and immerse them in the oil until golden brown. Fry only a few at a time. Drain on paper toweling, and eat while hot.

Four Gods Soup

If you have access to the special ingredients used in this recipe—many Chinese markets carry them—you are in for a beguiling experience. The longan, a litchi-like fruit but smaller, gives this soup its distinctive flavor. It is used dried (*gwei yuen rou,* or *gwei yen rou*) and is packaged in small, dense quantities of 4 ounces, often in little red boxes. At Chinese markets, ask for them specially, as they are sometimes kept behind the cashier. Lotus seeds and dates, especially the Chinese dates, contribute heady nuances of their own. Use any of the four different dates suggested; the taste will vary subtly with each, and all are appealing. Chinese red dates, also called jujubes, are lacquer-red, leathery skinned, light in flavor and in weight. Chinese preserved or "honey" dates are sweet and hard, not as flavorful as California. Chinese black dates, which look like prunes, have an almost smoky flavor and will give a stronger taste to the soup than the other three dates. The fourth "god" included in the original recipe is *chien shr*, sometimes called fox nuts (seeds from a type of water lily). Reputedly rich in nutrition, they add little by way of flavor and can be omitted. If you wish to include some, follow the same preparatory steps as for lotus seeds.

This is considered very nourishing for expectant mothers and offers wintertime invigoration for all. For refreshment during an afternoon card game, serve it in small, colorful bowls on plates with ceramic Chinese spoons. Or, as a special end to a dinner, this offers an exotic change from sweets or pastry. Serve up individual bowls in the kitchen or at the table from a steaming bowl. You can assemble the makings ahead, then time the steaming to coincide with your dessert hour. Or you can steam it completely ahead of time, then reheat by steaming before serving. It cannot really be overcooked. Lotus seeds only improve with extended steaming—as long as ten hours in some recipes.

Makes six small (½-cup) servings.

½ cup (125 ml) dried white lotus seeds

2 tablespoons (30 ml) (packed) dried longans

6 medium dates (Chinese red, black, or preserved; or California)

3–3½ tablespoons (45–52.5 ml) honey or ¼ cup (60 ml) crushed rock sugar

3 cups (750 ml) water

2 drops lemon extract (optional)

Soak the lotus seeds 8 hours in water to cover. Remove them to a pot of fresh water; bring to a strong boil, then drain and discard the water (this step purges the seeds of an unpleasant odor). Add fresh water to cover generously and simmer the seeds, covered, for 1 hour. Reserve the liquid and measure it. Pick over the seeds; remove green sprouts, if any.

Place the lotus seeds, longans, dates, and sweetener in a heatproof bowl. Add cooking liquid from lotus seeds and enough extra water to make 3 cups liquid. (The above steps can all be done ahead of time, even a day before. You can do an hour of steaming in advance, too.) Steam 1 to 1½ hours, or until the lotus seeds are very tender and the dates and longans have plumped up. Before serving, add two or three drops of lemon extract if desired.

Advance preparation: The soup can be reheated by steaming.

Steamed Sweet-Stuffed Buns

(A)

(B)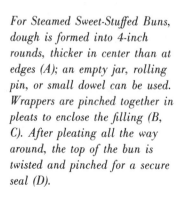

(C)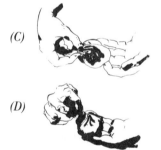

(D)

For Steamed Sweet-Stuffed Buns, dough is formed into 4-inch rounds, thicker in center than at edges (A); an empty jar, rolling pin, or small dowel can be used. Wrappers are pinched together in pleats to enclose the filling (B, C). After pleating all the way around, the top of the bun is twisted and pinched for a secure seal (D).

The Cantonese steamed sweet buns in dim sum tea-houses are quite doughy; these are much smaller, with more filling than dough. Use your ingenuity in providing tempting fillings for these plush little bundles. Sweet red bean paste is the most common Chinese choice. It is available canned in Oriental markets, along with the equally delicious black bean and lotus seed pastes. (Do not mistakenly buy a can labeled "sweet bean paste," a thick and pungent sauce.) Some pie fillings, such as mince, are also successful, as are other stiff fillings like date, poppy seed, and chestnut puree. These are available canned in gourmet shops or specialty sections of supermarkets. Some Chinese also use sesame paste, which is runny but firms up during steaming. (You can also use roasted sesame tahini.) Sweeten this, and any other fillings that may need it, with powdered sugar in proportions of about one to three; granulated sugar will be gritty. Of course, it's not necessary to make the whole batch with one filling. When using two or more fillings, dot the stuffed buns with a distinguishing mark (drop of food coloring, sesame seeds, poppy seeds, etc.).

It is possible to assemble these ahead, freeze (in a container so they are not touching), and steam before serving. If you are steaming them in a bamboo basket, you can bring it directly to the table, or transfer the buns to a plate for serving.

This recipe makes one dozen buns.

Dough:

2 cups (500 ml) all-purpose flour

1 teaspoon (5 ml) dry yeast

½ cup (125 ml) hot water

⅛ teaspoon (.5 ml) baking soda dissolved in ¼ teaspoon warm water

Fillings:

Sweet red bean or lotus nut paste, poppy seed or date filling, mincemeat

To prepare an all-yeast dough, add 1 teaspoon dry yeast to ½ cup hot water.

Add yeast mixture gradually to 2 cups flour in a mixing bowl. Turn out onto a floured board and knead 5 minutes. Replace in the bowl.

In a dry climate, grease the exposed surface of the dough lightly. Cover; let sit in a warm place until about double in size.

Turn the dough out onto a floured board. Make an indentation in the center and add the baking soda solution; knead, working in more flour as needed, to make a smooth dough—5 minutes. Roll the dough into a cylindrical shape, 12 inches long. Cut into 1-inch pieces. Shape these, cut-side up, into a round shape, then flatten them with the palm of your hand, turning them over three or four times. Wielding a pastry roller (or small rolling pin, piece of dowel, or an empty jar) under the palm of your hand, roll from the edge to the center, then back again, turning the piece of dough counter clockwise a little with your other hand after each roll, to make each into a 4-inch round (see illustration A). The center should be thicker than the edge in order to support the filling. You can stack these if you begin filling them immediately; otherwise they will stick together as they continue to rise.

Place 1 tablespoon (slightly heaping) filling in the center of each round. Gather the edge together to enclose the filling. One way of doing this is to hold the round on the fingers (inner side) of one hand (the left hand if you are right-handed). With thumb and fingers of your other hand, gradually pinch the edge together all the way around. Start with one pleat, then draw successive pleats to it as you revolve the bun in a counter direction; your thumb stays in position at the original pleat as you pinch the other pleats to it (see illustrations B and C). When using a generous amount of filling, it is also helpful to keep pushing the filling down in with your free thumb. When the filling is entirely enclosed, twist and pinch the center portion of dough to seal (see illustration D).

Arrange the stuffed buns ½ inch apart on a damp cloth inside a bamboo steaming basket; or, lacking this, use a flat, perforated rack or a heatproof plate (a plate is less desirable since steam cannot circulate as freely); the rack or plate also should be covered with damp cloth. Place well above the boiling water in a steamer for 15 minutes (allow an extra minute or two for frozen buns; do not defrost them first). Serve hot. These will stick to the cloth, but if you wash and reuse the same cloth each time, they will not stick as much.

Eight Treasures Rice Pudding

This is *the* classic Chinese dessert, for it can be magnificent not only gastronomically but visually. It appears as a dome of glutinous rice studded with preserved fruits and nuts. The preparation is akin to making an upside-down cake. Use your artistic flair in the selection of ingredients—any combination of nuts and dry, preserved, and candied fruits can be used. The list below offers a few suggestions. Use as few or as many as you like, in any proportion, for a dazzling multicolored mosaic or an elegant one-color scheme. "Eight Treasures" is a traditional reference to a combination of select ingredients. This is often a dessert for a special occasion, but small bowls of it are also served in restaurants in China that specialize in snacks and desserts. Such individual portions are quickly reheated. You, too, can assemble this ahead, even a day before. Start the final steaming an hour before serving time. The only catch is that you must procure glutinous rice. This "sticky" rice is sometimes labeled "sweet" rice, not for its taste, but because it is often used in desserts. It is available in Chinese and Japanese markets.

This recipe makes six large servings. If there is any left over, it is just as good, if not better, reheated. It is especially delicious with a hot sauce (see Variation).

2 cups (500 ml) glutinous ("sweet") rice

1¼ cups (310 ml) water

3 tablespoons (45 ml) sugar

3 tablespoons (45 ml) butter, margarine, or vegetable oil

Sesame oil to grease bowl

Prunes

Dates (California, or Chinese preserved)

Candied pineapple, citron, or kumquats

Glacé cherries

White lotus seeds

Raisins

Walnuts, toasted

Sunflower seeds, toasted

Pine nuts, toasted

Peanuts, roasted

Rinse glutinous rice until the water runs clear. Cover with water and let soak 1 hour. Drain and transfer to a greased heatproof bowl. Add 1¼ cups water to barely cover. Place on a rack in a steamer and steam 30 minutes (same procedure as On Steaming Soups, Chapter 7). Remove from the steamer and while still hot, stir in sugar, butter, margarine, or oil.

Consider color contrast, flavor, and texture in selecting the preserved fruits and nuts that will decorate the outside of your pudding. Lotus seeds must be precooked. Soak in water overnight; wash, drain, and bring to the boil in a pot of water; drain, add fresh water, and simmer, covered, until most are very tender (do not worry if a few stay crunchy). Check over the lotus seeds and remove any green sprouts, which are very bitter.

Choose a heatproof bowl that will just hold the rice and other ingredients. Grease it well with shortening. Line it with the fruits and nuts, then fill with rice. If the fruit-nut lining tends to tumble down while you are assembling it, add rice as you finish each level.

Cover the bowl with a plate or aluminum foil to prevent condensed steam from dripping into the pudding. Steam 1 hour or so.

Unmold the pudding by covering the bowl with a serving plate and upturning both together. Serve up individual plates at the table. Can be refrigerated and reheated by steaming.

Variation: Top individual servings of pudding with a hot sauce made according to directions in Lotus Seed Squares, Variation.

Fruit-Nut Confections

These are plump and crunchy with nuts. The chewy dough is made with glutinous rice flour. This comes boxed or packaged, also labeled "sweet rice flour" or "sweet rice powder," in Chinese or Japanese markets and many supermarkets. Check twice to make sure you aren't getting just "rice flour," which won't do. The dough is divided into nuggets, which are steamed and then topped with a piquant prune-nut mixture. In this case I prefer prunes over Chinese black dates, not only for the taste but because their moisture holds the mixture together. If you want to inject a bit of color, toss in some chopped candied fruit. It's possible to make everything ahead. Have the balls rolled and arranged for steaming, and keep them tightly covered with plastic wrap in the refrigerator. Then steam just prior to serving, and add the topping. Eat while still hot and soft (they harden when cool and do not reheat well). For a festive occasion, serve these with either of the two sweet fruit soups in this chapter.

This recipe makes one dozen small confections.

¾ cup (180 ml) + 1 tablespoon (15 ml) glutinous ("sweet") rice flour

¼ cup (60 ml) sugar

1 teaspoon (5 ml) vegetable shortening (Crisco)

3½ tablespoons (52.5 ml) hot water

4 prunes (large) or Chinese black dates

1½ tablespoons (22.5 ml) toasted walnut bits

2 teaspoons (10 ml) toasted pine nuts or sunflower seeds

glacé cherries, candied fruit, or citron (optional)

In a bowl, combine the glutinous rice flour and sugar; add shortening and hot water. Mix by hand, squeezing and pressing for several minutes to work into a ball. Moisten with water if the dough is too crumbly, or dust with more flour if it is too sticky. It will not be as cohesive as a wheat flour dough, but should just hold together comfortably, smooth without being sticky. During steaming, it should expand somewhat and the texture turn almost gummy.

Using the palms of your hands, roll the dough into a cylindrical shape, 12 inches long. Cut into 1-inch pieces; roll these into balls. Arrange them an inch apart in a bamboo steamer on a dampened cloth, or on a greased, flat, perforated rack or heatproof plate. Steam for 10 minutes or until cooked through to the center (this may take longer if you use a plate, which inhibits steam circulation). They will stick to the cloth, but if you wash and reuse the same cloth each time, they will not stick as much.

While the dough is steaming, prepare the topping. Chop prunes (or black dates), walnuts, and preserved fruit. Toss these together with the sunflower seeds or pine nuts. After removing the rice-flour balls from the steamer, press a little of the fruit-nut mixture onto each, and arrange on a plate. Since they are sticky, it helps to grease the plate lightly with a bit of sesame oil. Eat with the fingers or a small fork.

Litchi Gelatin

An American style fruit salad or refreshing summer dessert with the succulent white litchi. Some gourmet or Chinese sections in supermarkets supply these canned. This recipe yields eight half-cup servings. The Variation, which is mostly fruit with a minimum of gelatin, serves five.

1 can (20-ounce [562 g])
litchis

2½ tablespoons (37.5 ml) fresh
lemon juice

Water

2 envelopes unflavored
gelatin

6 tablespoons (90 ml) sugar

Drain litchis, reserving syrup. Add lemon juice plus water to the canned syrup to make a total of 4 cups liquid; bring this to the boil in a pot.

Meanwhile, toss gelatin with sugar in a bowl; pour in the hot syrup and stir until sugar and gelatin dissolve. Let cool. Add fruit at this point or wait until the gelatin is partially set. Refrigerate (in one bowl, or divide at this point into individual bowls) until set.

Variation: Drain one 20-ounce can litchis, reserving syrup. Measure the syrup and add water to make a total of 2 cups liquid; bring this to the boil. In the meantime, put one envelope unflavored gelatin in a bowl; sprinkle on a little cold water and mix until moistened. When the syrup boils, pour it into the bowl, and stir until the gelatin dissolves; let cool. Add litchis and refrigerate (in large bowl or individual bowls) until set.

Chrysanthemum Flower Tea

Tea-drinking customs vary widely in China. Pots and small cups are common, of course, but so are glasses or special small bowls, with lids. Like a pot, these also contain the loose tea leaves and can be refilled over and over throughout the day. The lid not only keeps the beverage hot but is useful when sipping to avoid imbibing any leaves.

Teahouses have always been popular gathering places in China. Some people go for a meal, others to while away the time, chatting with friends, discussing business, reading newspapers, and playing games like *go*. Food may be served, as at the dim sum houses. Others provide only tea and the ever-popular roasted watermelon seeds for snacking. These come in several flavors, including five-spice, soy sauce, and rose water. In some houses, you could leave your pot on the shelf and come back later in the day for a refill without extra charge—and bills might not have to be settled up till the end of the year.

"Kung fu" tea in southeastern China uses a tiny tea set consisting of a miniature pot and several cups that hold only a sip or two. The set rests snugly in a bowl filled with hot water to keep everything warm. The pot is filled repeatedly—each filling is enough for one round—and the brew is usually very strong. These pots are never washed, so that a potent and flavorful residue builds up with time. In really old pots, brews are made without even adding tea leaves. These aged pots are highly prized by connoisseurs.

Teas, of course, are many and the quality carefully graded. Some people mix their own blends, much as we do with coffee beans. Sometimes flavorings are added, such as litchi or tiny jasmine flowers. The ladies of Suchow used to add a few fresh rose petals to their jasmine tea.

Chrysanthemum flower tea occasionally can be ordered instead of jasmine or green tea in dim sum teahouses. It is a sweetened beverage that, according to the Chinese, has a "cooling" or calming effect on the system.

The tiny flower is a special variety of chrysanthemum sold in Chinese herbal shops and in some Oriental groceries. The yellow variety is preferred, but white may be used as well. You may have to experiment with the amount—some yield a stronger brew than others. I did not care for this tea at first until I hit upon the right balance between sweetening and flowery acridness, then it became a favorite after-dinner brew. Mid-afternoon, too, it gives a good noncaffeine pickup. If you cover the pot with a tea cozy or wrap it with a tea towel, it will stay hot during the steeping period.

This serves one. For more, increase the sweetener proportionately, but don't use as many flowers; for example, a *scant* ½ cup flowers is about right for 4 cups water.

2 tablespoons (30 ml) (loose)
dried chrysanthemum
flowers (20 flowers)

1½ teaspoons (8 ml) honey,
crushed rock sugar, or
granulated sugar

1 cup (250 ml) water

Put flowers and sugar or honey in a teapot; pour in 1 cup boiling water and steep 20 to 30 minutes.

Suggested Menus for One to Four Persons

It is probably a good idea to attempt just one or two recipes at a time until you're better acquainted with them as regards timing and taste. After that, if you're interested in putting together a whole meal, the following menus may be helpful. They are designed to minimize the time you have to spend doing last-minute cooking.

You can usually prepare relishes, cold dishes, and desserts ahead of time. If you want to be sure of having everything ready comfortably in advance of final cooking, it is also possible to cut up the ingredients for entrees and soup, sometimes even assemble the soup, and refrigerate. With presoaked dried, canned, and preserved foods this probably involves little or no nutrition loss. Cutting will often be your most time-consuming activity; once all the preparation work is done, the cooking will seem fast by comparison. While a soup and rice are steaming, you can complete one or two stir-fried dishes, which only take a matter of minutes. A complete meal for one or two persons can easily be prepared in an hour or less.

If you are cooking for just yourself, let one of the entrees, accompanied by rice, be the whole meal (the recipes in boldface are the best choices). For two or more persons, just add another dish per person, not necessarily in the order presented in the menu. Thus, any of these 43 menus will serve four people, or three if appetites are hearty. Serve rice with them, unless you are including noodles, potatoes, or a dish like potstickers. Finish up with fresh fruit or a dessert from Chapter 8.

In planning any menu, seek contrasts. An appetizing array of different textures and colors, and certainly flavors, helps make a successful meal. This is not as challenging as it may sound. Many dishes have variety built right in, combining crunchy with soft textures, for example. But if one of your dishes is strongly flavored or spicy, you would want to balance it with a lighter one. Try not to repeat ingredients, or the same type of food, such as two melons, or two varieties of beans. Tofu, of course, comes in different forms and you sometimes can combine them very successfully in one meal.

For an informal dinner with family or friends, present everything family style, for all to help themselves. This is also the Chinese way. And except at formal dinners, all the dishes, including soup, are placed on the table together or in quick succession as they come off the fire. They will usually keep warm long enough so that everyone can start eating together (though Chinese home cooks are sometimes still in the kitchen with one or more dishes in progress). Or you can keep things in a warming oven. And, if you prefer, you can serve up individual plates in the kitchen instead of using serving platters.

In the south of China, individual bowls of plain rice are an integral part of the meal. In the northern wheat-producing areas, other staples are also common, including noodles and an extensive variety of breads and buns. These may be tortilla-like, thin and unleavened; or laced with green onion and fried to a golden brown; or thick, chewy, and cut into pie-slice wedges. They might be round and dense, for breaking up and dunking in broth; or small and flaky with both savory and sweet fillings; or biscuitlike and stuffed with cold cuts. Dough is steamed into plain, breadlike buns *(mantou)*. Thick or thin doughs are stuffed and steamed into round buns, popular at any meal, including breakfast. A hearty noodle dish or platter of pot-stickers, with soup and relish, is often the whole lunch or dinner. Then, too, many people enjoy rice or congee at one meal and a wheat staple at another.

Rice is usually not served at parties or banquets in China since there is often wine, and the two seldom appear together; besides, rice is considered an "everyday" staple. It is sometimes offered before the dessert for formality's sake, but partaking would constitute a breach of manners, signifying that one had not had enough to eat. It is not likely you will want to attempt a formal Chinese dinner. The sheer logistics would be overwhelming. The number of guests at a table is usually twelve, and there are at least twelve dishes, served in succession. Furthermore, each course traditionally incorporates a different type of food and a different style of cooking. If you keep that in mind, the following menus should seem a snap by comparison.

Serve these menus with rice (unless noodles or a similar dish is included), and fruit or a recipe from Chapter 8 for dessert. Recipes in boldface are one-person meals. For more persons, add one extra dish per person, not necessarily in the order given.

Fried Noodles with Garden Vegetables
Szechuan Style Cabbage Relish
Clear Mushroom Soup
Lotus Seed Squares

Noodles with Sesame Sauce
Snappy Cucumber Relish
Asparagus and Mushroom Soup
Hashed Icicle Radish or Turnip

Bean Thread Noodles
Hot-and-Sour Soup
Pungent Bean Sprouts
Young Luffa Gourd with Gingerroot

Chinese Style Refried Beans
Spicy Asparagus and Mushroom Soup
Garland Chrysanthemum or Spinach with Wine and Soy Sauce
"Crystal Icicles" Relish

Chinese Pumpkin or Yellow Squash with Pine Nuts
Black Mushroom and "Meatball" Soup
Spiced Pressed Tofu with Peanuts
Braised Long or Green Beans with Black Mushrooms (Var.)

Tofu Dressed with Gingerroot and Green Onion or Savory
    Steamed Casserole
Tangy-rich Carrot Relish
Chinese Cabbage with Fried Gluten Nuggets or Bean Threads
Chowder of Fava or Lima Beans

Tofu with a Rich Sesame Sauce
Sun-Dried Watermelon Rind with Tender Mushrooms
Juicy Winter Melon or Cucumber
Tangerine Segments in Hot Juice

Easy Browned Tofu with Soy Sauce or Crispy Fried "Duck"
Sweet-and-Sour Relish Sticks
Hearty Bean and Black Mushroom Soup
Braised Chinese Cabbage with Delicacies

Savory Browned Tofu with Leek or Green Onion or Bean Curd Sheet Noodles with Garlic Chives or Leek
Sweet-and-Sour Chinese Cabbage Relish
Spicy Green Beans
Young Luffa Gourd Soup

Five-spices Browned Tofu and Black Mushrooms
Zesty Chinese Cabbage Stems
Gingery Fried Gluten Soup
Luscious Fava or Lima Beans with Bamboo Shoot

Crunchy Tree Ear or Snow Peas and Soft Browned Tofu or Sliced "Chicken Breast" with Tree Ear and Mushrooms
Green-and-Gold Relish
Succulent Black Mushrooms and Cashews
Open-face Steamed Dumplings *(Shao Mai)*

Tofu and Black Mushrooms Simmered with Lily Buds or Potato "Goose"
Green Peas or Soybeans in the Pod
Velvet Turnip Soup
Curried Broccoli Stems or Asparagus

Hot Pepper Tofu with "Pork"
Eggplant with Fried Gluten or Chestnuts
Garden Vegetable Soup with Bean Threads
Sliced Pears and Water Chestnuts

Honeycomb Tofu
Amaranth or Spinach with Garlic
Deep-fried Tofu or Fried Gluten Soup with Bean Threads
Mustard-hot Celery Relish

Tender Greens and Deep-fried Tofu or Greens and Bean Curd Sheet Noodles
Pungent Bean Sprouts
Spicy Three Shreds Soup
Taro, Yuca Root, Mountain Yam, or Potato Temptation

Three Delicacies and Deep-fried Tofu or Shredded Black Mushroom "Eel"
Sweet-and-Sour Chinese Cabbage Relish
Tomato and Tofu Potage with Golden Needle Mushrooms or Bean Sprouts
Fava or Lima Beans in Mustard Sauce

Eight Treasures "Meatballs"
Szechuan Style Cabbage Relish
Clear Mushroom Soup
Braised Long or Green Beans with Black Mushrooms (Var.)

Meaty Stuffed Cucumber
Green Peas or Soybeans in the Pod
Noodles with Sesame Sauce or Winter and Summer Bamboo Shoots
Litchi Gelatin

Stuffed Eggplant Ambrosia
Zesty Chinese Cabbage Stems
Spiced Pressed Tofu with Peanuts or Chinese "Ham"
Asparagus and Mushroom Soup

Boiled Pot-stickers
Snappy Cucumber Relish
Spinach and Tofu Potage with Black Bean Sauce
Succulent Black Mushrooms and Cashews

Open-face Steamed Dumplings *(Shao Mai)*
Braised Chinese Cabbage with Delicacies
Silken Tofu and Black Mushroom Soup
Fava or Lima Beans in Mustard Sauce

Chewy Stuffed Dumplings, Fried or Marvelous "Chicken"
Zesty Chinese Cabbage Stems
Braised Long or Green Beans with Black Mushrooms
Gingery Fried Gluten Soup

Spiced Pressed Tofu with Peanuts or Bean Curd
   Sheet Noodles
Sweet-and-Sour Relish Sticks
Fresh and Black Mushrooms with Delicacies
Luscious Fava or Lima Beans with Bamboo Shoot

Piquant Pressed Tofu Patties or Tofu "Cheese"
Tangy-rich Carrot Relish
Asparagus, Black Mushrooms, and Fried Gluten or Sweet Basil
Bean Thread Noodles
Litchis in Hot Syrup

Gingery "Meat Shreds"
Sweet-and-Sour Chinese Cabbage Relish
Eggplant Sautéed with Fried Gluten or Garlic
Baby Corn Spears with Mushrooms and Tree Ear or Green Pepper

Celery and "Meat Shreds"
Chinese Pumpkin or Yellow Squash with Pine Nuts
Chowder of Fava or Lima Beans or Broth with Winter Melon
Eggplant with Fried Gluten or Chestnuts

Crunchy Green Pepper and "Meat Shreds" with Green Soybeans or Peas
Young Luffa Gourd Soup
"Crystal Icicles" Relish
Sun-dried Watermelon Rind and Tender Mushrooms

Pressed Tofu and Mashed Tofu with Bamboo Shoots or Juicy Rice "Duck" Casserole
Sweet-and-Sour Chinese Cabbage Relish
Juicy Winter Melon or Cucumber
Spicy Three Shreds Soup or Three Delicacies Soup

Spring Rolls or Bean Curd Skin Rolls
Mustard-hot Celery Relish
Garland Chrysanthemum or Spinach with Wine and Soy Sauce
Hot-and-Sour Soup
Sliced Pears and Water Chestnuts

Peking Style Noodles with Bean Sauce and Mixed Garnish
Szechuan Style Cabbage Relish
Succulent Black Mushrooms and Cashews
Tangerine Segments in Hot Juice

Eggplant with Fried Gluten or Chestnuts
Tender Greens and Deep-fried Tofu
Spicy Green Beans
Velvet Turnip Soup

Eggplant Sautéed with Fried Gluten or Garlic Tofu "Cheese"
Green-and-Gold Relish
Tomato and Tofu Potage with Golden Needle Mushrooms or Bean Sprouts
Steamed Sweet-Stuffed Buns

Chinese Cabbage with Fried Gluten Nuggets or Bean Threads
Tofu with a Rich Sesame Sauce or Easy Browned Tofu with Soy Sauce
"Crystal Icicles" Relish
Spicy Asparagus and Mushroom Soup

Asparagus, Black Mushrooms, and Fried Gluten or Sweet Basil or Shredded Black Mushroom "Eel"
Tofu Dressed with Gingerroot or Green Onion
Garden Vegetable Soup with Bean Threads
Fruit-Nut Confections

Tofu "Meatballs" with Delicacies or Chestnut "Chicken"
Sweet-and-Sour Relish Sticks
Clear Mushroom Soup (Var.)
Fava or Lima Beans in Mustard Sauce

Deep-fried Tofu or Fried Gluten Soup with Bean Threads
Tangy-rich Carrot Relish
Young Luffa Gourd with Gingerroot
Taro, Yuca Root, Mountain Yam, or Potato Temptation

**Black Mushroom and "Meatball" Soup or "Chicken" and
    Tofu Ball Soup**
Snappy Cucumber Relish
Chinese Style Refried Beans
Garland Chrysanthemum or Spinach with Wine and Soy Sauce

Hearty Bean and Black Mushroom Soup
Zesty Chinese Cabbage Stems
Hashed Icicle Radish or Turnip
Curried Broccoli Stems or Asparagus

Chowder of Fava or Lima Beans
Sun-dried Watermelon Rind and Tender Mushrooms
Braised Chinese Cabbage with Delicacies
Piquant Pressed Tofu Patties or Winter and Summer
    Bamboo Shoots

Silken Tofu and Black Mushroom Soup
Green Peas or Soybeans in the Pod
Fried Noodles with Garden Vegetables
Cranberry Jelly Fritters

Spinach and Tofu Potage with Black Bean Sauce
Szechuan Style Cabbage Relish
Fresh and Black Mushrooms with Delicacies
Gingery "Meat Shreds"

**Tomato and Tofu Potage with Golden Needle Mushrooms
    or Bean Sprouts**
Mustard-hot Celery Relish
Luscious Fava or Lima Beans with Bamboo Shoot
Spring Rolls

Feast of Delicacies
Pungent Bean Sprouts
Honeycomb Tofu
Broth with Winter Melon
Eight Treasures Rice Pudding

Chinese Ingredients

This section lists all the special ingredients used for the recipes in this book, along with purchasing, preparation, and storing information. If an item is used only once or twice, you may be referred to the individual recipe(s) for details. In a few cases, when the ingredient is a frequently used one (such as tofu), the information appears in the introduction to the appropriate chapter.

Alphabetized arrangement here is according to the full name of the ingredient; for example, "rice wine" instead of "wine, rice." There are a few obvious exceptions, as when "dried" or "Chinese" is the first word.

When shopping for an unfamiliar ingredient, use this section in conjunction with the Shopping List at the end of the book. There you will find the Chinese names, sometimes useful when asking a shopkeeper for assistance.

Agar-agar: See Lotus Seed Squares. This product will keep indefinitely wrapped in plastic in a dry place.

Amaranth: See Amaranth or Spinach with Garlic.

Baby Corn Spears: See Baby Corn Spears with Mushrooms and Tree Ear or Green Pepper.

Baby Mustard Cabbage: Although this is different from a small bok choy, you will find some markets calling it baby bok choy. The stems are thinner, rounded at the base, and a light green in color. They fan out at the top into dark green, broad leaves. Some varieties also sprout little yellowish flowers. The heads are often quite small; sometimes several are bound together for marketing. The taste has a mild mustardy zest. Pictured on page 150.

Bamboo Shoot Tips, Salted-dried: See **Salted-dried Bamboo Shoot Tips.**

Bamboo Shoots:

Bamboo shoots are a favorite with Chinese vegetarian chefs. As Lin Yutang observed, ". . . a great part of the popularity of bamboo-shoots is due to the fine resistance the young shoots give to our teeth." In other words, their crunchiness adds something special to any dish, especially when they are combined with tender ingredients by way of contrast. To appreciate this extra dimension that they contribute, try including them in your own recipes for stews, sautéed dishes, casseroles, and soups. Unlike other crisp vegetables, they retain their texture even after prolonged cooking. Furthermore, they have a way of absorbing other flavors while imparting their own subtle sweetness to the dish.

There are reportedly over sixty genera of bamboo in the world, but finding a single fresh shoot at the market in this country can be a problem. The only ones I have ever seen are the "giant" variety, shredded and soaking in pails of water. Since these have an unpleasant sharp flavor, I much prefer a good canned shoot. Fortunately, some excellent brands are widely available. When you have a choice, buy them whole (the label will so indicate) or in chunks, not presliced. The canned article is always precooked, so needs only to be rinsed with boiling water—to rid it of the canned flavor—then under cold running water.

Winter bamboo shoots are preferred over other varieties for their crispness, fragrance, and sweetness. Small ones may be no bigger than a thumb, and are available canned, whole, or in chunks.

When you start comparing the various types and brands, you will notice distinct differences. Brands that use the "giant" type *(mao swun)* or its very large "tips" can be decidedly acidic in flavor and are not easily digested. The canned "green," too, frequently has these faults. Often, however, the label will not indicate the variety, and you must let taste be your guide.

Winter bamboo shoots are an exception. These will be labeled as such and usually come in chunks or whole. This type is generally preferred over others for its crispness, sweetness, and perfume. The shoots are dug up in winter before they have emerged above ground, and because all the sap has gone to the roots, they are particularly flavorsome and nutritious.

Of all the brands, I find Ma Ling the most dependable in quality. After opening, refrigerate shoots in water, tightly covered; change water every few days.

If you have access to good fresh bamboo shoots, do of course use them. In China the "winter," "spring" and "green" are often available at markets in the husk. The tips of an underground summer shoot, called *bien swun*, are also excellent; these are salted and dried to produce a special delicacy, salted-dried bamboo shoot tips. For more on these, see Chapter 5, where they are used in several recipes. There is also a thin, asparaguslike shoot called *gwei-ju swun*, which is more tender than crunchy, yet quite tasty. You can sometimes buy this canned (one label reads Slender Bamboo Shoots).

Ideally, bamboo shoots should be freshly cut the same day of use, although winter bamboo shoots keep well if properly stored. Some people have gone to outlandish lengths for the sake of freshness. The wealthy salt brokers of Yangchow, famous for their extravagant gormandizing, set up a relay system whereby bamboo shoots in the hills outside the city were popped into a cooking pot immediately after being cut. This was trundled forthwith down to the city on a portable charcoal brazier by bearers who changed hands every few miles. By the time the simmering pot of bamboo shoots and meat reached town, it was ready to be set right on the table.

When parboiling fresh bamboo shoots, leave them in their sheath to save as much flavor as possible, and boil until tender. The time will depend on size; winter shoots are often no bigger than a thumb and may take only a half hour. Then slice off the husk. Or they can be fried raw—julienned, sliced thinly, or diced—but this is not recommended, as they are not as digestible this way. In most cases frying would have to be done separately, before adding other ingredients. For soups, it is best to parboil the shoot first; if you do use it raw, the soup will have to be cooked longer. The "giant" *mao swun* should be soaked in water several days and shredded before using.

When slicing bamboo shoots, for maximum crispness do so from pointed tip to the base—lengthwise, not crosswise.

Bamboo Shoots, Dried: Do not confuse with salted-dried bamboo shoot tips. Sold in plastic bags in Chinese markets. Before using, soak in lukewarm water several hours until soft. Discard soaking liquid. The dry product will store indefinitely if kept in a dry place, wrapped in plastic.

Bean Curd: See introduction to Chapter 3.

Bean Curd Sheet: See On Bean Curd Sheet, Chapter 5.

Bean Curd Skin: See On Bean Curd Skin, Chapter 5.

Bean Curd Sticks: Dry, brittle, yellowish sticks derived from soybean milk. Sold in cellophane or paper packages in Chinese markets, the label reading "Beancurd Sticks" or "Dried Bean Curd (Sticks)." Soak in warm water 5 hours or until soft. The dried sticks will keep several months in a plastic bag in a cool, dry place.

Bean Sauce, Chinese: Also called brown bean sauce, yellow bean sauce, and ground bean sauce. Consists of fermented soybeans (or fava beans) with flour, salt, and sometimes a variety of seasonings. The beans may be ground, making a smoother consistency, or left whole. Use these interchangeably to give pungent bean flavoring to cooked dishes. They are a common shelf item, in cans and jars, in Oriental groceries. (Check the label for additional ingredients; the Szechuan variety contains chile and should not be used in these recipes unless you want a very hot taste. For better control of seasoning, it is probably better to use the basic bean sauce and add your own chile, garlic, sugar, etc., to taste.) These products will keep indefinitely in a tightly covered container, if refrigerated after opening. Japanese miso can be substituted.

Bean Sprouts: See **Mung Bean Sprouts.**

Bean Threads: Thin, translucent, noodlelike, dried strands consisting of mung bean starch (the starch is extracted from powdered mung beans by a water process). Sold in small cellophane packages (2 ounces, sometimes more or less) in supermarkets and Oriental groceries. The label may read "Saifun." Soak before using by covering with cold water for 3 to 4 hours, or boiling water for 15 to 30 minutes. Drain and, if desired, cut into shorter lengths. The dried product will keep indefinitely in a dry place.

Black Bean Sauce: A potent cooking sauce made of fermented black soybeans, sold in jars in Chinese markets. See Spinach and Tofu Potage with Black Bean Sauce for more information. After opening, store the sauce in the refrigerator, where it will keep indefinitely.

Black Dates, Chinese: Dried dates, resembling shriveled prunes, with a strong and smoky flavor, sold in plastic bags in Chinese markets. Store in refrigerator or cool, dry place in plastic bag or jar. Will keep indefinitely.

Black Eggplant: Pictured and described on page 131.

Black Mushrooms:

Fresh black mushrooms are sometimes available at markets, but it is the dried article that is used in most Chinese recipes. Chinese commonly call them "aromatic mushroom" *(syong gu)*. This delicacy is, deservedly, becoming available all over the United States in Oriental food stores. "Shiitake," a Japanese equivalent, can also be used. It is sold (at a high price) in the Oriental sections of many supermarkets and may be labeled "forest mushrooms."

The best variety of dried black mushroom has a thick cap with a pronounced pattern of white cracks, and thick stem. They are soaked in cool water before use, and the soaking liquid adds flavor to many recipes.

Your best buy is to purchase quarter-, half-, or 1-pound bags of dried black mushrooms at Chinese markets. A 1-pound bag contains over 200 mushrooms, and they will keep indefinitely if stored in a dry place, or in a tightly covered jar in the refrigerator or other cool place.

The range in quality for this product is great, and it is to your advantage to discriminate between inferior and superior, for it can mean a significant difference in flavor, aroma, and texture. Broadly speaking, three grades can be distinguished:

The commoner type has a thin cap with a dull brown, wrinkled top. The better variety—the winter mushroom, which takes three years to mature—has a thicker cap with a finely wrinkled, sometimes crackled surface and rounded edge. The most prized of the winter mushrooms are called *hwa* ("flower") *gu*. They are very thick and have a more pronounced pattern of white cracks on top; the stems, too, are very thick. (The Japanese equivalent is *matsutake*, grown on pine logs.)

The size of these mushrooms varies. It would be redundant to stipulate size in every recipe, and inconvenient for the reader to go by weight. So for our purposes, when a recipe calls for "black (or shiitake) mushrooms," figure on a diameter of 1¼ inches. If yours are smaller than this, use more; if larger, use less.

To soak dried black or shiitake mushrooms, rinse them first in cool water. Cover with cool water until soft; allow about an hour, depending on thickness. Warm or hot water draws flavor from the mushroom and should be avoided unless you are pressed for time, and then only if the soaking liquid is to be used in the recipe. After soaking, squeeze the mushroom, retaining the liquid, and cut off the stem. (Squeeze the liquid out of the stem, too, but discard the stem itself.) Use the soaking water in the same recipe if liquid is required; if not, save it for another recipe. If you find that you do not have the required amount, add water to make up the difference. In most of the recipes, you will probably have ½ to ¾ cup liquid after soaking. It is best to use the mushrooms on the same day of soaking, but if any are left over, you can store them overnight in the liquid, covered with plastic wrap, in the refrigerator.

To slice: With the presoaked mushroom flat on a cutting board, wield the knife at a slight angle to the board.

To cut: Sometimes, instead of slicing, the mushroom is cut into smaller pieces, in half or into thirds. For thirds, cut off one portion (less than half), then divide the larger remaining portion into halves.

Bok Choy: A vegetable with long white stalks culminating in dark green leaves, now available in many supermarkets.

Broccoli Stems, Chinese: Pictured and described on page 40.

Cassava: See Taro, Yuca Root, Mountain Yam, or Potato Temptation.

Cassia Blossoms: These tiny blossoms of the cinnamon cassia are used as a delicate flavoring, usually in sweet dishes. You may be able to buy the preserved blossoms (sometimes called cassia blossom "jam" or *gwei hwa jiang*) in small jars or containers, refrigerated, in Chinese specialty markets. If refrigerated in the tightly covered container, these will keep indefinitely.

Cedar Buds: Tender shoots of the fragrant cedar, *Cedrala odorada*. Use fresh shoots (not the salted, dried kind carried by some stores) as a flavoring in fillings and soups and as a garnish in cold-tossed dishes. See Tofu Dressed with Gingerroot and Green Onion for more information.

Celery, Chinese: See Mustard-hot Celery Relish.

Cellophane Noodles: See **Bean Threads.**

Chestnuts: Use fresh or canned. Chinese stores also sell dried chestnuts, which must be presoaked overnight, then simmered until tender (2 or more hours); however, these often lack flavor and tenderness and may not be worth the trouble. For directions on preparing fresh chestnuts, see Chestnut "Chicken," Chapter 5.

Chile Oil: Sold bottled in Chinese markets.

Chinese Bean Sauce: See **Bean Sauce, Chinese.**

Chinese Black Dates: See **Black Dates, Chinese.**

Chinese Broccoli Stems: Pictured and described on page 40.

Chinese Cabbage: Also called Napa cabbage. Available year-round in supermarkets and Oriental groceries.

Chinese Celery: See Mustard-hot Celery Relish.

Chinese Dark Vinegar: See **Dark Vinegar, Chinese.**

Chinese Eggplant: Pictured and described on page 131.

Chinese Icicle Radish: See **Icicle Radish, Chinese.**

Chinese Parsley: See **Cilantro.**

Chinese Preserved "Honey" Dates: See **Preserved "Honey" Dates, Chinese.**

Chinese Pumpkin: See Chinese Pumpkin or Yellow Squash with Pine Nuts.

Chinese Red Dates: See **Red Dates, Chinese.**

Chives, Garlic: See Bean Curd Sheet Noodles with Garlic Chives or Leek.

Chrysanthemum Flowers, Dried: See Chrysanthemum Flower Tea.

Cilantro: Also called Chinese parsley and fresh coriander. Oriental markets and many supermarkets, as well as Latin American and Middle Eastern groceries, stock this fresh, fragrant garnish. Used in soups and cold-tossed dishes. Will keep one week, refrigerated, in a plastic bag.

Corn Spears, Baby or Young: See Baby Corn Spears with Mushrooms and Tree Ear or Green Pepper.

Curry Powder: Madras curry powder is recommended. It contains other spices and is sold in jars or tins in Indian and many Chinese groceries.

Daikon: A long white icicle radish, now carried in many supermarkets as well as Oriental groceries. Use interchangeably with Chinese icicle radish and sometimes turnip. Will keep a week or longer wrapped in plastic and refrigerated. Pictured on page 14.

Dark Vinegar, Chinese: Try to obtain the bottled *Chen Chiang* ("Chinkiang") vinegar, sold in Chinese groceries. This has a most hearty, tantalizing savor, as pungent as it is piquant. Dark vinegar, distilled from rice, is sometimes called black vinegar.

Deep-fried Tofu: See On Deep-frying Tofu, Chapter 3.

Dry Mustard: See **Mustard, Dry.**

Eggplant, Black: Pictured and described on page 131.

Eggplant, Chinese: Pictured and described on page 131.

Eggplant, Japanese: Pictured and described on page 131.

English Cucumber: Also called hothouse. More slender and less seedy than regular cucumber, it is very crisp, with tender skin. Sold in many supermarkets, sealed in plastic.

Fava Beans: Also called broad beans or horse beans, favas are used in Middle Eastern and some European cuisines. Sold fresh in pods at some Chinese and Italian groceries, spring and fall. The fresh beans must be shucked, then parboiled or steamed for several minutes, and skinned. See illustration, page 35. Canned favas are sometimes available in Middle Eastern markets. Dried favas are stocked by Chinese grocers and must be soaked one day or more, then skinned and boiled till tender. The dried bean is often sprouted, cooked, and served as a side dish.

Five-spices Powder: A mixture of ground spices: most commonly star anise, fennel, cloves, cinnamon, and Szechuan pepper. Sold in jars or plastic bags at Oriental markets. Use sparingly as a flavoring. As with any spice, it will store indefinitely but loses flavor over extended periods.

Fried Gluten: See introduction to Chapter 6 and Fried Gluten Puffs Basic Recipe.

Garland Chrysanthemum Greens: See Garland Chrysanthemum or Spinach with Wine and Soy Sauce.

Garlic Chives: See Bean Curd Sheet Noodles with Garlic Chives or Leek.

Gingerroot: The kind most commonly in stock is "old" gingerroot. Sometimes fresh young gingerroot is available in Chinese markets as well, recognizable by ivory-yellow, almost transparent skin with pinkish tinge where shoots have been clipped. This has a lighter flavor than old gingerroot, so double the proportions when using it. Wrap gingerroot in brown paper and plastic, and store in the refrigerator, where it should keep for a couple of weeks or more. If you live in an area where it is not always in ready supply, you may want to freeze some: Simply wrap the knob, whole, in plastic. Defrost just enough to allow slicing. Defrosting is not necessary when grating: Just scrape with a knife (you can efficiently skin it this way, too). See also **Marinated Gingerroot.**

Ginkgo Nuts: When cooked, the small, oval, yellow-white nutmeats are tender and chewy, with a delicate flavor. They come shelled, boiled, and ready to use in cans at Oriental groceries. (Do not be put off by a bitter taste; this disappears with heating.) Some brands are labeled "white nuts," a direct translation of the Chinese. The ginkgo tree is occasionally seen in this country. Chinese markets and herbal dispensaries often carry the nuts in the shell, in bulk or in bags. Resembling a large pistachio, they must be shelled and parboiled.

To parboil: Shell the nuts. If the meat is fresh (not hard), simmer in water, covered, 45 minutes to 1 hour; remove the thin, brown skins. If the nut meat is dried and hard, soak overnight in water, remove the skin, and simmer 45 minutes to 1 hour.

Nuts in the shell can be stored indefinitely in a cool, dry place, uncovered. The canned nuts should be refrigerated in water in a tightly covered container after opening; if you change the water every few days, they will keep for several weeks.

Gluten, Fried: See introduction to Chapter 6 and Fried Gluten Puffs Basic Recipe.

Glutinous Rice: Sticky after cooking, the short type is also labeled "Sweet Rice," presumably because it is most often used in desserts. Japanese and Chinese markets carry it. Usually it should be washed till the water runs clear, then soaked 1 to 2 hours in water (room temperature) to cover. Drain, add required amount of water (usually twice as much as rice), and steam till done.

Glutinous Rice Flour: This is "sticky" rice flour, milled from glutinous rice. It is often used in making sweet confections, so it may be labeled "Sweet Rice Flour" or "Sweet Rice Powder." Packaged (sometimes in boxes), often sold in supermarkets. When shopping in Chinese markets, take care not to confuse this with regular "rice flour."

Golden Needle Mushrooms: So called because they have very slender, long stems with a tiny cap. Also called enoki mushrooms (Japanese). Available fresh in some Oriental and health food markets. Store in the refrigerator. Sold canned in Chinese and Japanese markets and in some supermarkets in small jars (Green

Giant brand). See Tomato and Tofu Potage with Golden Needle Mushrooms or Bean Sprouts for more information. After opening canned mushrooms, rinse them and store, refrigerated in water, in a tightly covered container.

Green Soybeans: An appealing addition to many dishes for their color, nutlike flavor, and crunchiness. Some Chinese and Japanese markets sell them frozen, both shelled and in the pod. (Canned are not recommended, being inferior in flavor and texture.) Do not substitute dried soybeans.

Icicle Radish, Chinese: A large, long, bulky white radish sold in Chinese markets. Use interchangeably with daikon, which is usually longer and more slender. Pictured on page 14.

Japanese Eggplant: Pictured and described on page 131.

Jujubes: See Red Dates, Chinese.

Lily Buds, Dried: Also called dried lily flowers and sometimes "golden needles" (from their Chinese name). Sold in cellophane bags in Oriental groceries. Before using, soak in cool water until soft (½ to 1 hour), squeeze out the liquid, and pinch off any hard stems. To retain as much flavor as possible, do not use warm water for soaking. Discard liquid after soaking. Store the dried buds in a plastic bag or tightly covered container in a cool, dry place; they will keep indefinitely.

Litchi: Also spelled lichee or lychee. See Litchis in Hot Syrup.

Long Beans: Also called foot-long beans and yard-long beans. Pictured on page 34.

Long Onion: See **Welsh Onion.**

Longans, Dried: See Four Gods Soup for more information. To store dried longans after opening, wrap tightly in plastic and refrigerate; they will keep indefinitely.

Lotus Seeds, Dried White: Also called lotus nuts. Sold in cellophane bags in Oriental markets. Expensive, requiring several steps in preparation, but superior to the canned, precooked seeds. See Lotus Seed Squares for parboiling directions. The dried seed will store indefinitely in a plastic bag in a dry place.

Luffa Gourd: See Young Luffa Gourd with Gingerroot. Pictured on page 147.

Marinated Gingerroot: Sold in tall jars (1 pound, 2 ounces) in Oriental markets. After opening, this will keep in the refrigerator for several months.

Miso: A Japanese paste of fermented soybeans, rice, and salt. The dark red kind is saltier than the yellow (or "white"). Use as a substitute for Chinese bean sauce. Sold packaged or in bulk at Chinese, Japanese, and health food stores. Will keep indefinitely in the refrigerator if tightly wrapped in plastic.

Mountain Yam: Pictured and described on page 43.

Mung Bean Sheet: See Bean Thread Noodles, Variation. This also comes in precut, dried strips. Will store indefinitely if kept dry and wrapped in plastic.

Mung Bean Sprouts: These are available fresh in most supermarkets as well as Oriental groceries. Buy them crisp, and use on day of purchase or within a day or two at most, before they turn brown and limp. Some cooks prefer to nip off the hairlike tips of the sprouts before rinsing for use. In Chinese markets these are sometimes sold side-by-side with soybean sprouts, which are larger.

Mustard, Dry: Sold in the spice section of supermarkets. To prepare, see Mustard-hot Celery Relish. Dijon mustard is a substitute but is not as hot.

Naga Imo: See Taro, Yuca Root, Mountain Yam, or Potato Temptation. Pictured and described on page 43.

Orange Peel, Dried: See Tangerine (or Orange) Peel, Dried.

Oriental Cucumber: Usually more slender, smaller, and crisper than regular cucumber. Called *kyuri* in Japanese, it is available in some Oriental markets during the summer and fall. Use unskinned and unpeeled. These may have a slightly curled shape. Do not confuse with small canning cucumbers.

Parsley, Chinese: See **Cilantro.**

Pine Nuts: Available shelled from Chinese markets, nut shops, health food stores, and Italian delicatessens. Usually sold in bulk by the ounce. Test for flavor before buying. If flavorless, or unavailable, substitute sunflower seeds in these recipes. Will keep several months in a tightly covered jar in a cool, dry place.

Plain Pressed Tofu: Sometimes called dry or dry-pressed bean curd. See introduction to Chapter 4 and Basic Recipe. The commercial product will keep several weeks in the refrigerator before opening. After opening, rinse, pat dry, wrap in plastic, and refrigerate; it will keep about a week.

Pot-sticker Wrappers: See Boiled Pot-stickers *(Shwei Jow)* for more information. The store product will keep a couple of weeks in the refrigerator if tightly wrapped in plastic, or several months in the freezer (it may dry out over long periods).

Preserved "Honey" Dates, Chinese: Hard, dried dates sold in cellophane bags in Chinese markets. Sometimes can be used interchangeably with California dates. Will store indefinitely in plastic bag or jar in refrigerator or cool, dry place.

Preserved Snow Cabbage: Sold canned or refrigerated, this is a fine-leaved mustard green preserved in brine. Crunchy, usually chopped, it gives nice saltiness and pungent vegetable flavor to dishes. Canned labels include "Snow Cabbages, Preserved in Brine," "Pickled Cabbage," or "Red-in-Snow" (from the Chinese name; red peppers are sometimes included). A more fresh-tasting and generally superior variety comes in plastic bags labeled "Pickled Mustard Greens" or simply "Mustard Greens." Look for them in the refrigerator section of Chinese markets. After opening, the canned and fresh will store several weeks in a tightly covered container in the refrigerator.

Pressed Tofu: See introduction to Chapter 4 and Basic Recipes for Plain Pressed Tofu and Spiced Pressed Tofu.

Pumpkin, Chinese: See Chinese Pumpkin or Yellow Squash with Pine Nuts.

Red Bean Paste: A sweetened puree of cooked red beans, used as a filling in desserts, sold canned in Oriental markets. After opening, this will store several weeks in the refrigerator in a tightly covered container.

Red Dates, Chinese: Dried, lightweight, with lacquer-red, papery, wrinkled skin. Sold in plastic bags or in bulk in Chinese markets. See Four Gods Soup for more information. Stored in a plastic bag or tightly covered container in a cool, dry place, these will keep indefinitely.

Red-in-Snow: See **Preserved Snow Cabbage.**

Rice Wine: Use Chinese brands (usually made from glutinous rice) such as Chinese Yellow Wine, *Shao-hsing* wine, *Lao Chiu*; or Japanese saké, sold at most liquor stores and many Oriental markets. Used sparingly, it imparts superbly subtle flavor and aroma to foods. See On Stir-frying, Chapter 2, for more information on use. Substituting other wines will alter the flavor and is not recommended.

Rock Sugar: A delicious sweetener. In lumps, it may be labeled "Yellow Rock Sugar," in plastic bags at Chinese groceries. See introduction to Chapter 8 for more information. Will store indefinitely in a plastic bag or jar in a dry place.

Saké: See **Rice Wine.**

Salted-dried Bamboo Shoot Tips: See On Salted-dried Bamboo Shoot Tips, Chapter 5. Store in jar or plastic bag in a dry place. Will keep indefinitely.

Sesame Oil: Buy the amber-colored kind processed from roasted sesame seeds. Usually a few drops is enough to lend pleasant aroma and slight flavor enhancement to a soup or other dish. Do *not* try to substitute the colorless, flavorless type sold in some supermarkets and health food stores. You will find the required kind in Oriental stores and with the Chinese products in supermarkets. Check the label to see if other oils (for example, soybean) have been added. This is acceptable, but pure sesame oil is preferable.

Sesame Paste: In jars at Oriental groceries, this may also be labeled Sesame Seed Paste. It consists of roasted, ground sesame seeds and soybean oil. Use interchangeably with roasted sesame tahini (not raw tahini) stocked by health food stores. For a sauce recipe, see Tofu with a Rich Sesame Sauce. After opening, the paste will keep indefinitely, tightly covered, in the refrigerator.

Sesame Seeds: These come both white and black. Oriental markets carry both, while health food stores have the white. To toast them, place in a dry skillet over medium or medium-high heat, and shake and/or stir continuously till browned; they will continue to brown after removing from the heat, so transfer to a bowl when just lightly tanned. If the recipe calls for crushing, use a mortar and pestle (lacking this tool, you can omit the step; its purpose is to release the oil). It is better to toast seeds just before use; but both toasted and raw will keep in a tightly covered jar in the refrigerator or a cool, dry place for long periods.

Shiitake Mushrooms: See **Black Mushrooms.**

Silken Tofu: See introductions to Chapters 3 and 7.

Soy Sauce: Soy sauce is made from fermented soybeans. The soy sauce used in the testing of these recipes was Kikkoman (regular, not light), mainly because it is widely available in this country and also because of its excellence. When using other brands, slight adjustment in proportions may be necessary to correct for differences in saltiness and potency. The imported Chinese brands include "thin" soy sauce *(sheng chou)* and the thicker "black" or "dark" *(lao chou)*. The former, which is very salty, is used when a lighter color and flavor are desirable, as in dips, dressings, soups, and fish or fowl dishes. "Black" soy sauce, which sometimes contains caramel or molasses, is more suited for cooking with meats, and is especially popular with Cantonese. Other cooks, among them Shanghainese, also favor a savory "mushroom soy," which comes in both thin and thick varieties.

Soybean Custard: See introduction to Chapter 3 and Silken Tofu and Black Mushroom Soup. Store this product as with regular tofu (see Chapter 3).

Soybean Sprouts: See Stock—Basic Recipe in Chapter 7. Use these as fresh as possible—no later than a day or two after purchase.

Soy-pickled Cucumber: Sold in 6-ounce cans labeled "Pickled Cucumber," in Chinese markets. After opening, store in a tightly covered container in the original liquid. Will keep for long periods in the refrigerator.

Spiced Pressed Tofu: See introduction to Chapter 4 and Basic Recipe. Before opening, the commercial product will keep several weeks in the refrigerator. After opening, rinse, pat dry, wrap tightly in plastic, and store in the refrigerator, where it will keep a week or so.

Spring Roll Skins: See Spring Rolls. Tightly wrapped in plastic, these will keep in the refrigerator for a couple of weeks. Frozen, they will keep longer but may dry out over an extended period.

Star Anise: A small, eight-petaled pod used as a spice (whole, in segments, or ground). Sold in Oriental markets, Chinese herbal dispensaries, and some health food stores. Will keep indefinitely in a tightly covered container in a cool, dry place but loses potency over long periods.

Straw Mushrooms: These come in cans in Oriental groceries, and sometimes in small jars (Green Giant label) with the Oriental products in supermarkets. Some are peeled, some unpeeled—use interchangeably. To remove canned taste, drain and rinse with boiling water before using. The flavor is delicate. When a recipe calls for fresh mushrooms, you can include a few of these for variety. After opening, store tightly covered in water; if water is changed every few days, they will keep for several weeks in the refrigerator.

"Sweet" Rice: See **Glutinous Rice.**

"Sweet" Rice Flour (or Powder): See **Glutinous Rice Flour.**

Szechuan Peppercorns: Also called "Wild Pepper" and Chinese peppercorns, available in Oriental markets and Chinese herb dispensaries. Do not substitute black peppercorns. Will store indefinitely in a tightly covered container if kept dry and cool, but like any spice, will lose flavor with time.

Szechuan Pickle: The knobby stem portion of a type of mustard plant is preserved with salt, chile pepper, and sometimes other spices to become very crunchy and hot. On opening the can, do not let the olfactory assault alienate you; the pickle is used sparingly to lend a peppery vegetable flavor and "crunch" to dishes, with very tasty results. To retain crispness, avoid overcooking. Available canned and in bulk at Chinese and

Japanese markets and some supermarkets. The label may read "Szechuen Preserved Vegetable," "Preserved Szechuan Mustard," "Preserved Mustard," "Mustard Pickles," or "Home Style Szechuan Pickles." Rinse before using if you want a slightly less hot flavor. After opening, store (unrinsed) in a tightly covered jar in the refrigerator, where it will keep indefinitely.

To shred: Slice very thinly, then stack slices and cut into shreds. To mince, first cut into shreds, then cut shreds into tiny dice.

Tahini: See **Sesame Paste.**

Tangerine (or Orange) Peel, Dried: Small chips of dried skin, available in plastic bags at Oriental groceries (may be unmarked, so ask for assistance). Used sparingly as a flavoring. Will keep indefinitely in a tightly covered container in a cool, dry place.

Taro: Pictured and described on page 43.

Tientsin Preserved Cabbage: Preserved Chinese cabbage, used in small amounts in soups, fillings, and other dishes. It comes already chopped, packed in cans or in a distinctive squat crock (earthenware, glass, or plastic). Some labels may read "Tientsin Preserved Vegetable." Named after a city in northeastern China, this type is garlic-flavored. There are other varieties, but not as commonly available in the United States. (Do not use the five-spices type in these recipes.) After opening, store tightly covered in the refrigerator, where it will keep indefinitely.

Tofu: See introduction to Chapter 3.

Tofu, Deep-fried: See On Deep-frying Tofu, Chapter 3.

Tofu, Plain Pressed: See Plain Pressed Tofu.

Tofu, Pressed: See introduction to Chapter 4 and Basic Recipes.

Tofu, Silken: See introductions to Chapters 3 and 7.

Tofu, Spiced Pressed: See Spiced Pressed Tofu.

Tofu "Cheese": "Preserved Bean Curd," "Preserved Wet Bean Curd," "Bean Cake (Fu-Yu)" and "Wet Bean Curd" are some of the names given this product on jars and cans in Oriental markets. See Tofu "Cheese," Chapter 1, for more information. After opening, store (in the original liquid, if any) tightly covered in the refrigerator, where it will keep indefinitely. The red type in brown crocks does not require refrigeration.

Tree Ear: Also called wood ear and dried black fungus (but distinguished from a smaller dried black fungus named *chuan erh*). Dried, sold in plastic or cellophane bags, the brittle, crinkled "leaves" are black or brown on one face and often gray on the other, but after soaking turn a deep reddish brown. The texture is springy yet strangely crunchy. The leaves are sometimes loose, sometimes connected ("1 tree ear" in these recipes). Size varies, so it is hard to specify accurately how much you will need to soak for the recipe. One dried, crinkled leaf, 2 × 2 inches, will yield, after soaking, about 1 tablespoon minced, or 1 heaping tablespoon shreds, or ⅛ cup small pieces.

Soak in cool or lukewarm water until fully swollen (½ to 1 hour); rinse, and cut or tear off the tough stem portion. If you have any left over, store it in the soaking liquid, covered, in the refrigerator, where it will keep another day or two. Do not use soaking liquid in the recipe.

The dry tree ears will keep indefinitely in a plastic bag or tightly covered container in a cool, dry place.

Vegetable Oil: Corn or peanut oil is preferred, but salad or cottonseed oil will do.

Water Chestnuts: Sold fresh (unpeeled) in Oriental groceries and some supermarkets, resembling small flower bulbs. Peel before using, then store in cold water, refrigerated, if not using right away. Canned (peeled, whole) water chestnuts are stocked by most supermarkets. After opening, rinse with boiling water, then cold water, to remove canned flavor. Can be stored in water in a tightly covered container in the refrigerator; will keep several weeks if the water is changed every few days, but tends to become waterlogged.

Welsh Onion: See Savory Browned Tofu with Leek or Green Onion.

Winter Bamboo Shoots: See **Bamboo Shoots.**

Winter Melon: See Juicy Winter Melon or Cucumber.

Winter Mushrooms: See **Black Mushrooms.**

Yam, Mountain: Pictured and described on page 43.

Young Corn Spears: See Baby Corn Spears with Mushrooms and Tree Ear or Green Pepper.

Yuca Root: Pictured and described on page 43.

Shopping and Mail-Order Sources

Here are the names and addresses of a few stores around the United States that carry the ingredients used in this book, including bean curd sheet and, in most cases, bean curd skin and salted-dried bamboo shoot tips. To facilitate shopping at Chinese grocers or ordering by mail, it might be helpful to make a copy of the Shopping List that follows this section. It provides the names of ingredients in Chinese, so you can be more certain of getting precisely what you need. If you do not live near any of the stores below, scan your local Yellow Pages under Food Products, Groceries, etc., for Oriental food markets. Also check your supermarket for Chinese and gourmet sections, and look into the local gourmet and health-food stores. You can even order by mail, as the majority of Chinese foodstuffs used in these recipes are dried or canned. Most of the suppliers below provide mail-order service.

Mandarin Delight, 1024 Stockton, San Francisco, CA 94108; Tel. (415) 781-4650.

Metro Co., 641 Broadway, San Francisco, CA 94133; Tel. (415) 982-1874.

Yee Sing Chong Co., Inc., 966 N. Hill St., Los Angeles, CA 90012; Tel. (213) 626-9619.

Pacific Mercantile Co., 1925 Lawrence, Denver, CO 80202; Tel. (303) 295-0293.

Da Hua Foods, Inc., 615-617 Eye St., N.W., Washington, D.C. 20001; Tel. (202) 842-1992, -1993.

Kam Man Food Products, Inc., 200 Canal St., New York, NY 10013; Tel. (212) 571-0330.

Shopping List

This is an alphabetized listing of the ingredients you might buy at a Chinese market. The Chinese name or names preceding each entry can be helpful since not every ingredient or product has a commonly recognized English name. Just show this list to your Chinese grocer when you are in need of assistance. It will also cut across most dialect barriers, as the written name is usually understood generally.

洋菜　Agar-agar

苋菜　Amaranth

玉米笋　Baby Corn Spears

青江菜　Baby Mustard Cabbage

竹笋　Bamboo Shoots

百葉,千層　Bean Curd Sheet

腐皮,鮮腐竹　Bean Curd Skin

元枝腐竹　Bean Curd Sticks

原晒豉　Bean Sauce, Chinese

粉絲,細粉　Bean Threads

豆豉醬　Black Bean Sauce

黑棗　Black Dates, Chinese

香菇,冬菇　Black Mushrooms

芥藍菜　Broccoli Stems, Chinese

桂花醬　Cassia Blossoms or Cassia Blossom "Jam"

香椿頭　Cedar Buds

芹菜　Celery, Chinese

栗子　Chestnuts

辣油　Chile Oil

白菜,紹菜　Chinese Cabbage

南瓜	Chinese Pumpkin	金針菜	Lily Buds, Dried
菊花	Chrysanthemum Flowers, Dried	荔枝	Litchis
香菜	Cilantro	長豆	Long Beans
咖哩粉	Curry Powder	桂圓肉	Longans, Dried
黑醋，鎮江醋	Dark Vinegar, Chinese	蓮子	Lotus Seeds, Dried White
油豆腐	Deep-fried Tofu	絲瓜	Luffa Gourd
黑茄	Eggplant, Black	和味子薑	Marinated or Preserved Gingerroot
蠶豆	Fava Beans	山藥	Mountain Yam
五香粉	Five-spices Powder	粉皮	Mung Bean Sheet
油麵筋	Fried Gluten	綠豆芽	Mung Bean Sprouts
茼蒿菜	Garland Chrysanthemum Greens	芥辣粉	Mustard, Dry
韭菜	Garlic Chives	小黃瓜	Oriental Cucumber
薑	Gingerroot	松子	Pine Nuts
白菓	Ginkgo Nuts	白豆腐乾	Plain Pressed Tofu
糯米	Glutinous Rice	水餃皮	Pot-sticker Wrappers
糯米粉	Glutinous Rice Flour	蜜棗	Preserved "Honey" Dates, Chinese
金針菇	Golden Needle Mushrooms	雪裏紅	Preserved Snow Cabbage
毛豆	Green Soybeans	豆腐乾	Pressed Tofu
磨原豉	Ground Bean Sauce	紅豆沙	Red Bean Paste
白蘿蔔	Icicle Radish, Chinese	紅棗	Red Dates, Chinese
		紹興酒	Rice Wine

冰糖 Rock Sugar

扁尖筍 Salted-dried Bamboo Shoot Tips

芝蔴油 Sesame Oil

芝蔴醬 Sesame Paste

芝蔴 Sesame Seeds

醬油 Soy Sauce

豆腐花 Soybean Custard

黃豆芽 Soybean Sprouts

醬瓜,花瓜 Soy-pickled Cucumber

五香豆腐乾 Spiced Pressed Tofu

春卷皮 Spring Roll Skins

八角 Star Anise

草菇 Straw Mushrooms

花椒 Szechuan Peppercorns

四川榨菜 Szechuan Pickle

舊陳皮 Tangerine (or Orange) Peel, Dried

芋頭 Taro

天津冬菜 Tientsin Preserved Cabbage

豆腐 Tofu

腐乳 Tofu "Cheese"

木耳 Tree Ear

菜油 Vegetable Oil

馬蹄 Water Chestnuts

大蔥,青蒜 Welsh Onion

冬筍 Winter Bamboo Shoots

冬瓜 Winter Melon

冬菇 Winter Mushrooms

山藥 Yuca Root

Index

About the Author

Martin Stidham, a graduate of Northwestern University, has lived in the Far East for over ten years, first as a student at National Taiwan University in the Graduate Institute of Chinese Literature, later as a translator of short stories, poetry, and novels (including *Yajio* and *Rollicking Heroes*). A long-standing interest in the cuisines of the region, especially vegetarian, has taken him into home, restaurant, and temple kitchens. He has studied privately with instructors from the area's well-known cooking schools, including Wei-Chuan and Pei Mei's, besides being tutored in special techniques by tofu makers and manufacturers of other Chinese specialty food items. Recently the author has been involved with two books on early-childhood education, *Little Earth School: Education, Discovery, Celebration* and a work-in-progress on starting and running a school. When not engaged in activities similar to the above, he can be found watching vintage movies, traveling, or thinking about traveling. Besides roaming throughout Japan, Southeast Asia, and New Zealand, he has traveled extensively in Western Europe, Morocco, Pakistan, and Uzbekistan (Tashkent, Samarkand, Bukhara, Khiva), as well as Outer Mongolia (MPR), with visits to Siberia, Moscow, and Kashmir.